Amazon Fulfillment Services
172 Trade Street
Lexington, KY 40511

Shipping Address:

Sandra R. Capen
1172 SW Pelican Crescent
PALM CITY, FL
34990
United States of America

YOUR ORDER OF JUNE 27, 2016 (ORDER ID 109-9926967-0830616)

Qty	Item
	IN THIS SHIPMENT:
1	**This is Who We Hire: How to get a job, succeed in it, and get promot** Groenendyk, Alex Paperback 1941142621 Amazon.com, LLC

This shipment completes your order.

DQpt26gMN

THIS IS WHO WE HIRE

*How to get a job, succeed in it,
and get promoted. The definitive career guide
from decision makers in the selection process.*

ALEX GROENENDYK

ISBN: 978-1-941142-62-2

http://www.amazon.com

For detailed information about your orders,
please visit Your Account. You can also print invoices,
change your email address and payment settings,
alter your communication preferences,
and much more - 24 hours a day - at
http://www.amazon.com/your-account.

Returns are easy !

Visit http://www.amazon.com/returns to return any
item - including gifts - in unopened or original condition
within 30 days for a full refund (other restrictions apply).
Please have your order ID ready. Thanks for shopping
at Amazon.com, and please come again !

	Item Price	Total
d.	$15.48	$15.48

NV   744   #2WGMH   20C5760
06/27/16   91634686

PRAISE FOR
THIS IS WHO WE HIRE

"Alex won our President of the Year award twice while competing with over a hundred of his peers at Fiserv, an organization of more than 22,000 employees. He is consequently well-qualified to provide a highly detailed and actionable guide of what employers search for when recruiting and promoting."

—Jack Bucalo

Jack Bucalo was Global Head of Human Resources at Fiserv, Inc., USA, a $4.1 billion international technology leader. From 1993 to 2005 he was responsible for over 22,000 employees worldwide. He has directed the recruiting campaigns for college and business school graduates at many top U.S. universities including Harvard, Chicago, Northwestern, Pennsylvania (Wharton), and Columbia.

FOREWORD

FROM FRANK MARTIRE
EXECUTIVE CHAIRMAN OF THE BOARD AT FIS

FIS is the world's largest provider dedicated to banking and payment technologies serving over 20,000 financial institutions in 130 countries with 55,000 staff.

For you to win our job selection process and succeed once on board, you have to be uniquely relevant and essential to *our specific needs*. This means you will have to convincingly demonstrate equally specific results, skills, attitudes, and behaviors that match those needs.

We look for people who know what they want to do with passion and ambition. This is because we know these drive your effort to both understand our needs and prepare yourself to a much greater level. The deeper your understanding of the priorities and consequences facing your current or future manager, colleagues, and customers—the greater your commitment to exceed their needs. This makes the difference between mediocre and great results.

This is true whether you are applying for your first job, attempting to succeed in the job you have now, or wish to be considered for a promotion. The earlier you identify how you would like to provide value and start building your ability to deliver it in a way that is applicable to specific employers, the better off you will be.

So find out where your passions lie, target the right jobs, and understand exactly what a future or existing employer wants from you. Then make the effort to develop and align yourself to be the ideal match. *We look for evidence that you have done so in the past and are continuing to do so every day.*

The recommended actions in **This Is Who We Hire** will help you maximize your value to an employer. Everything you learn in this guide can also be applied to what you should look for in others so that you can successfully select people and build your own teams. It also covers the basics on how to manage and lead them.

These are essential skills for you to land a job, expand your responsibility, and be promotable.

Good luck!

Frank Martire
Executive Chairman of the Board at FIS

INTRODUCTION

FROM PAUL JARLEY, PH.D.

Dean of the College of Business Administration with over 8,000 students at the University of Central Florida, which is the second largest university in the U.S.

It has become increasingly clear that the time has come for colleges to play a greater role in improving job outcomes. We can't just sit back and hope our graduates go on to greatness.

Our approach is a strategy of engagement. Getting people to talk, interact, and collaborate with each other. We created monthly events where our faculty talk about their research and interests with business leaders in the community. We created monthly events where our faculty talks about their research and interests with business leaders in the community. We created The Exchange, a unique 120-seat venue in our college where students and faculty leaders interact with business leaders every day. We added four, one-credit Career Professionalism classes to the curriculum to help our students weave these experiences into a compelling story to tell potential employers.

How we came to engage with **Alex Groenendyk** and his book, **This Is Who We Hire**, is a good example of how these initiatives work. It was our students who discovered his book and brought it to the attention of our Director of the Exchange and our Director of Professional Development and Placement. Alex soon became a favorite repeat speaker with our students, and a collaboration was born around the skills and actions that we believe have the most positive career impact.

The Career Professionalism classes, that all students in our college take, are unique in three aspects. First, they are not one-time experiences just before graduation. The classes are an *integral* part of the student's *entire* time in our college. Secondly, the classes are designed to be active, not passive. Students are assisted and incentivized to seek out projects, internships, networking conversations, and experiences that will help them discover what they want to do in their professional lives and secure an opportunity to do it *before* graduating. The emphasis of our courses is on doing, taking ownership, and developing interpersonal skills through as much practice as possible. Thirdly, the focus is not just on landing the right job, but also on how to perform well, exceed expectations of their employers and get promoted. This also facilitates our long-term collaboration with our students and their employers, which benefits all parties, including the next year students who follow their footsteps.

I am delighted that **This Is Who We Hire** will now be the text to drive the activities in all four of our Career Professionalism classes. It is also a book each student can and should take with them for continued guidance in their workplace. It provides an actionable and repeatable process they can use to manage their *entire* career.

Dean Paul Jarley, Ph.D.

CONTENTS

SETTING THE STAGE

MASTERING THE JOB CYCLE

The challenge. Some good news! Making the career breakthrough. The importance of having a process to guide you. How to get the most out of this book.

CHAPTER ONE
WHAT DO EMPLOYERS WANT?

The trouble with generic career advice. What management doesn't want you to know. Dinner with General Schwarzkopf brings clarity.

Why objectives are so important. Consequences are your motivators. Measurable expectations define your task. Everything starts or stops with relationships. The three things you must prove.

What is alignment? The key steps of alignment. How you fit in AND stand out. How to cross the "Suitable for hire" and "This is who we want!" thresholds.

CHAPTER TWO
HOW TO CONNECT AND FORM
PROFESSIONAL RELATIONSHIPS

Improve your dating skills! The basics of being likable. Lead with your face. Body language speaks louder than words.

Ask the right questions. Use words people listen to.

Understanding four common personality types and how to relate to them.

Connections are not enough. Why you need relationships and how to build them. How to fill "goodwill" tanks. Use relationship health checks.

CHAPTER THREE
FINDING A JOB!

Do you know what you want to do? Taking your personality into account. The most common strategies and why they don't work. Understanding how employers like to recruit.

What is networking? Why you should network. How to network. Whom should you network with. When to network. Three final tips on networking.

Is social media a better alternative way to find a job? Seven tips for successful job-hunting using social media.

CHAPTER FOUR
PREPARING FOR THE SELECTION PROCESS

CHAPTER FIVE
NAILING THE INTERVIEW

CHAPTER SIX
NEGOTIATING THE BEST DEAL

Should you negotiate? What a successful negotiation can be worth! When to negotiate. How to develop your negotiating power. Tactics and behavior to expect during the negotiation.

How to make a detailed negotiation plan. Watch out for the "let's split the difference" tactic. Defusing the angry interviewer. Get more by increasing the responsibilities. What else you should negotiate.

CHAPTER SEVEN
JOINING THE TEAM

The right way to start. Know why you were selected. Develop a professional relationship with your boss. First, make your boss your most valued customer. Second, turn your boss into a mentor. Five tips on being a good mentee.

CHAPTER EIGHT
KEY COMMUNICATION SKILLS

Why communication skills are SO important. The six steps of effective communication. Create a good listener experience. Dealing with angry people including your boss!

CHAPTER NINE
GETTING THE JOB DONE!

Just do it! Seven tips on becoming highly action oriented.

A 10-step process for achieving significant tasks. Always thank everyone and be generous with praise.

CHAPTER TEN
DEALING WITH PROBLEMS, BEING CREATIVE, AND MAKING SOUND DECISIONS

How to use the Achievement Methodology to solve any problem. Problem summary.

Creativity blockers, Four ideas for thinking outside the box. Creativity summary.

How to use the Achievement Methodology as a decision-making process. Decision summary.

CHAPTER ELEVEN
GETTING THE PROMOTION

Why? First succeed in your current role. The importance of internal connections. Three promotion strategies. How to win the promotion selection process.

What does managing and leading mean? Which comes first the management and leadership titles or the experience? Six tips to become a better mentor. Building a new brand. Stay aligned as you rise.

CHAPTER TWELVE
TOP TEN ATTITUDES FOR SUCCESS

What is an attitude? How attitudes are formed and how they can be changed.

I choose my attitudes. I want to. I can. I seek to understand. I seek to improve. I care. I adapt. I serve. I take ownership. My integrity is sacred.

SETTING THE STAGE

MASTERING THE JOB CYCLE

THE CHALLENGE

I would like to start by asking you three questions:

1. How do some people quickly land a job with great pay, enjoy it, succeed in it, and rapidly get promoted? And how do they keep repeating that success?

2. Why do others take over a year to land a job, only to hate it, feel underpaid, and lose it within months? And why does this pattern often repeat itself too?

This leads to the obvious third question:

3. How will you make sure you are in the first group—and how will you stay in it?

The following statistics indicate that your chances of landing in the first group, without a well-executed plan, will be quite a challenge.

For example:

The time it takes to find and land career jobs is stretching from months to years.

1

This is particularly true for recent graduates. According to an Accenture 2016 US College Graduate Employment Study, half of all graduates in the United States of America did not have jobs that required their college degrees *two years after graduating*. We refer to this as being under-employed—a polite term that doesn't begin to describe how people feel after spending between four to six years studying and racking up debts of between $25,000 dollars to over $100,000 dollars.

Meanwhile, holding on to a job long enough to succeed, get promoted, and start an upward career path appears to be just as difficult.

According to recent Gallup polls, some 70% of the *entire* workforce feels un-engaged. This is another polite term for saying they like their job about as much as going to the dentist. When you feel "un-engaged," you are clearly unlikely to be a top performer or get promoted anytime soon. In fact, studies from the Mercer consulting firm and The Conference Board indicate that at any point in time, approximately 30% of the working population is actively looking for a way out by searching for "a better job" elsewhere, rather than working toward a promotion with their current employer.

At the same time, business leaders are very focused on costs and efficiencies. Underperformers and poor "fits" are rooted out and discarded without hesitation. The Marketers Forum conducted a study showing that within just six months of landing a job, 20% of their sample of graduates had either quit or been terminated.

This is a problem.

Such a short time in a job is usually not enough time to develop new skills, achieve impressive enough results, or build the references you will need to help you land a better job.

To make things worse, many repeat job seekers lack a clear idea of what "a better job" looks like and therefore how to find it, land it, and be more successful in it than their last job. This can lead to a pattern and a subsequent drift into a downward spiral.

Taking a long time to land a job is clearly frustrating and depressing. However, to finally land a job after much effort and then not be able to perform in it, to hate it and lose it, is the definition of futility!

I could go on, but I think that's enough of the "downer" statistics. The point is—there are serious risks in the early stages of any career.

This book's purpose is to make sure YOU overcome these challenges and beat these statistics.

It teaches you how to get a job AND how to succeed in it.

SOME GOOD NEWS

There *are* good jobs available.

One thing many business leaders have in common is they must grow their businesses or risk having to look for new jobs themselves. The consequences of failure combined with lucrative bonuses for success means they are generally very committed to making this happen.

The good news for you, the job seeker, is that virtually no business can keep growing without employing more of the right people.

Senior executives *constantly* discuss the need to find, attract, develop, and retain good people because, without them, sustainable growth is not possible.

In fact, I have spoken to managers at many different levels, and they often complain that there is a *shortage of the people they are looking for* and that this is a *constraint on their ability to meet their objectives.*

They have to spend too much time and effort scanning resumes and online profiles followed by arranging and conducting too many worthless interviews with poorly prepared and unsuitable candidates. As a result, many managers also admit that when they finally do find the right person, they get a sudden rush of excitement as they decide, ***"This*** *is who we want!"* It's the moment in which a manager can clearly visualize exactly how the new recruit can help that manager achieve their corporate objectives, and as a result, their personal career ambitions too.

Your abilities to connect with a potential employer, understand what they are looking for, and trigger this reaction are therefore a key focus of this book.

However, in addition to the *"This is who we want!"* reaction, there is an equal and opposite emotion. It is the sick in the stomach feeling a manager gets when they think, *"We recruited the wrong person!"* Nothing disappoints and embarrasses a manager as much as one of their new recruits failing, having to terminate them, and start the costly recruitment process all over.

It is even more embarrassing and disastrous for you. As you look for your next job, if your next interviewer gets even a hint that this has happened to you, they will probably select someone else.

Note: Be aware that the start and end dates of your last positions are one of the *first* things a potential employer looks at when evaluating your resume.

This is why making sure you understand your manager's expectations and that you have the ability and motivation to exceed those expectations is an equally important part of this book.

MAKING THE CAREER BREAKTHROUGH

It can be done!

The flip side of the above statistics shows that there are just as many success stories:

- People who landed career positions before they graduated. Some are on their second promotions within two years. *What did they do differently?*

- People who lost their jobs but landed others within weeks. *How?*
- People who actually find their work enjoyable, and a 10-hour day flies by. *What is their secret?*
- People whose careers are alive with fulfilling relationships. Their bosses have become both mentors and references. *Were they just lucky?*
- Young people in management positions who oversee significant numbers of staff, including some who are much older than them. *What got them on the fast track?*

I will share with you what these people know and do, (and how employers view them), that makes the difference between rapidly climbing toward their goals versus spiraling away from them.

This is a step-by-step guide that teaches you how to genuinely develop and market yourself as THE candidate that employers of your choice want to hire. It also teaches you how to succeed in the job by making a positive and fulfilling impact, including how to become a future leader.

INTRODUCING THE JOB CYCLE

In order to get a job, succeed in it, and get promoted, there are a number of phases of activities that you need to become good at. Consider them a process you can follow and repeat in a cycle.

Phase 1 – Finding your direction

- Understanding your own personality and interests
- Connecting and networking with people who can describe jobs in detail to you
- Identifying target jobs and career paths that match your interest and personality
- Building a strong motivational vision of your desired future
- Targeting employers you are likely to enjoy working for and executing a sustained long-term networking campaign within them

Phase 2 – Preparing for a job

- Understanding how the target job creates value for the organization and how it is measured
- Understanding what skills, attitudes and achievements employers specifically look for when hiring for your target jobs
- Preparing yourself to be the ideal match for such jobs by building your relevance
- Developing your story and elevator pitch
- Documenting your relevance on social media profiles such as LinkedIn and in achievement folders
- Preparing a specific tailored high-impact resume that gets you an interview

Phase 3 – Winning the selection process

- Targeting specific actual live job opportunities
- Understanding the hiring process and who the key decision makers are
- Understanding what the decision makers care about most and what they will base their decisions on
- Preparing answers backed by examples for the most likely questions
- Preparing questions of your own to uncover needs you can match
- Connecting with the interviewer and matching your personality
- Question answering techniques and interview control
- Triggering a *"This is who we want!"* reaction

Phase 4 – Negotiating good compensation

- Laying the groundwork for the negotiation by building your value
- Prompting an offer
- Building your negotiating power
- When to negotiate and specific negotiating tactics
- Closing the deal

Phase 5 – Joining the team

- Key actions on your first day
- Forming the right relationship with your boss
- Strengthening your understanding of the business, culture, people, processes, and customers
- Aligning and integrating

Phase 6 – Performing well

- Understanding expectations in measurable terms such as key performance indicators
- Performing beyond expectations plus getting your over performance recognized and documented.
- Adding to your value by looking for additional opportunities to help and do more
- Continuing your relevant skills development
- Building career long references

After you have clearly performed beyond expectations for a while, you restart the cycle by going back to the activities involved in the first phase, which is targeting and finding your next job.

This could either be a promotion or another job that will give you the experience and skills you need to reach your next career goals.

You would begin your new cycle by transitioning from Phase 6 back to Phase1 as follows;

Phase 1 – Finding the promotion

- Networking within the organization to identify different promotion opportunities
- Learning what people in those positions do all day
- Understanding what types of personalities and skill profiles succeed most in those positions
- Deciding which specific promotion opportunities you want to target

Phase 2 – Preparing for the promotion

- Understanding how the higher position creates value and how that value is measured
- Developing your skills and relevance for the specific, targeted promotion opportunity
- Developing management and leadership skills
- Volunteering for tasks that provide *relevant* examples of skills, results, and leadership
- Repositioning your brand and reputation to match the promotion

The cycle continues with *winning* the promotion selection process, *negotiating* a new level of compensation, *joining* a new team, and *performing* at a higher level until you start your search to *find* your next promotion.

Each time you target a job to move your career forward, you repeat all the activities in each of the above phases at a higher level.

I refer to these activities collectively as the Job Cycle.

See diagram below.

The Job Cycle

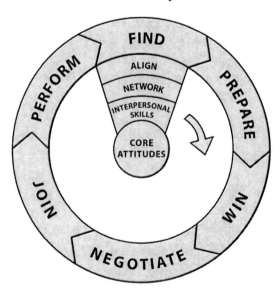

At the center of the cycle are the *top ten core attitudes* that will not only help you succeed but are the ones that employers increasingly base their hiring decisions on. Then come some critical skills such as your *interpersonal, networking, goal setting, and aligning* skills, which you need to be able to apply in each of the phases defined on the outside of the cycle. *Each of these skills is also specifically sought after by employers.*

Having a process you can follow to help you understand which phase you are in, which skills you need to develop, what actions you need to take, and how—is the most reliable way to take control and drive your career success.

IMMEDIATE SPECIFIC HELP

Depending on where you are in the Job Cycle right now, you may need urgent guidance on a particular subject. If you want, you can jump straight to your relevant topic, such as networking, resume writing, interviewing, negotiation skills, and so on. However each of these topics, when taken alone, become tactics, and as everybody knows, tactics are far more effective when they are part of an overall strategy.

A STRUCTURED APPROACH

The book is therefore designed to be a roadmap you can follow through the Job Cycle.

I have divided the chapters into short subsections and natural break points to make the journey easier.

Chapter One gives you a better understanding of how employers think, what they search for, and how to differentiate yourself in terms that are compelling and meaningful to *them*.

The second chapter covers the skills that lay the foundation for the rest of the book and indeed the rest of your career. This includes the interpersonal skills you need so you can build trusting relationships, understand people's needs and communicate effectively—*persuasively!*

Each chapter then follows the six key phases on the outside of the Job Cycle.

WHY DO WE NEED A JOB CYCLE?

To do anything consistently well it is very helpful to use a proven process. If you want to build fast and sustainable upward momentum in your career, *which is also something employers specifically look for*, then you need a *repeatable* process. Although this may seem obvious, most people *do not* follow a process or have the skills to do so. The statistics speak for themselves.

Let's look at each of the components within the Job Cycle and see what typically happens.

SKILLS

Many first-time job seekers, in particular, are missing key interpersonal, connecting, networking, goal setting, and alignment skills. These skills rarely occur naturally. They need to be deliberately learned, practiced, and applied constantly. Even a small improvement in any of these skills can have very positive consequences.

CORE ATTITUDES

Most people have a general idea of the importance of having a "good" attitude versus a "bad" one. Very few, however, can describe what that means in the context of a working environment. In fact, most have not thought much about their own attitudes and are not very conscious of how these affect themselves and others they come in contact with. They do not know how to get rid of detrimental attitudes or how to develop new desirable ones. In any case, they do not know what *specific* attitudes are expected from them by the employers they wish to join—or how to convincingly demonstrate that they do have the right attitudes when they meet those employers.

THE SIX PHASES

Find

Many people just don't spend enough time analyzing and thinking through what they want to do and what kind of lifestyle that would support. They certainly do not do so in a structured enough way to help them reach realistic and actionable conclusions.

According to an After College study in 2015, 85% of students graduate with no job lined up. They have no clear basis on which to select a job and therefore no way to prepare themselves to maximize their relevance for it. As a result, they do not build a compelling story. They use generic resumes that are not highly relevant to any job. This is why so many graduates take a long time to land a job—and when they finally do—it is often one they don't like.

Without a "dream job" in mind, it is difficult to find it—or know how to become the "dream candidate" for it.

Deciding what you want to do involves building a sufficiently large network of the right people and gaining specific information from them about what they do every day so that you can make an informed decision.

Prepare

Based on the information you learn from your network, you will decide which jobs to target, and you will then need to set goals to develop specific skills and experience to optimize your relevance.

The goals you set and achieve will define your future.

Not deciding what you want to do and therefore also not preparing yourself in any specific way is one of the main causes for underemployment. It can result in many wasted years of drifting and a common late twenties or early thirties "life crisis" as you feel increasingly left behind. Evaluating how you are performing now, deciding what you want to do next, and finding out how you will have to prepare—*to be able to do what you want next*—is a career long discipline within the Job Cycle.

At any stage in your career, when an employer asks "Why should we select you?" they want to know about the goals you set and achieved to build yourself into their ideal candidate.

Note: An absence of well-thought-out goals raises an immediate red flag during any selection process.

Win

Left to their own natural instincts, very few people will do anything beyond showing up for an interview, letting the interviewer take control, trying their best to answer questions, and then waiting to be told how they did. This section of the Job Cycle covers a whole range of techniques to help understand the selection process, who the key decision makers are, and what they will base their decisions on. It covers how you develop rapport with the interviewer, give and take control of the conversation, get feedback to guide you on target with your answers, and a simple four step structure to drive your way to an offer.

Negotiate

Many people are just too nervous to risk the job by going into the Negotiate phase for the pay they deserve. In any case, they have no idea *how* to negotiate. The financial impact can be very significant and affect your future earnings for years! The difference in pay over three to five years can easily make the difference between being able to save for a down payment on a house—or not.

Join

Very few applicants think ahead about how to integrate during the initial Join phase. It is *very easy* to get off to a poor start that disappoints everyone, especially your boss—often without you even realizing you have done so. It can alter how you are regarded and treated from then on.

This can impact your confidence and several of your other attitudes to create an immediate downward spiral.

Some people never recover from their poor joining phase, which is why they are soon on the job market again.

Perform

Likewise, many do not know how to succeed during the Perform phase. It doesn't seem logical to even worry about that yet. They believe they can cross that bridge once they are actually in the job.

This is a critical mistake.

Because of the significant impact of a poor recruitment decision, employers will ask questions, which you will only be able to answer in a compelling way if you have understood what it takes to succeed in the Join and Perform phases for the job in question.

Employers want to see that you have made the effort to find out and genuinely prepared yourself.

You will not be able to trigger a strong "This is who we want!" reaction unless you can make the interviewer clearly visualize you as part of their team, helping them successfully deliver their top priority objectives.

This requires a much deeper level of understanding of the job and its challenges. You will need to be able to bring up specific examples of your actions and capabilities that speak directly to the needs of the job in question.

Getting Promoted

Lastly, if you want your career to progress, you need to be promoted. There is no greater validation of your performance. Many people intuitively know this, however, relying *only* on your performance to get promoted is a mistake. Just because you perform well in a job at one level does not mean you are suitable for another job at a higher level. Even worse is expecting to be promoted just because you have been in a job for a significant period of time. These are *very common* mistakes.

If you want to be promoted, you have to employ the skills and actions in the Job Cycle to make it happen or it probably won't—regardless of how well you perform.

Note: Gallup has also identified that promotions lead to a disappointing performance 82% of the time! This clearly underlines the need to continue to use a process such as the Job Cycle to ensure you land the *right* promotion *after properly preparing for it*, start it in the right way, understand expectations and perform beyond them.

This book provides a solid process plus specific strategies and actions to help you get promoted. It also covers the basics on becoming a manager and a leader which you will need as you take on greater responsibility. Most people do not think about management and leadership (other than to complain and criticize) until *after* they have been promoted.

The time to learn and demonstrate management and leadership capability is during your campaign to get promoted.

Future employers will search for evidence that other employers judged you to be promotable, preferably twice within the same organization. They want to see that you were able to grow and succeed at higher levels. They also need to *feel your desire* to be promoted because they know it fuels your motivation to do any job well.

All other attributes being equal, employers will pick the candidate that can demonstrate a strong desire and history of being promoted.

SUMMARY

Those who succeed and move up fast are not born with extra talent. They're not just lucky. They are people exactly like you who have mastered the required skills in *all* the phases of the Job Cycle.

Followers of the Job Cycle have a clearer vision of their destiny and are proactively controlling more success factors in their journey toward that destiny.

Meanwhile, poor execution or omitted steps in any one of the Job Cycle phases can severely hold you back and even tip you into a downward spiral. Think "weakest link." You can be extremely talented and highly qualified, but if you fail to demonstrate the right attitudes, if your interpersonal skills prevent you from connecting with your interviewer, or if you fail to clearly align your focus and efforts with the objectives of your manager, you are not going far. Interviewers will begin to assess you in these areas within the first 10 minutes of an interview.

You need to master the ENTIRE Job Cycle in order to break into it, stay in it, and succeed in it at increasing levels of responsibility.

The skills, actions, and understanding in this book will be highly relevant to you for both your immediate success in the early stages of your career and your ability to sustain long-term success as you move up through different phases and start new cycles at higher levels.

Your mission is to jump on the fast track and Job Cycle to the top!

This book shows you how.

CHAPTER ONE

WHAT DO EMPLOYERS WANT?

Chapter Foreword by Lonny Butcher
Director of Professional Development and Placement, College of Business Administration at the University of Central Florida

WHY WILL AN EMPLOYER WANT TO HEAR *YOUR* STORY?

To find out what employers want we asked 50 local businesses to come together one afternoon at the University Of Central Florida. All of them either currently or previously hired graduates from our University. Many were alumni themselves. It was a great opportunity to get input and feedback on our graduates.

Our dean was facilitating the meeting, and it started out well. So our dean asked why they didn't hire more of them. This is what we got.

> *"Many of your students don't know how to tell their story."*

Their words still hang in the air like a neon "No Vacancy" sign—a harsh message.

> *"They just talk about themselves in mostly meaningless terms."*

This was by far the most prevalent shortcoming, even surpassing technical skills and conceptual knowledge.

"They can't relate what they've done to what we need."

Telling your story is simply a metaphor for the way you explain your value. For your story to hold the listeners attention, it has to be relevant, compelling, and unique. This has significant implications.

It means you can't drift through college (or afterward) and then create a "one fits all" story that's just a chronological account of your life. You have to "drive" your life to build the story you will need—to get the jobs you want.

You have to;

- Make decisions about what you want to do and target specific jobs and employers
- Learn what skills your target employers want from you and why
- Find ways to actually build the skills your target employers need

Based on this approach, you can prepare genuine stories that convey your strengths and learn how to tell them *in the context of each employer's requirements.*

So spend your time wisely. Network to decide what you would like to do and to verify the skills and experience employers want. Then use every opportunity to proactively build your relevance. Finally, learn how to rehearse and present your value to meet an employer's specific needs with maximum impact. This is how you trigger a "This Is Who We Want!" reaction.

Chapter One is the start of your journey.

Don't coast. Drive with purpose. Travel further and enjoy the ride!

Lonny Butcher

PART I

WHY THE USUAL QUALITIES WON'T GET YOU THE JOB

THE TROUBLE WITH GENERIC CAREER ADVICE

A great deal of career advice on what employers expect from you will come in the form of a list of qualities we are all familiar with. Unfortunately, without detailed context and specific actions to move you forward, these lists offer minimal help. And yet they are used everywhere, *including by employers themselves.*

Let me show you.

Take a look at the contents of a typical job listing. Below is an example that was actually used by an organization I worked for.

> **Ideal candidates will have strong ethics, have excellent interpersonal skills, and be team players with cool heads under pressure. Applicants must have successfully completed an appropriate university-level degree and be able to demonstrate relevant experience. They will have a strong focus on results, driven by high levels of motivation and creativity. They must be able to demonstrate a determined ownership attitude to solve problems and consistently get the job done well, regardless of circumstances.**

We've all seen these desired qualities listed in job postings and in hundreds of blogs on the Internet. They seem logical, but what do they actually mean? How do you develop them? In an interview, how do you demonstrate these qualities and prove you have more of them than the next candidate?

WHAT MANAGEMENT DOESN'T WANT YOU TO KNOW

The fact is most managers do not live up to these standards themselves!

I certainly never did. We often struggle just to describe these qualities clearly and consistently. Different managers will emphasize the importance of different qualities and often have very different interpretations of what they mean. Some are skills, and some are attitudes, and most are not easily measurable. Furthermore, most interviewers have had little, *if any*, formal interview training. As a result, many have no clue what questions to ask to accurately assess you in any of these areas. Somewhat shocking don't you think?

Unfortunately, merely SAYING you have these qualities proves nothing.

I look at resumes today and count the number of qualities listed. Nine times out of ten they are used throughout the resume, prefaced by "very," "highly," or even "extremely,"—but lack any supporting evidence. I am willing to bet that you have several in your resume right now.

I have interviewed many candidates who would suddenly put on their "earnest face" and say things like,

"Sir, I would just like to assure you that I am very honest, a fast learner, and a very hard worker. Oh, and I'm definitely a team player! And I'm extremely persistent, and I'm…"

The longer I stayed silent, the more qualities they would throw in.

I can assure you that I never felt assured!

At no point would this trigger my *"This is who we want!"* reflex.

Generic attributes with no relevant evidence to back them come across as overused, empty claims—mere buzzwords.

People also think that by using many such buzzwords or phrases, they might get lucky and hit one the interviewer appreciates *and actually believes.*

Even if they are not relevant, they all sound good so they can't do any harm—right?

Wrong.

Interviewers are invariably short on time and attention. Once you start using irrelevant, unsupported qualities, whether on a resume or during an interview, they are much more likely to conclude you are *not* a good fit.

Have you ever been in a shop where a salesperson goes on and on about benefits you are not interested in? Did it make you reach for your wallet or the exit?

Everyone you interview with or work for will have different interpretations of these qualities and a priority of which ones are most important to them.

Finally, just when you admit you're utterly confused, someone will tell you,

"Don't worry, dear. Forget all that. *Just be yourself, and you'll be fine.*"

As I will show you later, this can be the deadliest advice of all.

So how DO you prepare?

I experienced these challenges both as an individual trying to land jobs and as an employer looking to recruit. I spent way too much time thinking about which qualities were the highest priority and provided the most return. It made me look for a structured, simplified, and more

21

effective approach. Inevitably, I turned to my sales roots. Although employers refer to hiring as a *selection* process, it was clear to me that it is unquestionably a *sales* process for the candidates.

This may seem obvious, but many people are simply not comfortable with the idea of selling at all. Very few people have been through professional sales training early in their careers. Instead, they have mainly been exposed to the cheesy practices of unprofessional salespeople.

Selling is often seen as both distasteful by the candidates and something they do not believe they have the skills for.

As a result, job seekers attempt to maximize their chances by babbling on about as many generic qualities as possible. Their entire focus is on presenting themselves. They pass over the detailed context and the actual requirements of the job, including the specific needs and concerns of the person who is going to manage them. When this approach is combined with limited interpersonal and sales skills, job seekers are at a *significant* disadvantage.

Note: *Professional sales skills are regularly cited as being in the top 10 most desirable skills by employers when recruiting and also by top executives accounting for their own success.*

To be clear, I am *not* going to try to turn you into a salesperson in this book, but I will lean on a few of the most important selling principles as I show you how to understand and approach employers.

The first principle is that all good professional selling starts by making the effort to understand what the buyer actually wants and why.

To get some answers, I talked to other business leaders and my own management team. The ugly truth was that many companies, including ours, relied on managers who had little to no interview training to do the recruiting, especially for entry level candidates. They mostly relied on their gut instincts.

One unexpected dialogue had a significant impact on our thinking.

DINNER WITH GENERAL SCHWARZKOPF BRINGS CLARITY

I had the honor of sitting next to General "Stormin" Norman Schwarzkopf, who commanded the coalition forces in the first Iraq war. At the time, I was president of the fourth-largest business unit at a truly outstanding multibillion-dollar company called Fiserv. Due to the great efforts of my incredible team around the world, we had won the "Business Unit of the Year" award for the second time. As a result, I was invited to eat dinner with the company's founding CEO, the chairman, and the general at a company meeting on future strategic direction.

I found General Schwarzkopf very engaging, and we talked about East Africa, where I spent the first 20 years of my life. Through the course of the conversation, it became very apparent that he had a strong connection with the people reporting to him, even though he was often portrayed as a tough boss. (He was also known as "the Bear") The general clearly enjoyed these relationships and relished spending time with his staff, regardless of rank. It prompted me to ask what kind of people he surrounded himself with to make his incredible achievements possible. What did *he* look for?

His response was very short, simple, and direct. He said,

"They understand the objective, know what I expect, and deliver. Zero excuses. They know lives depend on it."

There was no mention of a single quality I was so used to seeing in every job description and resume!

This response had a powerful impact on me because it got me thinking about the importance of really understanding objectives and expectations. What does it take to know what is expected of you and to live up to those expectations? How does the relationship between you and your boss play into this? How does truly understanding consequences and genuinely believing excuses aren't an option impact your performance? And of course, what is the importance of all this when you are applying for a job?

It turns out that concepts like objectives, expectations, consequences, and relationships are at the HEART of what employers are looking for.

Let's take a look at these concepts.

PART II

GETTING TO THE HEART OF WHAT EMPLOYERS REALLY WANT

WHY OBJECTIVES ARE SO IMPORTANT

First, where do these objectives that General Schwarzkopf mentioned come from? I want to focus on two types. *BOTH are critical to your success.*

JOB RELATED CORPORATE OBJECTIVES

Most companies have a purpose or mission. Each company will decide what results constitute achieving their mission. These results are broken down into high-level objectives (think targets) to achieve specific results over a defined time period. Examples could include; within the current year reaching a certain market share, reaching a level of sales revenue, making a certain amount of profit and so on.

Corporate objectives are assigned to managers in departments such as production, marketing, sales, and customer service. All of these fit together like puzzle pieces to achieve the greater goals of the company. The managers will then further break down these goals into smaller and more specific ones for each of their team members. In this way, *all employees* should have objectives that, once achieved, help their bosses and anyone at the receiving end of their work reach their own objectives. There should be a chain of connected tasks and consequent results that can be followed from the lowest rungs of the corporate ladder all the way up to the mission at the top and vice versa.

To be selected and perform well once on board, you MUST understand the objectives of your desired role and how they fit into the overall objectives of the rest of the organization.

You need to know how your results affect your manager and anyone else dependent on your work, ideally all the way to the end customer.

Your objectives give you a focus and enable you to provide value. They determine which qualities you need. Therefore:

The only way to understand the real skills or qualities required to win a job is to know the details of the job's objectives.

Here comes the challenge.

There is a HUGE difference between organizations and individual managers in terms of how well they assign objectives.

This is yet another ugly secret!

Some organizations are very informal and rely on managers and staff to intuitively know what their jobs are, often based on very vague descriptions. In fact, the majority of job openings are in smaller companies where they may not have well-developed or documented objectives in place at all. You are just expected to learn on the job.

Even the larger, supposedly well-run organizations who have for years had "management by objectives" policies in place with a focus on key results and key performance indicators often struggle to get all their managers to set clear objectives and regularly review them for their entire staff. I was never once able to get 100% of my managers to do this. In many cases, lazy managers just take old job descriptions and re-use them for years, both for a contrived and very ineffective annual performance review and for recruiting purposes!

So it is quite possible that you will *not* be given a nicely prepared list of clear objectives prior to or even during your interview.

What are the implications of this?

Unfortunately, if you do not understand the objectives of the position you are applying for, you will have no basis on which to position yourself as the right candidate.

This understanding is critical to ensure you are on target when preparing your resume or answering questions during an interview. Without clarity on the position's objectives and how to deliver them, you will not be able to highlight relevant skills or previous achievements to demonstrate you can do the job. All you can do is guess. It only takes a few irrelevant statements to position yourself as the *wrong* candidate. This is one of the most common reasons candidates either fail to land jobs or fail to succeed in them afterward.

YOU will, therefore, need to find them out yourself!

For many positions, you may have to identify or even co-develop objectives and agree on expected results with your future manager *during the selection process*. As it turns out, this is an opportunity to differentiate yourself in the interview—and a great way to position you for a promotion if you continue to do so once you are in the job.

Just asking what the objectives are and clarifying them in detail will already set you apart from candidates who talk about themselves in meaningless generic terms or who just sit there passively answering questions.

I will cover how to really stand out in much more detail below.

PERSONAL OBJECTIVES—GOALS

Showing that you understand the corporate objectives of the job and demonstrating how your past achievements are similar to their expected results will go a long way toward convincing them that you can do the job. However, there is an old saying:

> **"People seldom do anything to the limit of their ability; they do it to the limit of their willingness."**

In other words, the will to win is as important as the skill to win! Interviewers therefore also need to be convinced that you have the motivation to *WANT* to complete your work objectives.

This is where your personal objectives or goals come in. They know that your personal goals, or lack thereof, play a major role in your drive.

Successful people have been studied for years. One consistent characteristic among them is that they have a very strong vision of where they want to go in their career and have *documented* plans for how to get there. *They constantly set themselves goals.*

Successful people are not just trying to get *any* job, nor are they just trying to survive in the one they have. They target *specific* jobs on a career path and feel highly compelled to excel in them because they are aiming for promotions to reach the next step in their plans.

They know how to identify key requirements along the way in terms of knowledge, skills, experience and results to achieve each step in their career goals. They also know how to break these down further into short-term deadlines and targets and are relentless in achieving them. The combination of a clear vision of desired long and short-term consequences with intelligent goal setting is a powerful driver. I will explain further below.

These people stand out in terms of their levels of motivation, energy, focus, and commitment. They thrive in jobs by delivering results, moving up, and repeating the process. Employers are looking for evidence that you are one of these *motivated* and *goal-driven* individuals with a career plan that you are clearly progressing along. This provides another great opportunity to differentiate yourself.

CONSEQUENCES ARE YOUR MOTIVATORS

General Schwarzkopf clearly alluded to consequences by stating that "lives depended" on objectives being reached. At first glance, this may sound as if it only applies to war and is way too extreme. However, there are plenty of industries and services where lives *are* on the line, the aviation, automotive, construction, food, and health industries to name a few.

Let's use a more day-to-day example, though. When you clearly understand that happy customers and their testimonials are absolutely essential for future sales (and therefore the future of the whole company, including *your* continued employment), it becomes hard *not* to do everything possible to achieve customer satisfaction objectives. This leads to an important behavioral conclusion:

Motivation is derived from understanding consequences.

Your motivation is maximized when you can see how the consequences of your actions move you toward both your corporate AND your personal goals.

For example, if you understand that in addition to the positive impact on the organization, a high customer satisfaction score also lines you up for the promotion you are after—and earns you a bonus—you will clearly be even more motivated.

Remember the general's reference to "zero excuses?" When you fully understand the *consequences* of your failure—to your manager, your team, and your own longer-term goals—very few excuses for failure will sound reasonable.

Conversely, when you have no clue of the consequences and no goals of your own, any excuse to quit or do the bare minimum, will do!

This is often the root cause of feeling disengaged and unfulfilled.

A good interviewer will, therefore, dig into both your corporate and personal objectives—and their consequences—so be prepared!

MEASURABLE EXPECTATIONS DEFINE YOUR TASK

General Schwarzkopf mentioned the importance of his staff understanding his expectations. Other people's expectations will play a *HUGE* role in your success because of the following:

It is other people's EXPECTATIONS regarding your results, NOT the actual results themselves that determine whether they are satisfied or disappointed.

Everything you do is perceived and judged by different people with different expectations. Therefore, both perceptions and expectations need to be clearly understood, especially your boss's, otherwise you could and most likely *will fail* to satisfy them regardless of your abilities.

It starts with how objectives are worded.

Objectives come in various forms. Some are just vague statements of a desired future. Others are very specific. For example, there is a huge difference between the following objectives:

"We wish to have the *most satisfied* customers in our industry."

"We wish to have a customer base that scores no less than 8 out of 10 on our customer satisfaction survey and for 100% of our customers to be willing to provide positive references."

It is easy to see how the first is susceptible to different interpretations, judgments, and therefore expectations. A single unhappy but very vocal customer (who might scream at your boss and threaten legal action) could skew the perception and get you fired, even though the majority of customers are very happy.

The second objective is much more specific and—most importantly— *measurable*. Perceptions as to whether you succeeded or failed are therefore much less vulnerable to *subjective* opinions.

So, the key, as you strive to uncover the important goals of a potential job, is also to understand how the results will be MEASURED.

Once you understand the measurements that define their expected results, you can use examples of where you have delivered similar results that were measured in the same way. *This will immediately get their attention.*

Note: Understanding the key objectives in a job and how they are measured should be a *critical* part of your preparation long before your interview. You can learn much of this from your network, and it plays a vital role in making sure your resume is on target and gets you an interview in the first place. However if you have not been able to build your understanding upfront, you *must do so* during the interview. Ask the questions!

EVERYTHING STARTS OR STOPS WITH THE RELATIONSHIP

Although relationships were not specifically referred to in General Schwarzkopf's statement, it was obvious from the way he spoke about his team that it was important. Many people misunderstand this.

Good managers do not want a cozy, "best friends forever" relationship because they believe this will lead to complacency.

However, there are specific skills and behaviors that can positively impact your likability when making first impressions and greatly improve your ability to connect and form professional relationships quickly. These skills are covered in detail in Chapter Two, but I will summarize their importance now.

It starts during the selection phase.

Interviewers can base as much as 40% of their evaluations on whether they like you, trust you and can visualize you fitting in with the team.

They need to decide whether they can stomach working with you 10 hours a day—and they often make this decision within the first 10 minutes of an interview. This is a pretty good reason to make sure you have the interpersonal skills to connect and build relationships quickly!

Earlier, we talked about the likelihood that you will *not* be presented with a clear list of objectives and measurements prior to an interview (or even once you're hired). Clarifying objectives and expectations requires substantial dialogue with both your interviewer during the selection process and ongoing with your boss once you join.

If the interviewers judge that you will probably not fit with them and the team, they will not bother to explain the objectives, and they certainly won't allow you the time to guess and spout generic attributes.

I repeatedly asked different managers whether they would recruit a candidate they disliked even if the candidate had the right qualifications. The answer was always NO!

In fact, interviewers specifically assess whether you took action to make sure you have a good relationship with your current and past managers. They want to know how well you understood their objectives and the impact of your role on them. Did you understand their expectations and what did you do to exceed them? There is widely held belief that;

"People do not leave the company they work for—they leave the manager they work for."

Interviewers, therefore, look carefully into this, and it is surprising how many people will severely criticize their current boss in interview situations to justify why they are looking for another job. Some interviewers will even encourage it to see how you react.

Past behavior is one of the strongest indicators of future behavior. People who do not get on with past bosses often do not get on well with future bosses.

This is because in their minds it is their bosses who are always the unreasonable ones in the relationship. Any such evidence in your past will inevitably make an interviewer discontinue your application.

Never criticize your current or previous manager, especially while talking to potential future managers.

They will only visualize you doing the same to them later.

So what did we conclude?

I regularly discussed these topics with my colleagues running other business units, senior corporate executives, including our corporate head of human resources, and those reporting directly to me. I also included my customers because we combined our staff with theirs to get large projects done. Between us all, we employed more than 40,000 people. We found that individuals who focused on actions listed below performed on a completely different level in terms of both achievement and job satisfaction.

- They made a conscious effort to build a specific type of relationship with their bosses and colleagues.
- They developed a detailed understanding of the objectives and results that were expected of them in measurable terms.
- They made the effort to truly understand the consequences of those results to their boss, everyone else *and* themselves. They understood the bigger picture and what was at stake.
- They strongly believed in their ability to improve. Therefore, they constantly worked on identifying and developing the strengths they needed to deliver better results.
- They had strong self-awareness, including an awareness of their impact on the people around them. They sought out feedback and willingly adapted, especially to change driven by new organizational needs.
- They developed detailed personal goals. They had long-term career goals and were able to achieve them by identifying and landing specific jobs and promotions along the path to their goals. They were extensive networkers who soon understood what results, skills, and behaviors were needed to succeed at each level and progress along their chosen path. Their vision of "career success" created a strong drive to succeed.

They had a strong sense of pride to exceed any corporate/personal targets and be good at anything they did. They wanted to win as individuals but not at a cost to the group. They liked being on a winning team with a

33

clear target to compete against. They understood consequences and truly hated to let the team down.

These six areas, therefore, had a significant impact on our candidate selection process, which can greatly clarify how you can prepare yourself. We grouped them into three key areas:

THE THREE THINGS YOU MUST PROVE

#1 Will you fit in? A company's culture is important. Do you share the same values? Will you be committed to the mission? Will you integrate with the organization, the manager, and their team? Will you adapt to the inevitable organizational changes? Will you ensure you do not let the team down? Will working with you will be a pleasure and effective. Will you listen, take direction well, and receive criticism with the right attitude.

#2 Can you do the job? Do you understand the position's objectives. Do you understand how your position adds value in terms of what results are expected and how you will be measured? Can you demonstrate you have the skills, knowledge, and experience to achieve the results they expect. Can you solve their problems? Do you have the potential to do more?

#3 Will you **do the job?** Do you understand the consequences of success and failure to all parties? Do you have the passion, commitment and perseverance to overcome obstacles and produce ambitious results? Do you have a strong desire to succeed that gives you the required energy to do so? Are you proactive and will you take the initiative? Do you set goals for yourself that drive you? How competitive are you? Do you want to take on greater responsibility? How do you react to failure?

This is high level and basic, of course. Not all interviewers will consciously structure their evaluations of you in these simple terms. Remember, many—if not most—have had no interview training. However, pretty much any area they cover with you, including any buzzwords *they* use, whether they realize it or not, will fall within one of the above three categories.

Now that *you* realize this, you can prepare and structure your responses around these categories for maximum differentiation. These are the three things you need to prove. Armed with this perspective, let's go back to that job listing excerpt from the beginning of the chapter. You will see how each ability falls into one of the above categories.

The following attributes clearly speak primarily to your ability to *fit in:*

> **"The ideal candidates will have strong ethics, have excellent interpersonal skills, and be team players with cool heads under pressure."**

The next refer to whether you *can do* the job:

> **"Applicants must have successfully completed an appropriate university-level degree and be able to clearly demonstrate relevant experience."**

The following cover whether you *will* do the job:

> **"They will have a strong focus on results, driven by high levels of motivation and creativity. They must be able to demonstrate a determined ownership attitude to solve problems and consistently get the job done well, regardless of circumstances."**

Now that you can see the context in which these attributes are important to an employer, you are no longer just trying to prove you have a random list of vague concepts. You can start building a list of *specific* and *relevant* examples that show how well you fit into *their culture,* and describe *how* you get the results *they are looking for, what drives you and why that is of benefit to them.* You can illustrate your high level of motivation through examples of relevant goal setting and achievements. When you are asked if you have a certain quality, you can decide which of the three categories it falls into and then raise the right pre-prepared examples, usually in the form of a *quick story about something that actually happened*, to support your answer.

Note: You will not just wake up in time for a job interview with handy examples of the attributes listed above. Looking backward and finding relevant examples in your past to prove you have these qualities is going to be much easier and much more convincing if you have previously set out to build such examples through setting and achieving goals.

You can start on this at any stage in your career, but, obviously, the earlier you start, the better. For example, many of these attributes can be developed while still at university or college which would have a great impact on the speed of landing a job after graduating.

In this way, you purposefully ALIGN yourself to what employers ACTUALLY WANT rather than having to rely on generics.

Aligning is an important concept that will prove invaluable as you target a potential job, land it, and succeed in it. It is one of the key skills central to the job cycle. Let's look at this in more detail.

PART III
ALIGN TO SHINE!

WHAT IS ALIGNING?

Think of "aligning" as a form of adapting. According to Charles Darwin's Theory of Evolution, a species survived more successfully if it adapted to its environment. It could do this by physically evolving over time or by changing its behavior. Failure to adapt often resulted in extinction.

Aligning yourself involves adapting to the specific needs of a job and the environment in which that job exists.

You do not have to strive for some generic idea of perfection. That's impossible, but you can strive to be the *"fittest"* for the job and career you want.

Different jobs at different companies managed by different people will require, you guessed it, different adaptations. We use the term "aligning" because a number of your characteristics—such as your appearance, interpersonal and professional skills, specific attitudes, previous achievements, current focus, and future goals—need to be *in line* with what management is looking for.

As with Darwin's theory, there are both short and long-term dimensions. The short term involves changes in behavior, particularly your interpersonal behavior so that you can connect with different personality types within potential employers and build relationships.

The longer term involves actually developing your skills and attitudes in line with the needs you have uncovered within potential employers. This involves long-term planning and commitment to what we call *targeted skills development* in Chapter Four.

Think of alignment as three key steps that you constantly work on throughout your career.

THE THREE STEPS OF ALIGNMENT

1. Align to connect and form relationships.

This involves using interpersonal skills to establish a good connection and score high on the "likability and trust factor" with *everyone* you meet. This should include people to build your network, your interviewer, your manager, colleagues, and anyone at the receiving end of your work.

Your prime objective is to maximize the degree to which people instantly like you and provide a foundation for clear, effective, and trust-based communication. Connecting and forming positive relationships is the first vital step that paves the way for any further interaction. You have to pass the *"like and trust threshold."*

We'll develop your connection and relationship-building skills in Chapter Two. This will include your ability to spot the signals to assess whether you have reached the threshold or not.

If you cannot connect well with other people, they will not open up to you to give you information or recommend you to other people. It generally makes everything more difficult. This is especially important during an interview.

You will not convince an interviewer of anything if you have not crossed this threshold first—they have to like and trust you before they will believe you and hire you.

2. Align your understanding.

A positive connection and relationship greatly improves your ability to identify the other person's likes, dislikes, and needs. When it comes to competing for a job or starting a new job, this means maximizing your understanding of your boss.

Specifically, it means identifying;

- The *results* your bosses will expect from you in order to meet their own objectives. This means you need to know how your results will be measured, along with the consequences of your success or failure. Finally, you need to know the specific skills and strengths required to make sure you can exceed these expectations.
- The behavior and attitudes your bosses will expect from you in order to fit into the organizational culture and team spirit.
- The motivations your bosses will expect you to have so that they feel reassured that you will do the job.

Your objective in this step is to cross the *"credibility threshold"*. You do this by showing that you fully understand the responsibilities and impact of your role in the context of their objectives and therefore what their requirements from you are across all three areas above.

People will not be convinced by anything you say until they are convinced that you understand and care about their needs first.

This step also defines your target for when you present yourself as a good match in step three. If you fail to define your target, you will be shooting in the dark when it comes to explaining your strengths. Your strengths will not be accepted and remembered unless they are tied directly to their needs. Plus as I said before, it only takes a few off target strength statements to position you as entirely the wrong person.

This step requires good questioning skills which I will cover in detail in Chapters Two and Three.

3. Match – Align yourself

There are two important aspects to this step.

First, you make sure that you *genuinely develop* yourself to be capable of satisfying the needs of an employer across each of the key three areas. This is the primary focus of the Prepare Phase in the Job Cycle.

Second, you make sure that you *present and communicate effectively* by linking every strength statement about yourself to one of their specific needs. This will be your primary objective during any interviews in the Win Phase.

3.1 Align your capability.

Once you have made the effort to understand the position's top priorities and the skills required to achieve them, you have to make sure you develop those skills. This is where long-term planning and targeted skills development become important. This is where you build your relevance to match up to the job. Your objective is to cross the *"capability threshold"*.

The earlier you actually meet people with jobs you are interested in (and their managers), the earlier you can really understand their skill requirements and start building them to differentiate yourself later. We'll go over how you can do that in Chapters Three and Four.

Note: This also means constantly evaluating what skills could be improved or added once you are *in* a job to make sure you grow and maintain the support of your boss and colleagues. Most candidates realize they need to prepare for questions on their existing skills. However, be aware that you will also be questioned on how you *continue* to improve yourself. i.e. What new skills have you learned *recently?* What courses have you been on *this year?* What are your development *plans?*

3.2. Align your fit.

A very conscious and focused effort is required to make sure that you exceed behavioral expectations once you understand them. This is where "just being yourself" can be very costly to your career success. Typical examples of behavioral expectations would include how you interact with your boss, team colleagues, and customers, plus your enthusiasm, can-do attitude, friendliness, helpfulness, willingness to learn and take criticism well, and being reliable and loyal.

I discussed this with Dan Lyons, who was previously the Chief Human Resource Officer for Darden Restaurants, responsible for ***more than***

170,000 staff! Prior to Darden, Dan was a Senior Human Resources executive with the Quaker Oats Company, now part of PepsiCo.

Dan and I are board members of venVelo, a venture fund that provides both capital and mentoring to start-up businesses in Florida. Finding the right people is a critical ingredient to the success of any business, so this is a frequent subject of discussion. He has also been a valuable advisor to me for this book.

Dan sums up "aligning your fit" as follows:

"Managers want to know that in addition to the job skills, you have the right personality, interpersonal skills, and attitudes to work well with your colleagues to achieve the overall team objectives. They look for a 'whatever it takes' commitment to ensuring the team succeeds."

This book covers your interpersonal skills, making sure your predominant personality traits do not clash with others, and the top ten attitudes most employers look for.

3.3. Align your drive.

We've discussed that successful people develop a compelling vision of their future plans and set personal goals to achieve them. You do this by networking with individuals who can help you decide which industries, jobs, and career paths appeal to you. Once you determine your path, these same connections can help you identify the skills and achievements you will need to qualify. This helps you set appropriate *goals* to achieve the *skills* you need—to win the *job* you want. We will go over this in Chapter Three.

Since your network is the most likely source of actual job opportunities, your goals will be well aligned. If not, you may be attempting to land the wrong job—one you will not enjoy or last in. Goal alignment provides you with energy and motivation through knowing that each positive result paves the way for the next goal.

To use an obvious example, if your personal goal is to become a professional athlete or entertainer rather than succeeding in the job you are applying for, then it is easy to see how your energy will be *diverted* from your job rather than reinforced. This will be spotted by a good interviewer or subsequent boss.

If you cross the thresholds of acceptability for each of the three areas above, then you cross an overall "suitable for hire" threshold.

The diagram below shows you how these three alignment steps work. They are the foundation blocks for any career strategy.

See diagram below.

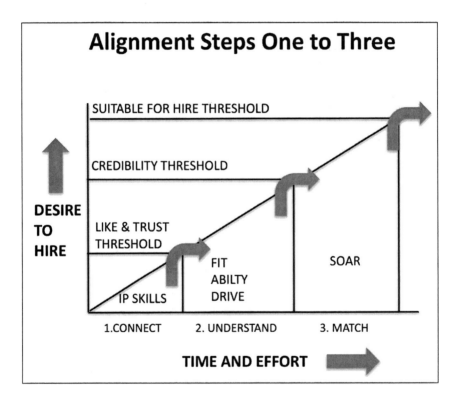

On the horizontal axis is time and effort spent with someone in your network or an interviewer. On the vertical axis is their increasing desire to help or hire you as you progress in time and effort going through the steps on the horizontal axis. Your objective in each step is to progress upwards along the diagonal line, crossing each threshold, and earning the right to move onto the next step.

ALIGN EVERY DAY

In any meeting, if a conversation is not going as well as you would like—check all your thresholds. Somewhere one of the thresholds was probably not reached, most often because you were not patient enough and started to talk about what *you* need or about *yourself* too soon.

Steps one and two are also very applicable to any information gathering networking meeting for example. Your contact will not open up until they like and trust you which is why you must always start with step one. Step two is perfect for you to gain all the information you need.

All three steps are applicable to an interview.

Getting people to like and trust you, then establishing their needs and then matching your strengths to those needs is the most simple and effective way to present yourself.

As stated earlier, an interviewer will not believe anything you say until they like and trust you. Any strength statement made before establishing your credibility is likely to be wasted or could even do harm. Only the strengths that you link directly to their needs will hit the target.

Make these steps a part of your daily life. Build the habit. Always ask yourself "do they like me, trust me, and believe I understand *their* needs?" *before* attempting to achieve *any* of your own objectives. Then ask yourself how your strength or what you want ties into *their* needs.

HOW TO CROSS THE FINAL "THIS IS WHO WE WANT!" THRESHOLD

Crossing the "suitable for hire" threshold is a major achievement but remember it is competitive out there! You are unlikely to be the only one to do so. You, therefore, need to stand out by differentiating yourself as far as possible. You have to be *the one* an employer wants out of many suitable candidates. This means you have to cross one more higher level threshold.

Earlier in this chapter, I described the process of breaking down an organization's mission into objectives and then delegating them. This defines the *top priority results* that *must* be achieved by every manager. Every manager should understand *the positive impact* from achieving their top priorities and the *negative consequences of failure*. Each manager then has to build and maintain a team with the right interpersonal skills, abilities, and attitudes to achieve the required positive impact.

Achieving top priority results always involves solving problems and overcoming obstacles. Managers often go to bed with these problems and their negative consequences gnawing at them. They can turn their dreams into nightmares. In terms of *corporate* objectives, examples of consequences of failure could include lost sales opportunities, lost customers, lost profits, legal exposure and loss of reputation. In terms of *personal* objectives, examples could include loss of credibility and respect, lost bonuses, career setbacks, and even lost jobs.

Making sure they can solve their problems defines their "needs" in terms of the most important capabilities and attitudes that they *MUST* have on their team—*and therefore from you as a new recruit.* Finding people who meet these needs so that they can achieve the deadlines on their objectives can easily make a manager feel under considerable pressure.

The more detail in which you understand this, the better you can position yourself to meet those needs and relieve that pressure.

Note: The *earlier* you develop a deep understanding of what problems and therefore what skills, attitudes, and experience are required in your jobs of interest, the more time you have to develop them and the more convincing you will be to an interviewer that *you are* the person they need. This is where targeting specific jobs in specific employers through long-term networking campaigns is so important. We will cover this in Chapter Three.

How well you prepare this way determines how effectively you can stand out on a resume or social media profile, connect with an

interviewer, and differentiate yourself as the most relevant and compelling candidate. It is also where your power to negotiate will come from.

If you can make the interviewer *clearly visualize* how you will help them achieve their priorities and the resulting positive impact on *both* their corporate *and* personal objectives—you will cross the ***"This is who we want!"*** threshold. This is the point at which you will get a job offer.

See diagram below.

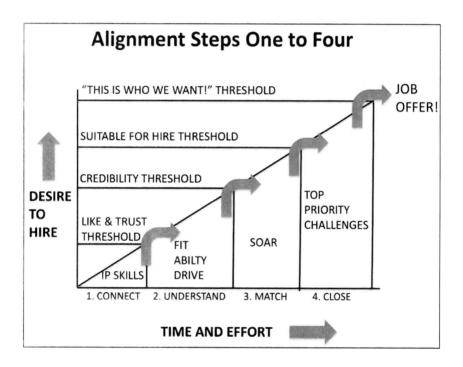

As you can see, it is the fourth step that earns you the right to cross the final threshold and start the conversation about an offer.

SUMMARY

You now have some insight as to what employers are looking for beyond the vague and overused buzzwords. Some job seekers merely incorporate these generic attributes into their profiles and resumes and use them to describe themselves during interviews, usually with no supporting evidence that is relevant to the needs of the employer. Others think they can just rely on their education to qualify them for a job.

As the statistics clearly show, there is much more to finding a job you will like, landing it, keeping it, and getting promoted. This chapter has covered a lot of ground, but it comes down to the three areas of *fit, ability*, and *desire* in the *context of the specific job* you are after—with a clear focus on measurable top priority results. These are what your resume, online profile, and the dialogue in your interviews need to be about.

THE KEY MESSAGE

You will find that corporate and personal top priority objectives, how the results are measured and rewarded, the types of obstacles encountered and the consequences of success versus failure—are at the root of everything!

Use the alignment steps as a structured way to analyze a job opportunity in the above terms. The understanding you gain will help you develop yourself to maximize your relevance, win the selection process, build your power to negotiate your salary and perform well in your job. *It will help you influence others and eventually lead them.*

Successful differentiation is all about identifying the areas an employer worries about most, and then positioning yourself as THE person who CAN and WILL make the biggest contribution to their objectives.

You will learn how you do this in the next chapters, and it will be a prevailing theme throughout the book.

Let's begin with the first step—developing the essential interpersonal skills to help you connect and build relationships with people—because everything starts (or potentially stops) right there!

CHAPTER TWO

HOW TO CONNECT AND FORM PROFESSIONAL RELATIONSHIPS

The purpose of this chapter is to provide you with the skills needed to carry out step one of the alignment actions, which is to form a positive connection and subsequent relationship with everyone you meet. Your objective is to cross the like and trust threshold.

I know you are eager to get to the Job Cycle chapters on finding, winning, negotiating, succeeding, and getting promoted. However, there are some basic interpersonal skills that will make putting those chapters into practice a lot easier and more enjoyable.

No matter how well qualified you are, a lack of the skills described in this chapter will severely hinder your progress. In fact, you may starve!

If you lack interpersonal capabilities, important people with high influence will refuse to meet you—or worse, refuse to help you once they *have* met you. Interviews that you have fought hard to gain will be lost in the first ten minutes. Good jobs will start off on the wrong foot and only go south from there. Promotions will be out of the question.

Note: Numerous studies (i.e. National Association of Colleges and Employers in 2015) have consistently shown that employers put good interpersonal skills such as effective communication and listening skills, relationship building and teamwork in their top ten lists of requirements.

So let's go, and let's make it fun.

> **"The quality of your life is the quality of your relationships."**
>
> **Anthony Robbins**

PART I

SPARKING THE INITIAL CONNECTION

IMPROVE YOUR DATING SKILLS

I have good news.

Many of these interpersonal skills are exactly the same as those required when dating! While the end goals are obviously different, there are many similarities in the required skills and process. I say this, not only to make my recommendations more fun and easier to relate to—*but because it is true!*

Note: If you think dating is a ridiculous concept to bring into the context of getting a job, consider the fact that eHarmony, one of the largest global dating services boasting over 44 million users and over 600,000 marriages, has announced it will be introducing a service to help provide a better match between job seekers and employers based on very similar algorithms to those used in their dating services.

So why are these interpersonal skills so important? As you will learn in Chapter Three:

The vast majority of people find their jobs through connections. These skills are vital to building a network of people who like you enough to want to help you, recommend you, or hire you.

Also, remember that one of the three main areas any employer will examine is whether you will fit into their team and be easy to work with. It is the *first* thing they will assess when they meet you and therefore the first "threshold" you have to cross. Many people tend to forget or ignore this, as they focus primarily on demonstrating attributes such as their qualifications and experience in their attempt to get over the "can you do the job" threshold.

Unfortunately, you will not be given a chance to demonstrate ANYTHING if your interpersonal skills put people off.

When you think about it, you are in fact unlikely to get an interview unless your resume already shows that you have highly relevant qualifications and experience. A potential employer is not likely to interview you unless on paper it looks very likely that you *can do* the job. Any subsequent failure to be chosen for a job is therefore much more likely to be caused by the interviewer not feeling comfortable with you in person than by what your actual qualifications are. Your interaction skills are therefore *absolutely critical*, and you have to demonstrate them *before* you go into the details of your abilities to do the job—usually in the first ten minutes of the interview.

This chapter teaches you some basic skills to help you create the best possible first impression, maximize your likability, and make any interviewer WANT to hear about your capability and desire to do the job.

It turns out that these are the exact same skills that during your first dates will either make the other person look forward to meeting you again or eliminate any further interaction!

THE BASICS OF BEING LIKABLE

Likability is your first objective. This may sound odd or even cheesy, but it is an underlying requirement for anyone to want to interact with you. If someone does not like you, they will try to shut down any further involvement and avoid you like a bad cold.

So what does likable versus dislikable mean in this context? Can we be specific?

We seem to have many labels for people we do not like. We often describe them as being at one extreme or the other of various characteristics. Some examples: aloof and unfriendly versus overly-famil-iar, uncommunicative versus blabber mouth, airhead versus over-opin-ionated, painfully shy versus overconfident and overbearing, too cold versus too emotional, and so on.

The list is endless, and although we all know examples of "other people" who fit one or more of these descriptions, many of us are in the dark about how *we ourselves* are regarded. This is because we're generally quite polite to each other. We walk on eggshells around most of the unlikable types and avoid them rather than confront them. As a result, most of us do not believe any of these extremes could possibly apply to us!

In fact, how other people view you also depends greatly on where THEY are on the scale of any given characteristic.

For example, even if you are genuinely in the middle between shy and extrovert, to a very shy person you could still appear overbearing. To an intense extrovert, you might appear rather dull. Hence the expression "Beauty lies in the eye of the beholder."

So, what should we do about this?

Some people simply insist on doing nothing: *"I am who I am."* These people cling to the view that they can only be themselves. Anything else is fake.

Do not be one of them!

If people generally do not like interacting with you, it will be *impossible* to build a network of useful connections, succeed in interviews, or work well with others.

Herein lies the secret.

It is not about who or what you ARE but how you make people FEEL. It is about what you DO.

And what you do is ALIGN to the other person.

A simple but nevertheless useful guide goes as follows:

People like people whom they perceive to be similar to themselves and who show genuine interest in them by actively listening, agreeing, and complimenting them. They also like people with whom they share common interests, experiences, and beliefs.

Such perceptions result in feelings that are often expressed in terms such as "relating to people," "having a good rapport," "having something in common," or "feeling a connection."

What this means in practice is that you should make sure you dress within *their* tastes, conduct yourself in a similar manner as *they* do, and show interest in *them* by asking questions. It means actively looking for common experiences and beliefs. It requires genuinely finding opportunities to *agree* with them and make *positive compliments*. These actions play to the three A's of common emotional needs—acceptance, approval, and affection.

For someone to feel good about you, you have to make them feel good about themselves first.

At this point, I often get comments that this feels insincere or manipulative.

Note: NEVER pretend to be anyone you are not. NEVER lie about what you have done or what skills you have.

As I stressed above, this is not about who you are.

It is about courteously and genuinely behaving in a manner that creates a comfort level for other people to WANT to continue the interaction.

Many years ago, this would simply have been considered good manners or etiquette, much of which has been eroded in today's society.

It can help to look at this from the opposite direction. What would make people *less inclined* to continue interacting with you?

Start by appearing uninterested and inattentive. Minimize your eye contact. A good way to do this is to be preoccupied with your cell phone when they speak. They will take an instant disliking to you if you interrupt frequently. Many people have no clue they are interrupters. However, when you do this, you are saying, "Look, I am not interested in listening to your opinion; you should be listening to mine instead." It is very offensive and destroys career prospects in exactly the same way it kills a date!

Note: Interrupting a potential connection means a connection lost. Doing the same to an interviewer means a job opportunity lost. Keep doing it to your boss and kiss goodbye any promotion prospects and even your employment.

The same applies if you strongly disagree, criticize, share overly-controversial opinions, or talk negatively about others. Another very common mistake results from feeling pressure to impress the other person. People talk far too much about themselves. If you do this, at best you will bore the other person; at worst you will appear a self-centered braggart. Oh, and last but not least, make sure you are never late for any appointment. Nothing communicates more clearly your lack of respect for other people and their time. All of these are absolute no goes, particularly during a first meeting while you are trying to make a connection, or early in an interview.

Is this false or manipulative? No, it is simply treating others the way you would like to be treated yourself.

ALL RELATIONSHIPS START WITH FIRST IMPRESSIONS

Be aware! From the second people meet you, they evaluate you.

The first judgment people make about you acts as a filter that causes them only to register and remember any additional information about you that supports the initial assessment.

This can be quite a problem if you get it wrong. As a result, there is a common saying:

"You rarely get a second chance to make a good first impression."

We all know this, yet so many people *do* get this wrong, and with significant consequences. Let's break it down into some basic skills.

LEAD WITH YOUR FACE

People will make surprisingly significant judgments about you from your expression. They will draw conclusions about your mood, energy, health, friendliness, likability, even honesty and intelligence—just from looking at your face!

Before you have said or done anything, your face can start positive or negative cycles that can help or hinder you throughout your entire career. So we need to get the face right to start with!

How many times have you heard or said, something like, "Oh, I hate that photo of me!" Guess what? That photo is often a good example of what you look like when you are not posing with your "best face" on.

Don't reserve your best face for photographs.

Many of us are surprisingly unaware of our daily expressions. However, because they have such a significant impact on how other people think about us, it is essential to increase our deliberate, conscious control of them. To make your face an asset and not a liability when interacting with others, I have found it helpful to divide expressions into two broad categories.

1. YOUR "AT EASE" FACE

This is the one that you wear all the time. It should make you look friendly and approachable. You should always have a faint smile with shiny eyes, which you can turn into a broad, genuine smile with full eye contact when you see and greet people. A popular song taught us that, *"When you're smiling, the whole world smiles with you."* Keep it in mind as you go about your day.

An at-ease face that is somber and lifeless, or reflects that you feel stressed, angry, or tired will not endear you to others. It will isolate you.

I have worked with people who have no clue that their day-to-day facial expression has settled into an unattractive, alienating liability. Most often, it is completely unintentional, but it has very negative consequences. Every time they meet somebody, their faces set a mood that undermines their objectives. People are often labeled as unfriendly, moody, intimidating, and unapproachable purely on the basis of their day-to-day expression.

We called this CBF syndrome. (It stands for "chronic bitch face.") Make sure you don't have it!

In particular, you should always appear happy to see people. Failing to greet people with eye contact and a smile can set off immediate negative chain reactions. They may think you do not like them, which subsequently alters their opinions of you and their behavior toward you, which in turn affects the way you behave toward them. It's cyclical.

Get some feedback!

Ask a good friend to give you honest feedback about your day-to-day face and what mood is usually displayed. I know of one individual who refused to believe the feedback he was getting until a friend secretly took some *candid* photos of him with a cell phone. He was shocked, but it worked. Put sticky notes in key places with smiley faces to remind you to stay aware of what your face is doing. Keep nudging yourself until your facial muscles get used to the new expression.

Also, become aware of the expressions of those around you. This will remind you to optimize your own expression. It will also make you less afraid of those severe or aloof faces because most people do not mean it. You will be bolder when approaching them.

People have a tendency to mirror each other, and if you are not careful, you will subconsciously match the stern expression of the people you are trying to connect to. Ironically they often have no idea that they suffer from CBF and will think *you* are the one who is disagreeable! Apart from certain obvious situations, nine times out of ten, if *you* smile, so will the other person.

Developing a positive facial impression is important to your whole life, not just your work life. It is very important as you try to build a network of connections, during interviews, or in any sales, customer service, or caregiving role. Your face has a big impact on the "customer experience," and as we will discuss later, there is a great benefit to treating everyone the same way you would treat a valued customer—*particularly your boss!*

Smiles radiate inwards, too.

There is compelling evidence that when you intentionally control your facial expression, it also has an impact on how *you* feel. Deliberately smiling and making your face look alert actually makes you feel better and more alert. Similarly, succumbing to feelings of frustration and fatigue by allowing your face to express those emotions tends to amplify them and make you feel worse. Try it and see.

2. YOUR "COMMUNICATION SUPPORT" FACE

Try a role-playing exercise in which you give someone a compliment with no eye contact and with your mouth turned down. You will see the impact immediately. At best, the recipient will think you're insincere—at worst, sarcastic. This demonstrates an important rule:

Your facial messages are often stronger than your words.

If your expression does not support your answer, an interviewer may not believe you. He or she may ask another related question to dig deeper, or merely score you poorly and move on. If there is a difference between your words and your face, your verbal message will always lose.

This particularly applies to your eyes.

Beware of how you subconsciously use your eyes. For example, looking away while someone is talking to you is usually a signal that you have stopped listening. It will certainly be perceived that way and interpreted as a lack of interest. People do not like that. Listening intently and visibly means keeping your eyes focused on theirs. The same goes for reinforcing sincerity when you say something important.

People feel a connection when their eyes are connected.

Shy people often have poor eye contact, which can make them appear insincere or even untrustworthy. Poor eye contact can easily cost you the job in an interview. If you suffer from shyness, try the old trick of fixing your gaze just between the eyebrows. It's less daunting, and the other person will not feel the difference. This is particularly important when you greet people. Everyone will advise you to shake hands firmly but not too firmly! Sure, that's important, but just as important is a confident look in the eye as you shake hands.

Nothing sends a more negative signal than greeting people without eye contact. It says "I am not interested in meeting you."

Many other nonverbal cues can be delivered through both facial expression and body language. Hands rising to the face, for example, especially if they cover the mouth or eyes, are an instinctive impulse when people are under pressure or not telling the truth. A hand over the mouth or a small cough halfway into a statement is a common involuntary sign of deception or discomfort. In fact, any hand-to-face contact—such as touching the chin, wiping the mouth, scratching the nose, eyebrows, ears, or scalp—is a similar indication.

Experienced interviewers watch for these signals. When you are asked a direct question, control any such impulse movements because merely the pressure of a difficult question can trigger you to disengage your eyes or cough or cause your hands to fly up—*even when telling the truth.* Those familiar with body language may suspect you are lying or at the very least think that you are uncomfortable with the question. They will wonder why.

YOUR BODY LANGUAGE SPEAKS LOUDER THAN YOUR WORDS

First, watch out for the other person's personal space. This invisible zone usually extends two to three feet—*stay outside of this space.* Ignore this, and anything you say will go unheard as the person will be entirely pre-occupied with whether or not to reach for their pepper spray.

Second, pay attention to other body movements, both yours and the other person's. Leaning slightly toward someone says, "I am alert and interested in what you are saying." Leaning back indicates boredom, fatigue, or disinterest, especially if combined with poor eye contact. The latter will instantly turn an interviewer off. It can also mean the listener is uncomfortable with the subject matter, particularly if accompanied by crossed legs or folded arms. Your optimum posture is a slight forward lean, just outside the other person's personal space. Keep your hands down, maintain good eye contact, and wear a ready smile.

Consciously adopt this position as you meet people to make connections and during interviews.

Last, eliminate distracting habits, such as jangling keys or coins in your pockets, jiggling your legs up and down, clicking a pen, or any other compulsive movements. This sounds so obvious, but at least half the candidates I have interviewed displayed one or more of these. It was often the *only* thing I remembered about them afterward. These are compulsive habits; most people do not realize they're doing them. Get some feedback. Ask friends to tell you to stop if they see you doing any of these things.

Your face and your body language are what people pay attention to FIRST.

It is vital to get this right before you say anything, or your words will not be heard. If you follow the advice in the above paragraphs, you will not go far wrong, so let's move on to *what* you say and *how* you say it.

PART II

HOW TO CONTROL THE CONVERSATION

ASK THE RIGHT QUESTIONS

Early in your career, there tends to be more going on around you that you do NOT understand than what you DO understand. It is, therefore, much safer to ask questions than to offer statements or opinions.

An ill-informed statement or opinion, combined with the wrong tone, can prevent you from building a useful relationship, can ruin an otherwise promising interview, and can easily get you scratched off the boss's Christmas card list. The good news:

Questions are the most powerful interpersonal skill available to you! They are the way to understand everyone and everything around you. They are also one of the most effective ways to influence people.

Questions make people talk, which gives you time to assess where they are on any scale, such as those mentioned in the section on likability above. For example, after a few questions, you can gain a sense of where someone is on a scale of introvert versus extrovert and then behave similarly to match yourself on that scale. This greatly improves *your* likability in the eyes of the other person, thereby increasing your chances of connecting.

Asking questions is a great way to show interest in someone else and avoid appearing self-centered, and above all, it prevents you from laying out an opinion that might be a turnoff.

It is much safer to ask if the other person likes something and why.

This is how you find out how people think and feel. It is how you discover common experiences and create opportunities to agree with and compliment them. Once armed with a better understanding of other people you can then decide whether or not to build on their answers by sharing a similar point of view to create common ground and deepen the connection.

Also, watch your tone. A genuine information-gathering question is usually presented with an "I am interested in you" tone. Reinforcing our words and opinions with complimentary tones is a habit we learn early in life. The stronger your opinion, the more likely you will cause offense with your facial expression and vocal tone if they do not like your opinion.

To avoid this, especially in an initial meeting, steer clear of offering up your own opinions until you understand those of the other person.

Asking questions is the best way to do that.

QUESTIONS FOR ALL OCCASIONS

Although there are many types of questions, the following two will serve as your building blocks for all situations, especially when you first meet someone.

1. Open questions

These are designed to encourage dialogue. They are structured to avoid yes or no answers that shut the conversation down. They come in two flavors.

- **Wide open** – These are general background questions and cover *uncontroversial* subjects. They are designed to generate relaxed conversation.
- **Targeted open** – Still open, but oriented toward gathering more specific information; often used for *clarifying* an answer from a wide-open question.

When you are meeting someone for the first time, you can use general, wide-open questions to get people talking about themselves and their background. This allows you to find and establish common ground on which to build the relationship. Wide-open questions typically take these forms:

"Would you please *tell* me a bit about your background?"

"Would you please *describe* what your organization does?"

"Would you please *take me through* a typical day in your role?"

By deliberately using phrases like "please tell," "explain," and "describe," you turn the questions into clear invitations for the other person to talk broadly about the subject that you have identified, such as where they live, where they work, what they do, their hobbies, and so on. Wide-open questions are generally asked at this neutral and safe level.

You can then use increasingly targeted open questions to focus on getting more detail in any area by using who, what, when, where, and why questions. Again, these are designed to encourage conversation rather than yes or no answers. They typically run as follows:

"So, *who* influenced you to…?"

"I see; *what* do you think you will do next?"

"*When* did you realize you wanted to…?"

"*Where* do you see these developments taking you…?"

"So, *why* did you at that point decide to…?"

These questions allow you to direct the conversation to specific subjects and find areas where you have a common experience. They help you deepen your understanding and keep the conversation flowing naturally.

2. Closed questions

These are used to confirm specific points. These questions are indeed designed to prompt yes or no responses, not lengthy discussions. They typically start with:

> "*Have* you…?" "*Are* you…?" "*Will* you…?" "*Do* you…?" "*Can* you…?" and so on.

The answer should be a simple yes or no.

CREATE THE RIGHT CONVERSATIONAL MOOD

The art of questioning includes knowing how to make your questions feel conversational with a natural ebb and flow. Do not begin with closed questions because too many of these will make it feel like an interrogation. A yes or no answer forces you to come up with another question, which can immediately make the conversation feel strained. You may need to practice this as most people who have not consciously developed the habit of asking open questions tend to use closed ones. It also helps to prepare and rehearse questions in advance for important meetings.

Make sure you respond to the answers someone gives to your questions. Don't just jump to the next one. This is where you get the opportunity to respond with some agreements, compliments, and common experiences. Instead of starting your next question with who, what, when, where, or why, structure the questions as follows:

> "This is very interesting…I would very much like to know *who* helped you to…?"

> "That is impressive. I would like to be able to follow a similar career path. *What* were the key steps you took to…?"

> "I had a similar experience with…. *When* did you realize…?"

> "This happens to be very relevant to me because….I would be very interested to know *where* you got…?"

"That is very helpful to me because….So *why* did you at that point decide to…?"

Remember the guide to likability at the beginning of this chapter. As your conversation progresses, you can use questions to gain insight into their thoughts, feelings, and opinions. Use questions like, "So what do you think about…?" "How do you feel about…?" "What is your opinion about…?" Each of these questions creates an opportunity to show interest, agree with them, draw parallels to your own experience, and give compliments.

Note: I am not recommending you falsely relate to people by pretending to have common experiences. Nor should you needlessly compliment them.

It has to be genuine. By using questions and showing interest in the other person, you will be able to uncover *real opportunities* to do so. Unless you have very proficient acting skills your body language will betray you. The chances are that if you try to fake this, you will come across as grossly insincere. Do not verbalize agreement if you do not agree. Do not do this robotically after every question or lay it on too thick.

However, do not disagree, either. Early in a relationship, especially in first meetings or early in an interview situation, there is very little to be gained from expressing your disagreement. You can either just say "that is interesting" and move on, or ask a clarifying question.

Instead of saying, "I think that is wrong because it will destroy XYZ," you ask, "That is interesting; how do you see that impacting XYZ?" Please note that when you say, "*That* is wrong," or stupid, or ridiculous, what the other person hears you say is "*You* are wrong, stupid, or ridiculous." I have met several intelligent people whose opinions are often correct but who disagree with others in a manner that offends them. As a result, they alienate themselves as other people avoid interacting with them.

Pointing out that someone is wrong, even when you are indisputably right, RARELY helps you connect or build a relationship.

Ask yourself first if the person's stated opinion in any way impacts your objective. If it does not—let it go. You do not have to correct everyone you meet all the time. If you are in a situation where you feel you have to, use the power of questions to help people come to different conclusions. Take your concern and turn it into a question. As they try to answer it, they will either convince you that they were right or realize there is a flaw and change their thinking themselves.

Note: Many interviewers specifically ask how you handle disagreement because it frequently occurs in day-to-day business life. If they do, you can now describe the use of questions to clarify and influence someone's opinion.

Certain topics, such as religion, race, politics, and sex, are danger zones. Stay well away from these! And remember to keep your language clean.

Remember, your objective at this stage is to be liked and to connect. Do not aggressively push closed questions in first meetings. As stated above, closed questions close the conversation while open questions open it up. You are trying to generate a flowing conversation to create a good experience. This, in turn, helps you find common ground and points on which you can agree, compliment, and elaborate further. Therefore, always begin with wide-open, general questions and uncontroversial subjects.

A NOTE ON ANSWERING QUESTIONS

It is important for you to recognize when questioning skills are being used on you, particularly during interviews. For example, you should now be able to recognize that open questions are intended to make you talk. Go with the flow and give descriptive answers that keep the conversation going. If you give short, monosyllabic answers to open questions, you will be perceived as moody, evasive, or hard to talk to. To appear friendly, open up a bit with descriptive sentences. Then ask an open question in return to keep the flow going. However…

Never talk longer than thirty seconds!

Make it a rule. Any longer and most people will get bored. The conversation will start to feel one-sided.

In interviews where pressured managers are short of time, keep your answers to open questions under 20 seconds, and then ask if your answers are what they were looking for to make sure you are on target.

If you get positive feedback, you can proceed for another 20 seconds before asking for feedback again.

When you receive a closed question, give a short, crisp answer *in less than five seconds.* Lengthy, meandering answers to closed questions will frustrate an interviewer who will think you are evasive. Closed questions are often used to confirm if something has been done or not. Look your interviewer in the eye and give a straight yes or no answer. This is the only way to engender confidence. The same applies to your boss once you are on the job. I have seen several talented (but overly talkative) individuals eliminate themselves in an interview, and from further progress up an organization, by failing to give short, direct answers when necessary.

Recognize when yes or no answers are being requested.

PREPARE AND PRACTICE

Many people, particularly those unaccustomed to asking questions, do not know what to ask about. They are afraid of asking a stupid question. It starts with preparation. Think about your objectives when you are planning to meet someone. Again, remember that initially we are focused on likability and connecting. The easiest approach is to start with wide-open questions around someone's background, and then use targeted open questions to clarify their answers. If you have the opportunity, do research prior to a meeting and find out specifics about your interviewer (things like previous positions, likes and dislikes even hobbies). This gives you a jumping-off point.

Once you are familiar with the concept of open and closed questions and how to ask and answer them, you will find the process surprisingly easy and enjoyable. These skills have wide applications—including, of course, first dates, with the added incentive that if you do this well enough, both parties may wish to drop the personal space rule!

In addition to brainstorming a list of potential questions ahead of time, build context in front of the question to set it up and make it seem natural. You can then follow a theme for a while. It's a practice you'll see among TV journalists.

For example, "I understand that you spent ten years in the military. How has that impacted your approach in business? What tactics and strategies from your military experience do you find applicable to the business world?"

Rehearse the questions out loud and see how they come across. It is worth role-playing important questions with someone. Some people find these exercises awkward and excessive, but role-playing immediately demonstrates if you are smooth or stumbling and gives you feedback on how the question felt. It gives you a chance to adjust it if necessary. When you ask it for real, it will sound much better.

DARE TO ASK

Many of us were discouraged from always asking "why" when we were young. If adults dampened our enthusiasm for questioning, they did us no favor. Having to memorize information in school may also have discouraged critical listening and questioning skills. As a result, we are often content to accept sound bites rather than digging deeper. Two techniques I use often are, *That is interesting, what **caused** that?"* and *"That is interesting, what is the **impact** of that?"* Variations of these two questions will help you clarify cause and effect to genuinely improve your understanding of any situation. They are also a great way to keep a conversation going.

Now is the time to bring back your curiosity. Ask questions, listen to the answers, and then ask more questions to clarify and confirm. Then relate and make a positive comment.

Note: Studies have shown that the failure to ask questions consistently ranks among the top 10 reasons candidates fail in interviews!

Questions are your best friends. Be aware of the different types, how to use them, and how to respond.

USE WORDS PEOPLE LISTEN TO

Assuming that we are interacting with agreeable facial expressions, body language, and vocal tone, let's talk about the actual words you use.

It has been well documented that people like to use certain words more than others.

Some of this is just habit. They use words they've adopted from their parents and other influencers in their lives such as teachers, culture, and peer groups.

Speech patterns can also relate to one of three senses: visual, auditory, or sensual. Some people want to *see* things, and they think with written words and diagrams. Others want to *hear* how things sound. They hear their thoughts and sometimes say them out loud to test them. Other people *feel* if something is good or bad, right or wrong. They talk about feeling things in their heart or gut.

Vocabulary can be influenced by the sense with which you most identify. For example, a visual person will use words like *appears, perceives, clarifies, sees, enlightens, vision, outlook,* and so on. An auditory person will use words like *listen, sounds like, telling,* and *I hear what you say.* A touch-oriented person uses words like *feel, grip, grasp, push, impact, firm,* and so on. Each has a vocabulary that is in tune with their predominant sense.

Why is this important?

Words are the building blocks of our thoughts, which drive our emotions and behavior.

We recognize, understand and pay more attention to words and phrases we regularly use ourselves. Therefore, if you use the same words someone else uses when you try to communicate a new thought to them, it is more likely they will listen and accept what you say. Such words, therefore, act as good "connectors."

There are a number of factors that shape your vocabulary. Organizations and departments within them can adopt certain phrases, technical jargon, and acronyms. Another source of different word use comes from different personality types as I will show you in the next section of this chapter. These differences are important to know and understand so you can adjust your language accordingly.

You can use this as an additional technique for building rapport. Ask open questions and listen carefully to the words they use. If you spot a trend, such as the frequent use of certain words, you can then respond and ask additional questions using similar words. This will make the other person subconsciously relate to you more easily.

When you "speak their language," other people intuitively listen more, understand better, and are more likely to accept what you say.

So for example, when you are in step two of the Alignment process, trying to uncover their top priority results, challenges, and consequent needs, listen carefully to the words they use to describe them. The more you use those same words, the more interviewers will subconsciously believe that you "get" their objectives and the easier it will be to cross their "credibility" threshold. Likewise the more you use their words as you go on to describe your own strengths and match them to their needs in step three, the more likely you will cross their "suitable for hire" threshold. Using their terms, phrases and acronyms as you describe how you can help overcome some of their top priority challenges in step four, will make you sound and feel as if you are already part of their team and make you fly over their "This is who we want!" threshold.

Note: There are also words you want to avoid using. Profanities are obviously out. However, many people develop a habitual use of redundant words and phrases such as *like, man, you know, um, sort of, really, cool,* and so on. Repetitive use of these words and phrases do not position you as an articulate communicator. I find myself counting the number of "likes" per sentence rather than paying any attention to what is being said.

PART III

HOW TO AVOID THE PERSONALITY CLASH

UNDERSTANDING FOUR COMMON PERSONALITY TYPES AND HOW TO RELATE TO THEM

There are a number of analysis tools available that can help you assess different personalities, including your own. These can help you significantly improve your interaction with others and help you assess your suitability for certain types of jobs. However, some of these have evolved to become quite complicated involving lengthy questionnaires and many subcategories that can combine to form many different personality types. These systems can be very accurate, however for the purposes of quickly aligning your behavior during a first meeting, I prefer the simplicity of the approach developed by psychologists Merrill and Reid.

Their system is based on four basic social styles, which we all have in varying degrees. It is the relative strengths of these social styles within each of us that produce certain personality and behavioral traits. These are easy to recognize within yourself as well as in others, especially during a meeting such as when networking or during an interview.

The objective of this section is to help you understand the most common behavior associated with the different predominant social styles and how the behavior of one social style can upset someone with a different social style.

Your first job is to recognize the predominant social style within yourself and how that affects your behavior. You then need to learn how to adjust your behavior to match the behavior of other people with different social styles.

This helps you avoid what is commonly called a "personality clash." It is just another way of aligning.

70

This approach will make your interaction smoother and will help you fit in. So let's look at the four basic social styles.

THE DRIVER

Drivers are characterized by a desire to get things done. They feel the pressure of time and therefore want to be in control. They like to focus on actions and results. They are usually strong-willed and decisive.

HOW TO RECOGNIZE DRIVERS: As people gain seniority, carry the weight of greater responsibility, and have less time available, they tend to develop Driver tendencies. For example, presidents or C-level executives (someone with "Chief " in their title) are likely to have a strong Driver aspect to their personalities. Their language includes words and phrases like *achieving tasks, meeting targets, deadlines, objectives, actions, results, measurements, growth, profit, cost control* and so on. They tend to lean forward when communicating and will interrupt the second you are off track. They frequently use phrases such as "I will" or "you must" when talking and tend to speak louder than average in a commanding tone. Everything is urgent and needs to be done now.

HOW TO RELATE TO THE DRIVER: Their time is short; wasting it will destroy your chances of developing a relationship or getting the job in an interview. I know a CEO with a strong Driver personality who has a brass sign on his desk that says in large letters "GET TO THE POINT!" Lean forward with good eye contact, use their words, talk about their tasks, actions, and challenges but never talk longer than 20 seconds. If asked to do something by a Driver, do not say, "I will try my best." Instead, say, "I will. Consider it done!"

THE ANALYTICAL

Analytical types are also task oriented but tend to be very structured and systematic. They want to understand the why and how of everything.

They want facts and logic. Analyticals try to see everything in black or white. (Shades of gray make them uncomfortable!) They like to plan and prepare in great detail.

HOW TO RECOGNIZE ANALYTICALS: You usually find Analytical people in the finance and technical sides of a business. Their shelves in their offices are often packed with reports, reference books, and technical manuals. They like to surround themselves with information. Their language is peppered with technical jargon, numbers, and logic. They like to become subject matter experts. They care about the reliability and comprehensiveness of their information. They use a quieter questioning tone.

HOW TO RELATE TO THE ANALYTICAL: They dislike drama, exaggerations, and people talking about themselves. Talk about their tasks and how they achieve them. When making a case, only use provable facts backed by evidence. Appear calm, balanced, and logical. Show appreciation for their analytical capabilities. When asked to do something, say "I will," followed by a brief explanation of how you plan to do so, to give them confidence in you.

THE EXPRESSIVE

Expressives are more people than task oriented. They too tend to talk in an above average loud voice. They are articulate, and they want to do the talking, mainly because they want to impress people. They have egos that need recognition. They like to use hyperbole themselves. They like high-energy, and creative people who like to win or be the best. They tend to be reactive rather than planners.

HOW TO RECOGNIZE THE EXPRESSIVE: You will usually find Expressive types in functions such as sales and marketing. They often dress well. Expensive suits, watches, shoes, and trophies are their symbols of success. Their offices often contain collections of trophies, photos with important people, awards, etc. They often talk about themselves and what they have accomplished. They are usually comfortable speaking in public.

HOW TO RELATE TO THE EXPRESSIVE: Match their energy and show them you are impressed. Not listening or ignoring their achievements will immediately upset them. Show confidence and a strong desire to succeed—just like them. Try to identify their terms and definitions of success, and use those when you answer their questions. If you see the interviewer in a photo with someone notable, make an enthusiastic comment: "You met the President? What was he like?" An Expressive will enjoy describing the occasion and in doing so, will give you plenty of opportunities to respond with compliments and agreement statements.

THE AMIABLE

Amiable types are primarily people oriented. Relationships are very important to them. In a networking meeting or an interview, they will try to make you feel comfortable and make it easy for you to connect. You *MUST* take advantage of that as they will be offended if you don't. They absolutely have to like you before you can move on. Although this is true of all the personality types in that none will recruit you if they *dislike* you; it is particularly important to Amiable types.

HOW TO RECOGNIZE THE AMIABLE: Amiable types are often quite tactile. They shake hands and can hold on for longer than other types. They will lay hands on your shoulder (note that Drivers and Analytics do not like this!). Amiable types like to talk about things relating to how everyone feels: staff motivation, team dynamics, customer satisfaction, and so on. They like to create harmony and dislike confrontation. They are often found in service-related positions. A key focus of their planning is to make sure everyone is in agreement with their plan.

HOW TO RELATE TO AN AMIABLE: Use their language to get through their filters to make sure you connect. They need to know that you care as much about them, and people in general, as they do. Take the time to make small talk and find strong connection points.

HOW THE DIFFERENT PERSONALITIES CAN EASILY CLASH

We all have personalities containing all four social styles but usually with a leaning towards one of them. If we are not careful, we can clash with people who lean towards another style.

Drivers can clash with all other styles including other Drivers. If you are a Driver by nature, you need to be careful not to instantly butt heads with another driver. They want you to be brief and to the point; but they do not want you to argue with them, especially in a networking or interview situation. Drivers can find Expressive types too flamboyant and distrust them. Likewise, they may find Amiable types too soft, too relationship-oriented, and not results-oriented enough. Drivers often feel that both Expressives and Amiables talk too much and don't get to the point quick enough. They like Analyticals because they are fact-oriented and to the point, but sometimes feel they lack drive and spend too much time analyzing rather than doing. Lean forward and behave like a Driver by being clear, actions and results focused. Drivers believe they control their fate, and they want to see that you do too.

Analytical types mainly like and trust other Analyticals. They tend to distrust Expressives and will dismiss any statements containing exaggerations. They are not particularly relationship-oriented, and strong Amiable types can make them uncomfortable particularly if they become tactile and invade their space. Your safest route is to behave like an Analytical by being very logical and fact-oriented.

Expressive types have egos that are easily offended. They do not like Drivers and Analytical types ignoring their achievements, interrupting, or brushing aside their overstatements. They can clash with other Expressives who compete with them for the limelight. Your safest bet is to appear Expressive by showing high levels of energy and passion, but not in any competitive way with them. Visibly demonstrate that they impress you through compliments. They like to be surrounded by people who want to be like them.

Amiable types trust mainly their own kind. They can find Drivers overbearing and bullying, Expressive types too self-centered, and Analyticals too cold. Your safest bet: appear Amiable. Show interest in them personally, and really make sure you connect well first before going on to any business.

It may sound hokey, but there are decades of research that supports this approach. It is very easy to hinder your ability to relate well to another person if you do not understand the effects of your social style on their social style.

There are substantial businesses based entirely on teaching other organizations how to take social styles into account when recruiting, team building and promoting their staff.

You may, therefore, find yourself having to take a personality test. It is certainly a common interview question to ask you to describe yourself. This approach gives you a professional way to respond. So take the time to think about which social style is most dominant in your personality. See if you recognize any of the associated behavior I have described coming from yourself. Then practice analyzing others around you and see which of the above social styles their behavior matches.

Remember that people like other people who resemble themselves. Your safest bet is to assess who you are interacting with in terms of their strongest social styles and then adjust your behavior to be similar to theirs.

This will make connecting and developing a relationship much easier.

Many managers (often without realizing or being prepared to admit it)—like to recruit people who they perceive as versions of themselves.

PART IV

GROW CONNECTIONS INTO RELATIONSHIPS

WHY CONNECTIONS ARE NOT ENOUGH

So far, we have worked on your ability to connect with other people. We have covered how to be accepted and liked by others based primarily on first impressions. This was designed to maximize your instant "like and trust" impact. Let's take it to the next level by developing skills to build relationships that are mutually beneficial and sustainable over time.

The fact that we have made a connection and established our acceptance and likability with someone only means that they are *open* to helping us. Simply knowing someone, even after creating a favorable, initial impression, is not enough.

For a person to spend significant time with you to give you advice, introduce you to others, and even hire you themselves, they require a POSITIVE RELATIONSHIP.

Beyond networking, relationships are also vital once you are in a job because they exist whether you like it or not. They are often created through organizational structure and the duties of the job. The only question is if they are positive or negative. The answer will significantly affect your enjoyment and performance.

For many people, even a single poor relationship in the workplace can become a major distraction, drain their energy, and spark feelings of isolation.

This is especially true if that relationship is with the boss.

The number one reason why so many people do not enjoy their jobs or perform up to expectations is because they failed to build the right relationships with their managers.

Interviewers, therefore, base a significant part of their decisions on whether or not they feel you have the long-term relationship-building skills to work effectively with them, their team, and their customers. They know that your inability to get along with your boss and colleagues does not just affect *your* well-being and performance, but also that of *everyone else* you do not get along with.

You need to be able to genuinely build the right relationships with the people around you.

FILL GOODWILL TANKS

You may find it useful to think in terms of everyone having a tank where they store their goodwill for you. Everything you say or do will either add to or detract from the goodwill tank. Look for opportunities to add to it by smiling, saying thank you, asking how they are, offering positive comments and compliments, giving credit or encouragement, being loyal, being humorous and upbeat, and offering genuine help.

Being down emotionally—frowning, criticizing, complaining and gossiping, exuding pessimism or cynicism—and always appearing tired and reluctant to help, will empty the goodwill tank and undermine your relationship. With each and every connection, visualize the goodwill tank and ask yourself if you have been filling or draining it.

For example, if you ask someone for more favors than you give, you create an imbalance that becomes detrimental to the relationship. Over time, this brings about emotions of resentment and anger. It takes only *two* consecutive instances of this nature before these feelings start to take root.

Volunteering to help others is a good way to build genuine goodwill in relationships BEFORE ever asking for anything yourself.

As you build a relationship, look for areas where you can help. Targeted open questions such as "What are some of the challenges you are facing?" or "What problems keep you awake at night?" can uncover opportunities for you to help. When I say "help," I *do* mean help—something you can actually do, not just advice. Make yourself available to actually do something for the other person even if it is just an introduction to someone else that can help them.

ADVICE ON GIVING ADVICE

When you develop expertise on anything, it can become very tempting to give advice to others. You feel they need it, and you think you are helping them. It seems like a great way to add to their goodwill tank. Unfortunately, if you are not careful, this can make you seem overbearing and actually drain the tank.

People simply do not appreciate advice unless they specifically ask for it.

Even then, keep your sound bites short, no more than 20 seconds, then check to see if you are making sense and if they agree or have had enough.

In fact, asking others for advice, followed by showing your appreciation for the advice, is a far more effective way of cementing relationships.

By asking for advice, you have indicated that you think they have expertise, which is a compliment. Their advice gives you opportunities to agree with them and to thank them, all of which contribute toward good interactions. This also offers opportunities to come back later and say, "Hey, I did as you recommended, and it really worked out. Thanks again!" You just added another positive interaction.

Meanwhile, you only have to give unsolicited advice once too often or for 10 seconds too long before you're labeled a "know-it-all." Additionally, you have also made the other person feel inferior and risked the possibility that the person disagrees with your advice. *None of this makes for a good experience that will add to the goodwill tank.*

MAKE EVERY INTERACTION A POSITIVE EXPERIENCE

Positive relationships are created and then sustained by ensuring *consistently* positive experiences. Sounds obvious, however:

All it takes is ONE poor interaction to make a relationship questionable.

Leave all of your judgments—opinions, grumpiness, and desire to "be right"—at the door. Align yourself to ensure *everyone* has a positive experience when interacting with you, not just the first time you meet but *every* time you meet. *Remind yourself of this before each meeting.*

An important factor in deciding whether to meet you again and embark on a relationship or whether to continue a relationship—is TRUST.

People want to be confident that you will not criticize them behind their backs. Therefore, avoid the THREE C's: *criticizing, condemning, and complaining* about anyone (or anything). Instead, be visibly ethical and loyal to the key people around you, as this will reassure everyone. People only have to observe you dishing out behind-the-back criticism or take advantage of someone once, and then they will always wonder if you will do it to them, too.

It takes only one breach of trust for your connections to disconnect!

Note: One of the quickest ways to lose a job is to criticize your manager in front of colleagues. There will always be people who think they can benefit from telling your boss. There goes the job and any chance of counting on your manager as a reference to get another one. Avoid participating in any negative discussions and encourage people to talk to the boss about their issues instead.

USE RELATIONSHIP HEALTH CHECKS

Relationships can turn sour without you even realizing it. Under pressure, you might say something insensitive, or someone else could make a comment that undermines your relationship. Sometimes outside influences or conflicts of interest can force you to compromise something that has a negative impact. Life is unpredictable. Things happen.

Regularly sit down with the important people in your life, such as your boss and the people you plan on using as references, colleagues, and customers to check the levels in their goodwill tanks.

Here are two useful relationship maintenance tips:

USE A CHECKLIST

Go through each of your relationships and consider the following:

Can the person relate to you easily? Have you assessed their strongest social style? Have you aligned your appearance, behavior, face, body language, tone of voice, and choice of words?

Have you connected? Have you found common ground in terms of experiences and opinions?

How is the person's interaction experience with you? Are you smiling, welcoming, courteous, humorous, agreeing, complimenting. *Always?*

Do you have sufficient quantity and quality of communication in place? Are you spending enough face-to-face time and not distancing yourself?

Have you built enough understanding about that person and vice versa? Have you asked enough questions? Do you understand their priority needs? Have you created an even ebb and flow in your conversations by volunteering information about yourself too? Do they understand your priorities?

Are you trusted both ethically and in terms of reliability? Have you made a point of appearing trustworthy? Avoided any disloyalty, been punctual, and delivered on what you say you will?

Are you adding value? Have you volunteered to help or introduced the person to anyone else of value? Are you building expertise that they might need?

Do you have relationship-eroding behavior? Criticizing, complaining, or being too needy? Do you put more in their goodwill tank than you take out?

Imagine the person was rating you on a scale of 1 to 10 on each of the above. What do you think you would score? Is there anyone you would *not* feel comfortable actually asking to rate you on any of these questions? If so, chances are that relationship is not optimal.

GET INSTANT FEEDBACK

Develop the habit of asking for instant feedback after any interaction. Ask questions such as:

> "Did this conversation go as you expected?"

> "Did I answer your questions?"

> "Are you comfortable with how this meeting went?"

> "Do you have any other concerns?"

> "Is there anything else I can help you with?"

Especially with Amiable and Expressive types, preface the above questions with "How do you feel?" It gives them an opportunity to express any discomfort that could erode the relationship. This way you can deal with it up front rather than allow it to fester without realizing. Watch their body language as some people are too polite or shy to voice their feelings. With Drivers and Analyticals it is better to use "What do you think?"

SUMMARY

IS ALL THIS CONNECTING AND RELATIONSHIP STUFF REALLY NECESSARY?

Throughout my entire career, I never once landed a job by applying to an advertisement. Every job, every promotion, every major business deal

I was involved in occurred because of the help I received from relationships. However, you cannot build good relationships if you cannot connect with people first, and such relationships will not last long if you do not nurture them. I can also trace the root cause of most things that did not go well in my life, to relationships I failed to build or nurture properly.

To prepare yourself to meet people, both to make valuable connections and to pass the "do we like and trust you?" threshold in interviews, take note of how other people appear, sound, think, and behave, and then adapt your behavior to align yourself with them. Do this by managing your facial expressions and your words, plus your tone. Use open questions to find opportunities to relate, agree, and compliment. This will give you an excellent chance of connecting and building rapport, which makes any further communication easier and much more productive. Then sustain those relationships by paying attention to the levels in their goodwill tanks, and make sure that every experience with you is a positive one.

Note: It is not just the big events in your life that depend on relationships.

Everything that goes on around you in an organization revolves around relationships, too. Some people think there is no place for feelings or emotions of any kind in the workplace. They believe people are obligated to do their jobs by fulfilling their tasks, and that's it. They view it in terms of black and white; relationships just complicate things.

Businesses are constantly evolving, trying to catch up to changes in the markets and new strategies coming from the top. As a result, objectives that were previously defined up and down the organization often don't fit together as they should. (In many cases they were never properly defined in the first place.) Management regularly changes people's top priorities, often failing to make sure that everyone who is dependent on those results is fully informed. Things are rarely black and white—and are usually *far* from perfect.

Also, never forget that organizations are made up of people. None of them are perfect in terms of their skills, attitudes, or priorities, either. They have emotions, including fear of change and failure. They have needs for belonging, recognition, respect, and courtesy. Some are downright lazy while others desire growth and success. There is jealousy, resentment, greed, and hunger for power.

Ignore any of this at your peril!

There is only one way you can succeed inside imperfect organizations made up of imperfect people.

If you want to understand what results are expected and how to deliver them, especially with the cooperation of others, you need to have the best possible professional relationships with all of the key individuals involved, especially the boss.

In fact, a good way to look at any organization is to view it as a network of people all supposedly cooperating with each other to get things done. How well *you* can get things done in this environment depends a great deal on how well you are connected within this network—and your ability to connect depends entirely on the interpersonal skills described in this chapter.

Good interviewers will expect you to understand this. They will challenge you to articulate how you build and maintain the critical relationships around you. *They will expect examples.*

Now let's put these interpersonal skills to use as we start looking for a job.

CHAPTER THREE

FINDING A JOB!

PART I

WHERE DO YOU START?

**"Dreams are extremely important.
You can't do it unless you imagine it."**

George Lucas

DO YOU KNOW WHAT YOU WANT TO DO?

These are important questions at *any stage* in your career.

Firstly, "Why do you want *this* job?" is a very common interview question. Employers want to know what your motivations are, how those drove you to prepare your relevance, and how they will drive your performance.

Secondly, employers will continue to ask you the same question once you have the job. They want to know that you have the motivation to keep developing new skills and keep improving your performance.

An inability to answer with clarity and conviction why you want a new job will very likely cost you the opportunity. The same inability in an existing job will soon affect both your attitude toward the job and the attitude of your boss toward you. This will certainly impact your chances of promotion and possibly your longer term employment too.

Unfortunately, most people spend far too little time really thinking about this in enough detail. This is absolutely a root cause for long periods of unemployment or underemployment, why many people end up in jobs they do not enjoy and end up quitting or being terminated.

When they do start thinking about their career, especially early on, they focus almost entirely on what they think they would enjoy doing, is interesting to them, and will be fulfilling. They want a job they have a passion for. There is nothing wrong with any of that.

However;

Beware of the over-hyped recommendations of "Just follow your passion."

What most people forget to take into account is the market need for what they want to do, their current ability vs. the competition, and what an employer would be prepared to pay for these activities.

The world is littered with disillusioned and penniless individuals and companies who just followed their passion without taking other things into consideration. To answer the what and why of your career direction in a meaningful and helpful way, you have to work through quite a comprehensive set of questions that cover not just your present situation but your longer term future too. What you enjoy now may leave you in a very poor position later. Conversely, being prepared to do something you do not enjoy much now could be a requirement for you to be able to do what you really want later.

For example, a key additional dimension to the above three areas of what you would consider enjoyable, interesting, and fulfilling is your desired lifestyle.

- What kind of lifestyle do you want in terms of family, house, car, meals and entertainment, hobbies, sports, holidays, education for children, health coverage, etc.? How does this change over time?
- What does your desired lifestyle cost and how will that change over time?
- Which jobs involve doing the activities you like and what do they pay? What career paths do such jobs put you on, and will they support your long-term lifestyle desires?
- What lifestyle sacrifices are you prepared to make as you balance short and long-term goals?

In Chapter One, we stressed our emphasis on finding individuals who had an ambition that drove them to perform well. We looked for people who defined their future by setting themselves goals. Sadly I meet people in their thirties and forties who don't enjoy their jobs and who still don't really know what they would prefer to do instead. They have no goals. It is no surprise that they are rarely the top performers or the ones being promoted. The good news;

It is never too late to start defining a new vision of a new better future and plotting a course to get there.

However, there is a clock ticking. The earlier you start, the more time you have to reach your goals. The later you leave it the harder it becomes. Therefore, I want to begin by addressing students—however the principles in this section can be applied at any stage in your career.

I start most of my speaking engagements at Universities or Colleges by asking for a show of hands to indicate who clearly knows what they want to do when they graduate. Usually, less than 20 percent of the audience will raise their hands. I then ask them to keep their hands raised until they are no longer quite so sure while I ask some more questions to see how specific they are. For example, I ask:

How many people with the job "you want" have you spoken to in detail about what they do all day?

Including;

- Why were they interested in the job?
- What strengths most helped them get the job? Why?
- What do they like doing most in the job and why?
- What do they dislike or find most challenging in the job and why?
- What results will be expected of them and how are they measured?
- What is the impact of success or failure—what are the consequences and to whom?
- What are they learning on the job?

- What career path will the job take them on? What is the next level job up?
- What is their lifestyle like now? What lifestyle do they anticipate later in their career?

How many managers of the job you want, have you met and asked the same type of questions?

Including what should the profile of the ideal candidate look like?

Such as;

- What are the top skills most needed?
- What attitudes are most sought after?
- What work experience is required?
- What personality types succeed and what types fail?
- Based on what my profile looks like now—what do I need to do to improve my chances of being selected for this job? What are my gaps?
- What is the salary range of this type of job
- What promotion opportunities does this job qualify you for?

As I go through the above questions, most hands start coming down.

It has been my experience that most people do NOT know what they want to DO. Those who claim they do know—tend to think in terms of job titles that they have heard or read about. They don't really know what the job actually DOES or what attributes they need to maximize their chances of winning the selection process and succeeding in the job.

Once most of the hands have come down I ask;

"Who has been told not worry about the fact that they don't know what they want to do?"

Usually, most people in the room raise their hands. I ask the audience to tell me what they have been told by whom. The most common answer is very consistent. It comes from parents, teachers and family friends and goes something along the following lines.

"It's okay, don't worry. I had no idea what to do either when I was your age. You'll figure it out soon enough."

Here comes another important message in the book.

Not knowing what you want to do—is not okay!

Unless you take specific actions, you may not figure it out for a long time. This can have very negative consequences.

Let me explain.

According to Complete College America, over 64 % of students switch majors and take an extra 2 years to complete their degree racking up over 20,000 dollars in extra costs per year—often added to their already ballooning student debts.

According to After College, 84% of college students have no job lined up by the time they graduate.

As I have quoted before, according to Accenture, half of all graduates then take over 2 years to land a career job.

Let's look at the impact of these statistics combined.

If it takes you two extra years to complete college and another two years to land a job, you can start a degree at the same time as a friend and end up FOUR YEARS behind them.

While you are struggling to land your first pay check to cover your debts that have extended by over $40,000, your friend is landing their second promotion. Over that four-year-period, your friend will have earned between $120,000 and $150,000. This can become a continuing pattern. If you end up choosing a job that you don't enjoy (which can easily happen out of desperation), before long you may be back at square one looking for another job while your friend is on their third promotion. As stated earlier, this pattern can result in a serious "life crisis" in your late twenties and early thirties as you feel totally left behind.

How and why does this happen?

Sure we can blame the education system for requiring too many credits and not having critical courses available when you need them. We can blame the economy for a shortage of suitable openings. However as I will repeatedly stress, the theme of this book is that you own your own future.

Some people clearly do complete within four years and land a job of their choice almost immediately. How?

Here is one of the reasons—one that *YOU* can control.

When you clearly know what you want and why, you develop a much higher level of energy and focus on getting it.

Therefore, you have to have a dream of your desired future—a detailed and vivid one!

Think back to when you last wanted a new latest and greatest watch, cell phone, laptop, or a new car. Maybe it was some critical equipment for your favorite sport or hobby or a new pet. You go on the Internet to look at blogs, forums, and websites. You research pros, cons and prices. Once you decide what you want, you can't help imagining what it is like to already have the item. In your mind you see the watch on your wrist, you see yourself driving the new car with your friends in it, you hear the incredible sound of that new guitar, you feel the warmth and love of that new puppy.

You want it! Your vision sparks an obsession to get it.

Your new heightened awareness causes you to start seeing other people with your chosen item everywhere. You talk to strangers to ask them if they like their choice, and they seem happy to tell you. Suddenly you are willing to hustle to get it. You don't see yourself as a hustler, but there you are justifying it and cutting a deal with your parents, your spouse or your boss for approval. Next, you are negotiating with different sources to get it at the lowest price. You are prepared to drive incredible distances to get it. It's not long before you have it.

Sound familiar?

So how is this relevant? Here is a universal principle.

The strength of your vision for the desired future will determine your level of focus, energy and commitment to complete the actions required to turn that vision into reality.

I recommend you read that sentence a couple of times!

The key to a vision's strength is the level of detail. The more details you have about feeling part of a team of people you like, doing something worthwhile, and enjoying the rewards in terms of a nice lifestyle, car, house, spouse, and interesting holidays—the more desirable and compelling the vision becomes and the greater the priority becomes to achieve it.

The following alignment activities will start to happen naturally:

- For students, you will search for greater relevance and interest in what you are studying. You will be able to select your courses more wisely and study with greater motivation and intensity. Your number of credits per semester and your grades will go up. You are significantly more likely to complete your degree inside four years.
- Networking will become less something you are told you must do and instead become something you enjoy doing as you find out more details about what you want to do and where you can do it.
- You will be able to target relevant internships that will provide worthwhile experience and have a greater chance of landing them.

You will put more effort into them and therefore get more out of them.

- You will start to associate with people who are doing what you want to do. You will become "like" them by building similar experience, speaking the same language, even dressing similarly.

By the time it comes to the interview, you will appear to be *a natural fit into their culture.* Your focus on building your relevancy will ensure that you have *the capability for the job.* You will be able to talk knowledgeably about their challenges to trigger a "This is who we want!" emotion. Everything you have been doing can be positioned as preparing for the job because *you wanted it!* You will clearly demonstrate that you have the *passion and ambition employers look for.*

In fact, you will already appear as if you are part of their team.

This is how you can secure a job before you have even graduated!

Those who postpone "figuring out what they want to do" until after graduation are often the ones who will take much longer to graduate and land their career job.

Without a vision driving you to take the above actions, you will *NOT* appear like you are already part of the team when you go for interviews. You will overwhelmingly look, sound and behave like a student—*one who still has to find their ambition.* This is *not* what employers are looking for.

All other attributes being equal between two candidates in a selection process, the individual who has a dream and has prepared sufficiently by setting and achieving goals to make it a reality—will win every time!

Note: This applies throughout your career. Whatever job you are in, if it is not on a path to your vision, the chances are that you are drifting rather than powering forward. Sooner or later this will negatively affect your enjoyment and performance which in turn will affect your chances of retaining the job and getting promoted.

Consistently successful people do not drift and stumble into their future achievements. One of my favorite quotes sums it up.

"The best way to predict your future is to create it!"

Abraham Lincoln

Successful people build a vision, break it down into goals and do the work to create their future.

So where do you start?

There is a widely held belief that the first thing you should do is to "look within yourself" to find out your personality type, what you like to do and what you are good at. Then you can start your journey by looking for opportunities that play to those strengths.

TAKING YOUR PERSONALITY TYPE INTO ACCOUNT

In Chapter Two we referred to four different personality or social styles. They are the Driver, the Analytical, the Expressive and the Amiable. There have been many studies that have accurately linked how well these different social styles perform in different jobs. Let's go through a few obvious examples to illustrate this. A strong Analytical type would do better in jobs that require a large amount of detailed analysis without involving much interaction with other people than say Expressive or Amiable types who are very people oriented. Meanwhile, an Analytical is less likely to do well in jobs that require extensive interpersonal interaction such as sales or customer service. Amiable types don't do well in jobs involving a great deal of confrontation. Drivers are not well suited to caregiving roles.

In fact, if someone has succeeded over a significant period of time in a particular role, you can often predict their dominant social styles just by looking at the requirements of the job.

Employers are increasingly taking this into account and will, therefore, try to assess your personality type to make sure it is suitable for the job they are offering. Many are resorting to personality tests. It is worth making the effort to think about your own personality and the type of jobs that you are more likely to enjoy and succeed in.

However, do not do this self-assessment in isolation for too long. This is not a one-time exercise that you need to make as comprehensive as possible at the start. This is a journey in self-awareness, rather than a one-time assessment to determine who you are and therefore what you should or shouldn't pursue in terms of a job for the rest of your life.

Build your awareness of the different personality types including which one you are. Then make it part of your research when you network to find out which jobs interest you. Always ask what type of personality is believed to be most suited to the job you are researching.

Ask specific questions about the position that speak to the strengths and weakness of your personality. For example, find out whether the job involves primarily detailed analytical work or people facing work. If you find a difference between what social style your connections say is best suited for the jobs you like and the social style that best describes you, then you need to discuss this and understand what the implications are and make doubly sure that you want to pursue those types of jobs. A significant part of why graduates do not last in their first jobs (20% are terminated or quit within six months) is because of a mismatch between their personality versus those best suited for the job.

So yes, I do recommend some upfront, high-level self-analysis, but I have listed three reasons below on why you should also just get out there, meet people and learn about different jobs firsthand, as soon as possible.

Do not make self-analysis another justification to stay at home.

This is especially important for Analytical types!

1. You *WILL CHANGE* your views.

Although several authors claim studies show that your results from per-sonality tests do not change much over time, *I believe they can.*

As you leave a college environment and start the first few years in the workforce, you will be exposed to many different activities and experiences you had not even considered when you first looked within yourself. Even though some tests prompt you to consider a range of activities and choose between them, in the absence of *real experience*, I think it is unwise to rely too much on the results.

In fact, asking people before they have had any experience in the workforce, what they think they are likely to enjoy and be good at is a bit like asking caterpillars the same questions before metamorphosis. Few caterpillars would rate flying as their preferred activity and strength.

If you adopt the steps of alignment, develop the right attitudes and commit to well-structured training, you will go through very significant changes—that for many come close to a metamorphosis.

I have witnessed this repeatedly.

I have seen people join our organization absolutely convinced they know what they want to do, but 18 months later they are immersed in something completely different and loving it.

2. Will your initial likes and strengths be *RELEVANT*?

The danger, especially early in your career, is that "what you like to do and think you are good at" may not be very impressive or relevant to many potential employers.

What really matters as far as getting a job and succeeding in it is that you do something well that a prospective employer is prepared to pay you for.

This approach of looking within yourself is in my opinion, very helpful to give you some direction and particularly to eliminate areas you feel 100% sure you do *not* like. It makes sense that if you feel hopelessly numbers-challenged, don't become an accountant or an actuary. Just be careful you do not limit yourself too much in the process as it is incredible what you can become good at—and really enjoy—if you motivate yourself to do so. More on this in point 3 below.

The "looking within yourself" approach says, *"This is who I am; what opportunities are out there that fit me?"* This can be quite limiting depending on your analysis. The approach I recommend says, *"What opportunities are out there that I like the sound of and what strengths do I need to develop to fit them?"* This extends your range of opportunities considerably.

Use your connections to find out what you need to learn to do well in order for you to ace the interview and succeed in the job. Then research what it will take to develop those skills. Only then start narrowing down your choices.

3. *You CAN CHANGE* your strengths and likes.

I will show you in Chapter Twelve how your perceptions of your strengths and likes are affected by your thoughts and consequent attitudes. If you control your thoughts and commit to a structured learning approach, you can significantly improve your capability in most activities. In his book "Talent Is Overrated" Geoff Colvin makes a compelling argument that many of the absolute top performers in their field got there through something he calls "deliberate practice" rather than natural talent.

As soon as you start to improve your performance in any activity and get a compliment from your boss, you will also LIKE that activity more.

This starts a positive, self-reinforcing cycle that can completely change your views of your strengths and preferences.

QUICK STORY

We had people whom we thought were extreme introverted, analytical types in our accounting team. This was an issue because we wanted them to present our financials to us at our board meetings. They would have rather died than speak in front of an audience, especially a senior and sometimes intimidating audience. However after some training, practice and genuine appreciation from executive board members they found that they really enjoyed giving presentations. Suddenly Expressive tendencies were starting to surface! I would find them in our boardroom eagerly waiting to present how a certain part of our business was performing. They changed!

So don't lock yourself in your bedroom immersed in endless self-analysis tests. I have met more than a few recent graduates who in the absence of real-world experience, either became unnecessarily depressed or unjustifiably optimistic about their career prospects. Too much self-analysis in isolation can be counterproductive.

Get out there and meet people at all levels in all types of jobs. Find out exactly what they do all day and how they got good at it.

This is the only way you will get firsthand, reliable information from which you can make a decision on how closely the requirements of the job fit your existing preferences and talents. It is also the best way to get a sense of what it will take to develop yourself into the ideal candidate.

Not making the effort to get the information to be able to target specific jobs results in many people staying at home and adopting the following very flawed strategies to find a job.

THE MOST COMMON STRATEGIES AND WHY THEY DON'T WORK

SPRAYING AND PRAYING

This approach usually begins with a sudden urgent realization that it is time to do something about getting a job.

Unfortunately, this is usually a direct result of people not knowing what they want to do—so they do nothing for way too long.

Then someone recommends some self-assessment and based on the results a resume is then hastily put together around what the candidates now believe their strengths are and what they think they want to do. This is then emailed in the largest quantities possible. Doing this is relatively easy, which makes job seekers think they are "comprehensively covering" the market. In their imaginations, their life summaries and strengths end up on the screens of decision makers who can't wait to read them and who will immediately fire off a return email to arrange an interview. They rarely feel the sting of any specific rejection and certainly no unpleasant feedback on why they were not suitable. It all feels highly productive and satisfying when they count up how many they have sprayed across the Internet.

Does this work?

No.

It is generally thought that only about 5% of people find a job this way.

Why?

In the first chapter, we talked about the importance of *aligning* your capabilities with the *specific objectives* of the organization.

Sending the same resume to many different organizations in the hope of a hit is the exact opposite of alignment.

Organizations are bombarded with generic, poorly written, irrelevant resumes full of overhyped generic capabilities that most candidates do not live up to.

Employers concluded long ago that selecting interview candidates from the incoming resume pool is mostly a waste of valuable time and expense. Yet this remains one of the most popular strategies. More than a few readers are likely thinking, *"Damn!"*

Note: Although this strategy rarely produces any specific rejections and therefore feels good initially, *there is a danger.* After a significant period of minimal responses, many people conclude that either nobody wants them or that there are no opportunities out there. This can develop into a very counterproductive and often self-fulfilling mindset that prevents job seekers from taking other, far more productive actions.

If you ever get tempted by this approach, repeat after me:

"Spray and pray doesn't pay!"

CHASING JOB LISTINGS

Other job seekers search company websites and employment boards responding to specific listings. That seems to make more sense, right? At least they are targeting official job openings. Again, they can cover a lot of ground with minimal strain from the safety of home, and there's little immediate rejection involved.

Does it work?

No, not really, and for pretty much the same reasons the first approach doesn't. It is basically just a variation of the spray and pray approach.

Companies are fed up sorting through resumes that do not address their needs. As with the above process, only about 5% of people who actually landed jobs did it that way. Another reason the percentage is so low is that not all companies publicly advertise their job vacancies. Many jobs are filled without ever being advertised.

There is an often-quoted statistic that says less than 30% of jobs are publicly advertised, and more than 70% are filled through word of mouth.

Given that 90% of applicants focus on the 30% of jobs that are advertised, applying to an advertised job puts you in the most-competed-for section of the market. This is where "your resume has between 5 and 10 seconds to make an impact, or it's in the shredder" really does apply!

If you are using a resume that has not been tailored to stand out in a very relevant way, you may have a higher chance of winning the lottery.

Do not send a generic resume to a job posting!

HOW EMPLOYERS LIKE TO RECRUIT

Let's take a step back and understand how employers tend to recruit, particularly the differences between large and small organizations.

Bigger organizations have human resources departments that specialize in finding the right candidates. They have well-developed relationships with colleges and universities for entry-level staff. They work with large national and global headhunters for more senior recruits. They often run extensive personality tests and interviews, after which they prepare short lists for managers with vacancies who then interview the candidates again. This can be a lengthy and arduous process for both sides.

The top end is *very* competitive because many people want to be part of a prestigious company with good training programs, one that is going to be around for a long time and provides seemingly limitless upward potential. These employers can, therefore, select candidates with the absolute top grades, preferably from well-known universities, and with the most impressive extracurricular involvement (think internships, presidents of fraternities or sororities, captains of sports teams, various societies, and so on.)

To really have a chance to break into the large organizations, you need to understand what it's going to take very early.

The decisions you made and the results you achieved in high school will already have opened or closed critical doors to these opportunities.

If you were not getting top grades in high school and lining up relevant programs of study in the right universities, your chances are quite limited. Once at the university, if you are not getting top grades, demonstrating leadership, and maintaining a high level of contact with your target organizations, you will struggle to get the internships and subsequent permanent job offers. The challenge is tough, but the prizes are great at the big-name organizations.

However, they are not the only game in town, and not everything bigger is always better.

In a large, multilayered organization, you can find yourself in a rigid structure with lots of rules, regulations, and seemingly inflexible pay grades. You can easily get stuck in a specialized role with little exposure to senior executives or the bigger business picture. And just because a large organization is going to be around a long time, it does not mean your position will.

At the other end of the scale, small companies often find people through connections such as existing staff, family, friends, and customers. They rely on the premise that a recommended friend of the family is likely to fit into the company culture. They are quicker to make offers with less process, acting on input from the team, and have a probation period to vet and rapidly exit candidates if they do not work out.

In smaller organizations, you are more likely to get early exposure to senior executives, and experience less red tape. You can be closer to the business objectives and are more likely to encounter a variety of business challenges. They may not have the formal training programs, but this experience can make you well-rounded, self-sufficient, and much more business-savvy than someone who has only been in a highly specialized role, surrounded by a comprehensive support system in a large organization.

Last, a great way to make some serious money is to join a company while it is small, perform well, get promoted, and earn some equity through stock options or buying stock. In this way, you can rise to a senior executive position in a company that by then has grown into a substantially larger one in which your stock options are much more valuable!

These differences in recruiting practices create a range of job openings. At one end you have the highly competitive, process-driven opportunities in large, well-known organizations. At the other, you have unadvertised jobs in smaller companies that quietly recruit through their networks.

The good news?

It is the smaller companies that create most of the entry-level jobs in the market.

This means your best approach to land the majority of jobs in the market is to build a network of connections to smaller companies. With the right skills and effort, this is something anyone can do.

"All right, then!" some people react. "We can keep drinking until we scrape through graduation, and then we just network with smaller organizations!"

On the contrary, this is not the time to ease up. Competition is fierce at *all* levels. Do not delude yourself into thinking that by forgetting about the big brands and aiming for the smaller ones that you will have it easy. For one thing, smaller companies also want the best and brightest they can get. Second, all the top-level graduates who did not make it into the big brands will be competing with you for jobs in the smaller ones.

Another question I often hear is whether networking applies when targeting the larger organizations since their recruiting is much more process-driven. In fact, some of them are quite strict in directing you to follow their processes rather than encouraging any informal dialogue. Their human resources departments want to control the process to ensure the overall organization does not end up with lots of inconsistencies.

However, some of their managers can be tempted to recruit quickly to meet the pressure of growing workloads when they are presented with a good candidate through their networks. They will try to avoid lengthy internal processes and make a fast decision. This is particularly true within large organizations that are made up of many smaller subsidiaries that still demonstrate some of the independent behaviors of smaller companies. Networking, therefore, *can* pay off.

You may not be able to avoid the centrally controlled process entirely (or at all), but at least you will have found your way into the process and gained inside knowledge—and support from your contact—on how to win it. This is a HUGE advantage!

So regardless of the size of the organization you target, nothing beats networking when targeting and finding a job. It is believed that as many as 70% of people land jobs this way. You should, too, so let's look at networking next.

PART II

BUILDING A PROFESSIONAL NETWORK

WHAT IS NETWORKING?

This is *not* just about collecting names and numbers.

Your objective is to build a genuine network of people who have both the ABILITY and the DESIRE to help you target, align and land a job.

This is where you put the interpersonal skills you learned in Chapter Two into action. You have to identify people who are in a position to be able to help you, and then build positive relationships with them. This will nearly always involve face-to-face meetings where you use your skills to be instantly likable and find common ground to relate to them. You have to find ways to put some goodwill in their tanks and develop relationships in which they are happy to help you.

WHY YOU SHOULD NETWORK

IN A NUTSHELL

Connections can help you understand what specific jobs are actually like, so you can choose a direction and ultimately target specific jobs. They can help you understand what the top priorities in such jobs are and therefore what qualities are required for these jobs so you can develop them and align yourself to be a good match. They can help you locate live opportunities by alerting you to what jobs may already be open—or might be soon. They can then give you details on how to position yourself during the selection process. This is known as the "inside track." They can introduce you to other people who have useful knowledge, or they can influence hiring decisions or even make the decision to hire you themselves.

Let's look at the key reasons to network in detail.

FINDING YOUR DIRECTION – TARGETING A JOB

Initially, networking will help you get genuinely useful information about day to day life in different jobs and career paths. It is a great way to explore options and help develop your interest in particular types of organizations and specific roles within them.

Start by making connections across a wide variety of jobs and industries. If you feel drawn to a certain type of job, try to meet as many people in that function within different industries as you can. For example, marketing roles within one industry can involve the same marketing principles as in another, but how such principles are applied and the actual feel of the job can vary enormously. If you like what you hear about an organization, you can focus on getting more contacts inside it. Think about similar organizations, such as competitors, suppliers, and customers. These are a great source of additional contacts and can give you a valuable perspective on what the people in the primary organization you're targeting are like to deal with. This broad approach will give you a comprehensive understanding of any industry and any attractive roles within it.

I meet many students and graduates who have no idea what they want to do. Every time this happens, I ask whether they are seriously networking. Sadly, the answer is *always* no. Networking is really the only way to build a detailed enough understanding of the different jobs out there so you can choose a direction. The more people you meet, the more likely you will find roles that appeal to you. You will be utterly amazed at how many different types of jobs there are that you had never heard of. The earlier you start networking, the earlier you will identify your target dream career job and the more time you will have to turn yourself into "THE" dream candidate in the eyes of the employer.

FINDING, LANDING, AND CREATING INTERNSHIPS

Your connections can advise you whether their organizations offer internships. They can put you in touch with previous interns plus the managers responsible for running the program. They can advise you on what they are looking for in an intern so you can align accordingly.

It is worth targeting organizations who offer internships to make connections there LONG BEFORE you apply.

In other organizations, it can also be worth trying to sell the idea of opening an internship specifically for you. If you have built a great relationship with a number of people in an organization and have shown them that you are serious about aligning to *their* requirements, they may take you on for a summer or even multiple summers while you are still studying, even though they have no formal program. Use the questions and answers in the section on choosing the right internships to structure the position so that it is worthwhile to both you and your employer.

ALIGNING TO WIN

Does this process sound at all familiar? It should! These are the basics of *aligning.* You're making connections and developing relationships. Through these relationships, you build an understanding of the missions and objectives of your target organizations and managers. You discover what they look for when filling specific jobs by getting into their top priority results, biggest challenges and consequences of failure. You then look at your own strengths and see how they could be positioned to match the requirements of any particular role. You may, in the process identify gaps which you can immediately start working on so that you are a closer fit when it comes to the actual selection process.

If you align well by adjusting to make yourself a closer fit based on the information from everyone you meet within an organization, *this will get noticed*. I talked earlier about how medium to smaller companies recruit. The first thing they do when looking to fill a position is to ask everyone internally whom they know that might fit. It is therefore quite possible that at some point you will be invited for an interview without even asking for a job! Once in the interview, you will be very well prepared to explain how you can add value. You will have all the inside information you need to pass their thresholds to gain an offer.

GAINING INTERVIEW PRACTICE

Think of networking as an opportunity for you to rehearse for an interview. You can practice achieving the four thresholds by creating a good first impression, connecting, and starting a relationship in which you are liked and trusted. You can practice your questioning skills to gain an understanding of the needs of the organization and the people you talk to in order to build your credibility. You can practice relating to people by describing relevant common experiences and matching some of your strengths to their needs. You can practice listening carefully and communicate using their words and corporate phrases.

If you have no experience meeting anyone in the workplace until the day you finally get a formal invitation for a job interview, chances are you will be very nervous. Your ability to work your way through their selection thresholds are slim to none! I have said it before, but it is worth repeating;

Graduates who have not networked are immediately apparent because they still sound like students.

Those who have networked and developed interpersonal and aligning skills immediately have a much better chance of getting past the "will you fit in" threshold. So use networking meetings to practice these skills with business executives. Remember that each person could be a potential employer or a good reference, so always prepare with research and bring your "A" game. Listen carefully to the feedback and take action to improve.

GETTING THE PROMOTION

The connections you make within your targeted organization to help you align and zero in on a job opportunity will also become highly valuable to you after you have joined. They will do wonders helping you fit in and enjoy the job, and they will provide advice and help on difficult tasks.

Your connections can also give you insight into higher-level jobs, thereby helping you target your next promotion AND help you win it.

It is vital that you continue to maintain these connections and build more of them inside the company once you start your job. Never stop networking!

HOW TO NETWORK

START EASY

Many people are nervous as they begin networking. The thought of reaching out to some stranger in a senior position paralyzes them. Start by practicing with your parents, their friends, and your friends' parents. Begin with friendly, familiar faces and get each to introduce you to the next.

Every day you are in contact with numerous people who have connections that could expose you to incredible opportunities. Consider this: At the time this was published, people on Facebook and LinkedIn averaged around 100 connections each. Think of the possibilities. Each person could theoretically introduce you to 100 people who in turn could each introduce you to another 100, totaling a possible 10,000 connections. Another round of this, and you're up to 1 million people, and all this took was just three layers of connections from a single person!

Recently, the University of Milan studied 720 million Facebook users with 69 billion friends between them to prove, using mathematical algorithms, that it took only five connections to link any one person to another, and that the number of links is shrinking. *The implication is HUGE!*

It means that anyone you meet is only five or fewer connections away from people who could make the decision to employ you.

Get into the habit of using your best interpersonal skills on absolutely EVERYONE you meet because they could be a connection to a potential employer or customer.

Early in your network-building activities, position your meetings as information and advice seeking only. Make it clear that you are *not* asking for a job. This takes the pressure off of meeting you, and it makes the process of connecting easier. If you fail to make this clear, some people, especially those in larger organizations, will not agree to see you, or they will refer you to their human resources department instead.

THE QUESTIONS TO ASK

Once you get in front of potential connections and have passed the like and trust threshold, apply your questioning skills, particularly the *open* ones. Ask them to talk about how their careers developed and what they studied and why. What kind of jobs have they done in the past? Ask about their current job, their organization, and why they joined it. This gets the conversation going easily.

Then apply the "Will you fit in, can you do the job, and will you do the job" type of thinking we covered in Chapter One. This creates a structured line of questioning for you to follow and will provide great information to help you cross their thresholds if you apply for a job in the same organization later. This is how you pick up the details of how to subsequently align yourself, your resume and how you prepare for the interview.

Fitting in

Ask what the organization's mission is. (Do prior research to see if there is a mission statement.) Ask them to elaborate on it. How do they feel part of it?

Ask what the culture of the organization and the department is like. Are there any particular types of values or behaviors they encourage or specifically discourage?

How would they describe the management style? Is it a heavy-handed hierarchical structure with strict boundaries of who talks to whom, or a flat and open structure? Is it driven by rules and reports or more by communication and example?

What is the team like? Do people work closely and supportively with each other, or do people mostly work on their own? Are there any politics?

What do they like or dislike about all the above and why? What makes them a good fit? What would make anyone a bad fit? Ask which social style (personality type) is most successful in the job and why.

Note: If possible, ask for a tour of their business environment. This may not be possible in the first meeting, especially as many such meetings are likely to happen outside of the office. However, at the right time, a tour can give you a real sense of what it might be like to work there and also provide an opportunity to make more contacts.

Ability to do the job

Start with their key objectives. What are their top priorities? How are they measured? What are their most challenging obstacles? What consequences of failure do they worry about most?

What specific skills have they had to develop in order to succeed in their jobs? What do they see as their biggest strengths for the job? How did they develop those strengths? What else will they have to learn? With hindsight, would they have studied or qualified in any different way?

If you are talking to a manager, you think you might want to work for, ask what key skills, attitudes, and experience the manager looks for in members of his or her team. Ask why? Ask if they use "key words" to search for candidates, and if so, what are they?

Motivation to do the job

Ask your connections about their passions—how did they find and develop them? How do they apply them to the job? What do they love about the job? What specific activities do they love to immerse themselves in most? Why? What do they find rewarding?

What drives them? What motivates and what demotivates them? What really upsets them in their current jobs? Ask them to explain their career path. What jobs did they have to do to earn the one they have now and why? What jobs are they targeting next? What are their long-term career paths? What kind of lifestyles do they enjoy now and anticipate in the future?

Putting it together

This kind of information, from a number of different people in different jobs in different industries, will help to develop a picture of what you may or may not like to do. Get into the details—such as the amount of time they are working by themselves, sitting behind computers, working as part of a team, traveling, face-to-face with clients, solving problems, under deadlines, doing routine work, dealing with conflict and stress, etc. As you progress, you will increasingly develop a sense of what you think you will like and dislike doing. Remember to keep your predominant personality type in mind as you go through this. You can then specifically ask how much of any particular types of activities are involved in a typical day when you meet other people.

General information

Do prior research so that you don't ask questions a 14-year-old can find on the Internet. Ask which aspects of the business are growing or declining and the main reasons why. Ask about their growth strategy, what they see as threats and opportunities for the business, who the most dangerous competitors are and why. Ask who their typical customers are and why those customers chose them. Ask what makes their customers really happy versus what upsets them and what their main customer satisfaction initiatives are. Ask about the organization's efficiency initiatives and its challenges in those areas. Ask who their suppliers are and which ones are better than others and why. Ask which recruitment companies are most often used and why?

Get down to their top priorities and challenges in each of these areas. The notes you make will provide excellent talking points when you meet again, meet someone else in the organization, or are in an actual job interview. This kind of information will also give you an opportunity to think about how you can develop and position yourself as someone who can help with such challenges.

All this gives you a wealth of information about that organization and industry to help you think about your direction, where else to develop connections, and how to prepare yourself should an opening come up.

Other connections

Last but in no way least, ask if they can think of anyone else who would be prepared to meet you, both inside and outside their organization such as their customers and suppliers including recruiters. If you are talking with managers, ask if you could meet one of their most successful team members. Ask if you could meet recent recruits that are doing well.

For your network to grow, you MUST ask for at least TWO additional introductions.

When your connection gives you names of other potential connections, try to get a briefing on them. Ask about their background, likes and dislikes, achievements, weaknesses, challenges, and strengths. This will help you when it comes to making an appointment with them (see scripts below) and give you openings to start a dialogue when you are face to face.

These are some of the questions to ask. Make your own list and keep it on your phone. Give it a quick glance before you head into that lunch or coffee meeting. Before long, you will know it by heart. Remember to use predominantly open questions, and do not forget the techniques you've learned about maximizing your likability. Show that you are listening by asking further clarifying questions.

Ask for advice. What would they do if they were in your shoes now?

Don't forget to thank them afterward!

It leaves a VERY BAD IMPRESSION if you ask someone to take time out of their schedule to help you and you don't thank them. Do so at least twice. Once at the end of the meeting and once again by email.

MAKING APPOINTMENTS

Many people struggle with the idea of calling others out of the blue to make appointments. In sales, this is often referred to as "cold calling," and the mere thought of it stops some dead in their tracks.

The best way to get past an activity you fear or dislike is to become good at it.

The answer lies in preparation and practice as described below. It starts with writing down what you plan to say.

SCRIPT YOUR CALLS

If people have to listen to you hesitate and stutter, and they cannot get an immediate clear idea of who you are and what you want, they will not meet with you.

I recommend using a structure to help you write out a clear script. A repeated theme of this book is the benefit of structure, as it provides a basis for consistent performance and a way to analyze what works and what does not.

Note: Having structures also gives you a tremendous advantage during interviews. Many questions will be targeted to find out *how* you do things. For example, "How do you approach asking for something important? How do you approach making appointments? How do you defuse angry people? How do you approach complex tasks?" Having a structure in mind that allows you to communicate very succinctly how you do something, supported by examples, will give you confidence and make you articulate and convincing. You will blow right past the candidates who have no structure to guide their responses.

The following structure will help you ask anybody for anything!

As with all structures, they initially feel cumbersome but after a while, they become how you operate. This one prompts you for an introduction, an opening, a compliment, a request, a benefit, and a close. When you become good at using this structure, it will significantly improve your chances of getting appointments (and positive responses to any requests). This helps you not to become discouraged or waste valuable opportunities.

You usually don't get a second chance to make an appointment with an influential contact. Making unprepared calls of this importance can leave a bad impression about you and is a terrible way to waste vital networking opportunities!

Try something along the following lines:

The Introduction

"Good morning, Mr. Smith, my name is John Brown. I was given your name by Ms. Jones in your marketing department who recommended I speak to you."

Immediately explain who you are and use the name of your previous contact to provide some context and put the listener at ease.

The Opening

"I am studying [insert field of study here], and I would like to be considered for a job in your organization when I graduate."

This immediately makes it very clear what your objective is.

The Compliment

"Ms. Jones indicated you are experienced in the area of [insert area of expertise, e.g. customer service] and therefore might be able to give me some useful guidance, as this is where I would like to start my career."

Remember, everyone loves a compliment. It helps bring down defenses and improves the chances of a person feeling like helping you.

The Request

"I would like to get some advice from you because I want to make sure I develop the key skills that you and your organization typically look for."

Simply state exactly what it is you want. Any confusion over what you want results in a refusal to see you. Note that studies have shown that by adding a reason with the word "because" results in a higher rate of agreement to any request.

The Benefit

"I believe this would make me a significantly better candidate for you should you be recruiting in the future."

The response rate will go up further if the reason is to the other person's benefit. Always think through what is in it for the person to help you. If you are targeting successful and expanding organizations, then their managers are always on the lookout for promising new candidates.

The Close

"I only need about 20 or 30 minutes and can make myself available at whatever time or place is most convenient for you. Is there a time that would work for you?"

Then stay quiet and wait for your potential contact to suggest a time.

DEALING WITH OBJECTIONS

"I do not have time."

It is extremely unlikely that anyone will be unpleasant to you. However, you may get the objection that they would love to help you but they "do not have the time."

Do not just give up. I know a senior individual who always said he had no time, just to see what the caller would do. It was his first test.

Here are some options:

If the person you are trying to meet is a friend of an existing connection, chances are the time excuse was genuine. Let's assume people are not going to reject you if a friend recommended you talk to them. In this case, it is worth fishing for a date further out into the future when the person might be a little less busy. Say something like this:

"I totally understand. Is there a time next month, or the following month, when you might be available? I don't mean to be pushy, but I believe your input could make me a significantly better candidate for your organization in the future. I promise not to take up more than 20 minutes of your time." Then stay quiet and let the other person come up with a date. *Note that you repeated the benefit of seeing you.*

If you have cold called this individual without any connection to whom you can refer, then it is possible the person may be giving you the brush-off. First, respond the exact same way as above. We will call this Plan A. Try asking for a date in the future. You can use the exact same wording. If the person says they will *always* be too busy to see you, go to Plan B by asking if there is anyone at a lower level who could help you. Say something like this:

"I understand. Is there anyone else in the organization, below you in [customer service], who might be prepared to spend the time? I just need a few minutes to make sure I am doing everything possible to match up to your future requirements. Hopefully, that will be in your organization's interest, too." Then stay quiet and wait for a name. If you get a name, you can then call that person using the same script above. In the introduction, you can use the name of the more senior individual with whom you were just speaking as the person who recommended you to speak to them. By using the more senior name, there is a good chance the other person will accept! (This is why you ask for another name *below* the person you are talking to when you go to plan B.) If the next person does not grant you a meeting, try Plan A and Plan B on them too. Eventually, you *will* get a meeting!

Note: Do not get too pushy with any specific individual. Remember, there are many ways into an organization. If you fail with one, there will be another. However, once you are into an organization and building up your contacts, you could easily run into these individuals again, and they may remember you.

DIFFERENT SCRIPTS FOR DIFFERENT SITUATIONS

Obviously, there are many variations of this script, depending on your circumstances. The key is to be clear and concise. Follow the structure of having an introduction, an opening, a compliment, a request, a benefit, and a close. When you close, stay silent, so the other person clearly recognizes the need to answer. You may think this is obvious, but you would not believe the rambling calls I have been subjected to. The entire call should not be more than a few minutes.

I used the example above to show the ease with which you can start building a network while still studying because I want to encourage you to begin as early as possible. Many students who put off networking until after graduating fail to recognize that the *easiest time* to get networking appointments is while you are still a student.

If you need income now because you have already graduated or have just lost a job, then you will need to change the opening and the request. The introduction and the close can remain largely the same.

Again, the objective of this call is *not* to establish if the organization has a job for you *now*. This is because when there are no immediate jobs available, your meeting request will most likely be turned down, at which point you have lost the opportunity to make a connection and gather any information to help you cross their thresholds later.

Your real objective is to get a meeting so you can connect with people inside the organization and form a relationship in which they feel comfortable to advise you how to align, to introduce you to others within the organization, and to alert you when there *are* openings coming up.

So even if you know there are jobs available, you should still state the objective of the meeting as advice-seeking only. You FIRST want to be able to develop a coach who can guide you.

You also want to avoid sounding desperate.

Current job seekers may want to consider the following script.

The Introduction

"Good morning, Mr. Smith. My name is John Brown. I was given your name by Ms. Jones in your marketing department, who recommended I speak to you."

If you do not have a previous contact, then go straight to the opening after stating your name.

The Opening

"I am a recent graduate in [insert your field of study here] and very interested in being considered by your organization *in the future.*"

Note that you are NOT asking for a job now.

The Compliment

"Ms. Jones indicated you were very experienced in the area of *[pick something specific that Mr. Smith knows well, such as the area he works in or manages]* and therefore in a good position to provide good advice."

Again, if you have no previous connection, go straight to the request. Passing on a compliment from someone they know usually works. However, DO NOT attempt to make your own compliment to a complete stranger within the first 15 seconds on a cold call. It will most likely come across as very contrived. Have you ever dealt with any of those overfamiliar cold calls using your first name just as you sit down to dinner? Don't be one of those. Stay formal and to the point.

The Request

"I would like to get your advice because I want to make sure I have all the skills your organization typically looks for the next time you are recruiting for your department."

Keep it simple and make it clear you are not asking for a job now.

The Benefit

"Hopefully, it is also in your organization's interest to ensure there are candidates available with the right skills to match your future requirements."

Again, you are emphasizing the future to take the pressure off.

The Close

"I only need about 20 to 30 minutes and can make myself available at whatever time or place is most convenient for you. Is there a time that would work for you?" (*Then stay quiet and wait for him to suggest a time.*)

REMEMBER THE OBJECTIVE OF THE CALL

This is an appointment-making telephone call only. Save your objectives to connect, understand and align for when you meet face to face. Do not attempt to gather information or try to sell yourself during the telephone call. The only way you will genuinely connect and start a longer-term relationship that could help you in the future is to meet in person. Getting that meeting is your objective. Stick to the structure and the script.

You may get, "Well, what sort of information are you interested in?" This could trap you into an extended phone conversation.

A telephone call may give you some insight but will not be remotely as effective as a meeting. It will not start a relationship.

Respond with something high-level like, "Ms. Jones indicated that you are already successful on the career path that I am very interested in pursuing and that you might need people in the future. I would really like to meet you to understand how you approached your career and what you now look for in others. I believe you could give me valuable career advice and help me make sure I am a more suitable candidate when you need someone. If that is acceptable to you, would you by any chance have 20 to 30 minutes anytime next week or the week after?"

Again, note the combination of providing a compliment and offering a potential benefit to encourage this person to meet you. Then pause for a second and go for the close.

REHEARSE, THEN REHEARSE SOME MORE!

For many people, this is a little nerve-racking and does not feel natural. The answer is to rehearse by role-playing. Write out the script in short sentences so you can practice out loud without becoming short of breath. If the sentences are too long (and especially if you are nervous), you may run out of breath and stumble. By repeatedly saying it aloud, you will alter the script until it sounds natural. Do it over and over until you can do the call without having to read the script. Reading while on the phone will again have you sounding like those awful telemarketer calls you get at night. Practice on friends, your parents, and friends of your parents to get feedback.

JUST DO IT

There comes a time when you simply have to get on with it. With a good visual of success in your mind, just go for it!

Stand up and smile as you dial.

This helps your breathing and makes a difference in how you sound at the other end.

So what if a few go wrong? Do not waste emotional energy on getting offended or discouraged.

Every call is a learning opportunity. I promise, if you keep following the above structure, people will agree to see you. Start with people you know because they are unlikely to reject you. Then go for their friends for the same reason; if you mention their friends' names in the introduction, they are unlikely to turn you down. If they give you names, remember to ask them for a briefing including what their strengths are so that you can use that in the compliment section of your script. In this way, you can expand your network indefinitely. Eventually, you will also gain the confidence to call complete strangers without any previous introductions or references and make connections of your own.

USE A CALL PLANNING & REPORTING FORM

In most sales organizations managers will require members of their team to use sales planning and reporting forms to help them prepare and set specific objectives for a call, guide them through all the important topics that need to be covered, document the key points of the discussion, and list the agreed follow-up actions.

I highly recommend you adopt this practice. At the top of the form, it has a field for the individuals NAME and DATE of the meeting. Then a BACKGROUND heading for any relevant information about that individual and the organization they work for. Filling this out forces you to do some research on Google, the organization's website and places like LinkedIn to learn as much as you can. Your notes here can provide jumping off points for open questions to look for opportunities to agree, compliment and find common ground.

The next heading is OBJECTIVES. Under this heading list the key things you want to achieve in the meeting. This could include detailed information under the areas of Fit, Capability, and Motivation. It could include information on some of their specific challenges. It could be a request for help or advice. It could be a request for introductions to additional contacts. It could be all of the above and more.

Then have a section on NOTES where you document the meeting. I prefill this section with words or phrases signifying key questions I want to ask leaving space in between for my notes. This ensures I don't forget important questions.

Finally have a section for FOLLOW UP ACTIONS. Here you document what you are going to do for them to fill their goodwill tank, names and contact details of additional people you will contact, new skills you are going to learn to fill a gap that was identified in the meeting, etc.

I have not created a sample document for this form in this book as this is so simple. Create something that works for you. I bring a printed form to the meeting as I prefer to write quick notes as I can do that more quickly and openly while keeping engaged in a flowing conversation rather than typing into a pad or computer. I ask for a business card which I staple to the form and keep in a folder. I then type out more comprehensive notes combined with further ideas for next steps and create digital files along with entries in my diary for the follow-up actions.

Using a call planning and reporting form helps you prepare, look professional, make the most of any meeting, plus document and schedule follow-up actions. Not doing so can cause you to waste vital networking opportunities.

From time to time review these reports, especially before a second meeting, to remind you of what was discussed. Finding something to revisit or compliment from a previous meeting is a great way to reestablish the connection quickly when you are meeting someone again.

Note; Some people think notepads are ancient and would prefer to use an electronic pad or computer. Just be careful, particularly with the older generation. They consider note-taking professional but feel that focusing on a vertical screen between them and you is rude.

Remember, you are trying to "connect" to the other person, which requires a lot of eye contact.

THE DISCIPLINE YOU WILL NEED

Ask everyone for suggestions of people you should meet. Start out just meeting as many as you can. Each will give you valuable practice, and one contact will lead to another. Build a portfolio of connections by imposing a discipline of systematically reaching out and connecting with a number of people per month.

Set a target.

The target can vary depending on your situation. In your last year of high school, you might set a target of one or two people per month. In college, you should sustain a higher target, especially in your last year before you hit the job market. I recommend an absolute minimum of one meeting per week in the first years of college. That only amounts to 55 contacts over a year. You should be meeting at least two people per week in your final year. Once you have graduated and are looking for a job, you simply need to meet as many as you can! Try to meet someone every day. This process only works if you have a significant number of contacts.

EXCUSES, EXCUSES!

The number one reason people struggle to find jobs is that instead of building a network, they make excuses and just stick to emailing resumes. There are two main reasons:

1. I Don't Have Time.

This *has* to become a priority in your life. It takes 30 minutes a day to make appointments. It can help to set aside the same time every day to focus on your network. When it comes to scheduling appointments, consider arranging them over breakfast, coffee, lunch, an after-work drink, or evening meals. After all, you have to eat anyway—and so do they!

Note to students!

I often hear "I am too busy studying to do any networking."

It is AS IMPORTANT to build your network as it is to study while at college.

Please read this twice!

The time and effort you spend on each should reflect that. Remember, it is the people in your network more than anything else, who will help you target a job, prepare and align yourself, find actual openings, and win the selection process. A clear vision of your target dream job will help you focus on studying relevant material and get more out of it. The vision will ensure you are more motivated to study and *graduate faster*. Your network is also most likely to be the best source for internship opportunities to give you some relevant experience.

It is immediately apparent to any potential employer who has been networking and who has not.

They want the networkers.

I have met many graduates who decided to postpone networking until after graduation and they frequently describe themselves as falling into an abyss with no jobs in sight while debts mount. Networking from day one as a student ensures maximum relevance to a good job pipeline by the time you graduate. In fact, many will graduate with a job already secured this way.

Failure to network is the number one reason students

- *do not know what job they want*
- *fail to land internships*
- *drift through college taking longer than 4 years*

- *become part of the 50% who take over 2 years from graduating to land a job*
- *do not enjoy the job they finally land and end up leaving within 6 months.*

This is one of the most important messages in this entire book for students.

2. I Don't Like Networking

The most common underlying **real** reason people do not network is in fact, "I don't *like* making appointments to meet people over the phone, and I am *nervous* of actually meeting them."

Many people feel uncomfortable phoning to ask for a meeting with a complete stranger, especially when they have no prior connection. There is no getting around this, especially if you have not built any network prior to needing a job. As I stated above – start with easy ones and build from there.

But start now!

Most jobs will regularly require you to call and set up appointments to meet people for any number of reasons. Interviewers will look for evidence that you are capable of doing so.

Describing your networking discipline, your call structures and the size of your network is a great way to provide such evidence. This is a fear you *must* overcome.

VISUALIZE SUCCESS

It is worth asking yourself,

"What exactly are you afraid of?"

If you have been courteous in your request, what is the worst thing that can happen?

A person with a personality disorder might be rude to you? Most people, especially the successful ones, will either agree to see you or politely turn you down. Remember, successful people are excellent networkers themselves. They recognize when someone is making the effort to network and know that networkers are also likely to be successful. Success attracts success. They *will* want to meet you. You might be someone they want on their team. So get that painful vision of rude rejection out of your mind. It paralyzes you unnecessarily. The chances of it happening are lower than you think.

If it does happen—so what? In fact, the sooner it does, the better, because you will then realize it doesn't matter in the slightest. You will simply learn and move on.

With a bit of preparation, planning, and practice, you can GREATLY increase the odds of anyone accepting a request to meet you. This will be a HIGHLY valuable attribute throughout your entire career.

WHO YOU SHOULD NETWORK WITH

Once we get beyond family and friends, who should we target for our network?

SAFETY IN NUMBERS

Although I recommend that you target organizations, do not pin all your hopes on any one organization only. No matter how promising things appear, in the end, you still may not get an offer. Even if you do, it is vital to have other offers for comparison and to give you some negotiation leverage. When you decide you like an industry, approach multiple companies within it. Although this too may sound obvious, one of the most common mistakes is to stop networking elsewhere when things start to look good with one organization. As a result, candidates end up with limited options at best and often nothing at all!

AIM HIGH

The more senior the people you are connected to, the higher the quality of your network. Senior employees have better information and can more easily position you to meet other senior people. However, do not be paralyzed if you are struggling to get top-level contacts. Keep connecting and meeting people regardless. In fact, diversification is a very good way of getting different perspectives. For example, it can be very useful to find out what it is like to work for a certain manager before applying for a job by meeting people lower down who report to that manager.

Higher-level employees often offer a wider perspective on what is going on and can also act as role models for your end goals. When you meet senior executives that you really connect with, you can find out how they got there and create a similar career path in terms of your goals. Such people can become great mentors to help you at each step.

In fact, these kinds of mentor relationships can turn out to be life transforming.

Based on personal observation, there is a *very* high correlation between successful people and those who surround themselves with mentors, and vice versa. Those who are struggling, invariably have no mentors and no idea how to get one.

If you think of mentors as coaches, can you name any top-performing athletes who don't have one?

Make finding and developing a profile of mentors a top priority. In Chapter Seven, I will show you how to turn your boss into a mentor.

AIM FOR SUCCESSFUL PEOPLE

Be aware of the power of association. In addition to aiming for high-level people, ask to meet those who are *perceived* to be successful at any level. Not only will they give you good input on how to do well in the organization, but they will introduce you to other successful people.

Winners associate with each other. You want to be associated with them too as this will give you an advantage in any future selection process. This is worth paying attention to because it also works the opposite way. Losers tend to stick together too. Don't be associated with people who are perceived negatively.

USE EXISTING NETWORKS

Now that you have the interpersonal skills to make connections, and you are clear about what you are trying to achieve, it is time to join existing networks. These come in many forms, but the more obvious (and most likely to be helpful) are professional associations.

Nearly every profession—from marketing to accounting—has national and local associations. Join several that look relevant and start attending meetings. Arrive armed with business cards, set shyness aside, and introduce yourself to as many people as you can. Use the same network-building approach as described above.

Note: It is not the overall association that will help you. It is specific individuals within the association who might. Get lots of meetings, and apply your interpersonal and aligning skills to build people's inclination to help you.

The main benefit of joining an association is that it makes meeting people easier. You are all members, and the whole purpose of the network is to help each other. Associations are particularly useful in helping you meet more senior people, so keep that at the forefront of your objectives. I have spoken to several individuals who also strongly recommended volunteering for committee work in associations. It dramatically accelerated their network building efforts, especially with senior people, and helped create references. It also allowed them to add another achievement to their resumes to discuss during interviews.

Of course, there are numerous groups and forums you can join or follow online, including organizations you want to work for. They can also be an excellent source of information, contacts, and a place to get noticed.

Also, take a look at asaenet.org, which is the website for the American Society of Association Executives. It has a ton of information on jobs, job fairs, other associations, education, and recruiters.

THE IMPORTANCE OF RECRUITERS

By now you may be wondering why I haven't mentioned headhunters and recruiters.

"These people know what job opportunities are out there; so I should send them my resume, right?"

No, not really.

When people email their resumes to recruiters, it is usually part of a "spray and pray" campaign. It tends to fail, yet again, for all the same reasons as when you blanket-email companies for jobs as we discussed. Standard resumes that do not position you for any specific job are not very helpful to recruiters. If you are going to do it, make sure your resume is targeted and aligned with specific job opportunities as I will show you in Chapter Four. However, even then do not expect instant results.

Job seekers often make the mistake of thinking they are customers of the recruiter and will be treated as such. They *expect* recruiters to make an effort to find them a place. Recruiters are very polite people who will not tell you this, but the fact is that they do not view the candidates as their prime customers. Why? Because job seekers are not who pay the recruiters. It is the organizations looking to fill positions that pay recruiters. Consequently, the organizations are the valued customers, not you. At best, your resume, especially if it is nonspecific, will go into a filing system where it is unlikely to see the light of day again. In fact, larger recruiters use digital scans to filter out any irrelevant resumes just the same way larger organizations do.

So are recruiters relevant? The answer is—absolutely yes!

Not as a quick way to get you a job at the time when you need one, but as an immense source of help in a long-term relationship. Allow me to explain.

Begin making connections with people in recruitment companies throughout college. Talk to your parents and their friends to get names of recruiters they have dealt with and get introductions. Look them up on the Internet and approach them directly. Ask every connection you make for names of people they know in the recruitment business, especially ones who helped them get jobs. You can use their names in the introduction when you make appointments. You can use the same scripts.

"Mr. Briggs told me you were very helpful to him in landing him a job and advised me to reach out to you for advice on…." *(It provides an immediate opportunity for a compliment.)*

Then use your interpersonal and aligning skills from Chapter Two to connect and form a relationship. Focus initially on the smaller and more local recruitment firms as they tend to be more approachable. The very large global organizations tend to be so focused on the more senior placements you may find it harder to get an audience unless you already have some connections there. *Do make sure* you network in the larger organizations as you become more senior yourself.

Recruiters tend to be very knowledgeable and can really help you understand the job market. They know which organizations are growing and recruiting and which have the best training programs. They know what qualifications are sought after and which are considered a waste of time. They also know the various salary levels each role commands and which companies are the most generous. They know which managers are developing their staff and which ones burn people out.

This type of information is invaluable!

Recruiters are also networking masters themselves.

Having your resume on file and knowing you personally are completely different.

Their ability to get to know people, remember them, and position them for potential opportunities in the future is what defines them. They have learned to think long term. If they conclude you are likely to succeed and move up in an organization, they will pay attention. This is because they know that sooner or later you will be recruiting yourself. They want to be the person you turn to for candidates *throughout* your successful career.

So do not just randomly send resumes to recruiters.

Instead, make an effort to make as many connections in the recruitment community as possible. Then pick a few of the most successful relevant recruiters to your chosen industry and build deep, long-term relationships.

They can provide a wealth of knowledge and potential contacts throughout your career. Keep up the relationship and they can provide you with excellent candidates to build your team as you move up. As they get to know you, and see your success, they will bring outstanding career opportunities your way, too.

WHEN TO NETWORK

The earlier you start, the better, ideally in your last year at high school. Apart from helping you establish contacts, networking will provide feedback that can be invaluable when you try to decide what to study in college. Going into your freshman year with a clearer view of what you want to do later will provide motivation that will significantly increase your chances of graduating with good grades and in the minimum time frame.

Students without a career vision typically meander from major to major, often taking two years longer to graduate and with significant extra costs. They are also much more likely to fail to graduate!

THROUGHOUT COLLEGE

Networking while in college can help you decide on what to study and what to specialize in, and also alert you to what transferable skills certain jobs need. This gives you the opportunity to differentiate yourself further by building those, too. Networking early also increases your chances of landing an internship. In fact, the earlier you start, the more time you have to complete *several* internships while still a student. Of course, having a large contact base by the time you graduate will get you off to a much faster start in your job search afterward. In fact, this can result in landing a job *before* you graduate.

Note: A good way to get relationships going with successful senior executives while still in high school or college is to invite them to give guest lectures with the cooperation of teachers or professors. A senior-level exec who might balk at an individual request will sometimes respond to a more formal invitation. You can then maintain those contacts afterward on your own.

Or make it easier. Asking your intended guest to make a speech to the whole class requires prep time a busy exec may not have. Instead, set up a lunch or breakfast with a few other students.

Volunteer to organize and manage such events as this will make it easier to maintain the connection. The calling practice with senior executives is good for you. Write the call script using the structure you learned, and practice a few times beforehand. Act as their chaperone and make sure the experience is positive for them. Thank them afterward. If it has gone well and they seemed to enjoy it, ask if they will do another one in six months. It's the beginning of a relationship!

Many colleges arrange for senior executives to visit campus. For example, the University of Central Florida has an excellent program where executives are invited to speak to students every day.

Make sure you attend these sessions, engage, introduce yourself and ask if you can reach out to them afterward.

AFTER COLLEGE

Many of you, however, will have left networking until after college when you need a job. As I said above, then you simply need to start now with maximum intensity. Use both social media and face-to-face meetings. Discipline yourself to spend a significant part of your day, every day, to find people and connect to them. Set yourself a minimum target of getting out of your house and meeting one person per day. It will take you some time to reach that number, but having a target will increase your chances of doing so.

Note: Many people after college think they should only focus on getting job interviews. After all, time and money is running out and they need a job now. Anything else is just a waste of time. By all means try to get interviews but as the statistics show, that is not easy and will result in you spending most of your time at home. Lack of rapid progress can make you feel desperate. When you do land an interview, your lack of interaction with working executives will show. Your chances of rejection are high. Your chances of choosing the wrong job out of desperation and lack of detailed information are high too.

You are most likely to end up getting an interview through your connections.

So go out and network to build relationships and to work on targeting the right jobs and your alignment. The interviews will come, and your chances of performing well in them will be much higher!

WHEN YOU ARE IN A JOB

Make sure to continue your networking both inside and outside the organization once you have a job—always. These connections can help you get things done in your current role. They can help you get promotions and even find another job if things go wrong. You never know what is around the corner in this fast-moving world.

You should work every day as if, at the end of it, you will be judged as to whether you should be allowed to come back the following day. You should also be building and maintaining the contacts you will need should the answer be no!

Once you are in the workforce, people are also much more comfortable opening up to you and building a relationship when they can see that you are successful. It is also when you are most likely to be in a position to provide some value to your contacts and put some goodwill into their tanks.

The best time to connect to those around you is when you are performing well. Everyone loves a winner! You become the desired connection for others.

No one wants to connect to a poor performer or someone who immediately makes demands.

THREE FINAL TIPS ON NETWORKING

1. Always try to close any interaction with some positive actions. For example, plan on sharing information or introducing each other to additional contacts. This keeps the connection active and expands your network. Do not overload your new contact with too many requests early on. Remember the goodwill tank. Fill it first!

I was recently discussing this with Mel Haskins, one of my first bosses and now the owner of a successful recruiting and consulting company in London, England.

Mel is the best networker I know, so I asked him to contribute.

"A common mistake, and one that can damage your reputation, is to connect with people purely on the basis of using them—usually as quickly as possible. Connections made this way do not last long and tend not to be very beneficial. I look at connections as friends in a long-term relationship. Many of

my connections have been going for over 30 years. We have matured in business together and watched each other's families grow up. This approach has resulted in friends in over 30 countries around the world, with many in very senior positions now. Because the relationships are based on genuine care, we proactively pass opportunities to each other. We don't have to ask for favors."

2. Whenever you meet people, *always* follow up with an email. Thank them for their time, and refer to something discussed in the meeting in a positive way. This is a reminder of who you are and reinforces that you connected on something constructive. Then refer to any agreed-upon actions. If for example, you settled on making introductions to other people, you can suggest times and places to do so. Be sure all your contact information is in your email signature for their convenience should they wish to reach you. Doing this step creates a positive professional image of you that is often saved and kept on file by the other person.

Point 2 is NOT an option; it is a discipline you must follow!

3. Write the name of the person on a day in your calendar about a month out from the day you met, talked on the phone, or Skyped. When that day comes, it will remind you to think about that connection. Did you thank the person? Did the agreed-upon actions take place? Ask yourself whether there is anything else you could do. Is there any information of interest you could share? Think about more recent connections you have made since the meeting and decide if there is any benefit to bringing these people together. Before long, you will end up with names written in every day of your calendar. This will create a daily discipline to ensure that the number of your relationships keeps increasing and that individual relationships do not fade away. Keep looking for things of value to do for your contacts to maintain the level of goodwill in the tanks.

PART III

SOCIAL MEDIA

IS SOCIAL MEDIA A BETTER ALTERNATIVE WAY TO FIND A JOB?

I often get feedback that telephoning people just seems old-fashioned. No one does that anymore!

"I don't want to make calls and meet with people; I just want to interact through LinkedIn, Facebook, email or text."

Many people feel this is the modern digital way.

Be careful and honest with yourself here. While there are significant benefits to using social media, this is also a common response to the unease of making telephone calls and having to leave the comfort of home to actually meet people in person. It feels much safer to sit at home behind a computer screen imagining that the unlimited power of the internet is working for you.

I deliberately covered the above more physical networking strategies first because, although these may appear to be old-fashioned, they involve some timeless principles of interaction that also apply to social media. Don't forget that many of the influencers and decision makers on whether you get hired are likely to be older than you. Some will be just as uncomfortable in the digital world as you may be with phone and face-to-face interactions.

It is also important to remember that, in the end, it WILL require physical meetings to land and succeed in most jobs.

As I said earlier, do not make the interviews the first time you physically meet any executives. The sooner you start actually meeting people to build your face-to-face interpersonal skills and your confidence, the better.

With that said, let's look at how you can use social media as it continues to transform how you can find people, connect and communicate with them, and find jobs.

SEVEN TIPS FOR SUCCESSFUL JOB HUNTING USING SOCIAL MEDIA

Because of the incredible speed of evolution of these networks, I will not go into any great detail of specific functions in any of the different networking services. By the time you read this, the chances are it will be out of date. In any case, I have yet to meet recent graduates who do not know their way around these networks. The purpose of this section is more about laying out principles than details.

1. *Do not* think of physical interaction and social media interaction as two alternative strategies. Use them together.

Let's look at a simple description of what is involved in traditional marketing to see how and when digital and physical interactions apply to marketing yourself. Marketing starts with research on needs and potential opportunities. This information is used to assess the size and location of those opportunities and to make sure that any product or service genuinely meets those needs. Marketing also makes sure that key features and benefits are communicated to the market as fast as possible to build interest and trigger a "buy" reaction.

This view of marketing is ENTIRELY applicable to your approach of finding and landing a job.

You can use both physical networking and digital research to find out what jobs you may be interested in. CareerOneStop.org is an example of a digital source full of such information.

You can use both your physical network and digital sources to help you understand what skills are required for the jobs you like. This helps you align yourself through "targeted skills development" to make sure you genuinely meet the needs of your market. I will describe this in detail in the next chapter.

Nothing will beat effective digital marketing tactics for reaching as much of your market as fast as possible. It will also help you find specific openings, especially with larger employers who rely increasingly on digital searches to find people.

This approach is all about optimizing your profile so that you can be FOUND.

Both digital and face-to-face interactions will help you find jobs in smaller companies. However, especially among nontechnical companies, the smaller the company, the less it will rely on sophisticated tracking systems to find people. Face-to-face networking will be more effective.

Meanwhile, nothing beats face-to-face meetings for getting through all the thresholds, especially the final "This Is Who We Want!" threshold prior to getting an offer. This is true regardless of the size of the organization

Social networks are an incredible way to find and link to people. However, it is more difficult to build up a genuine connection with enough goodwill for people to WANT to make any effort to help you or actually HIRE you if you do not physically meet them.

Therefore, once you have made the link on a network and established a good dialogue with a promising contact who lives locally, ask for a meeting. Do *not* do this right away, and *be careful!* Consider using Skype, especially for long-distance contacts. It is not as good as face-to-face, but it is a big step closer.

Note: When using Skype, treat the situation exactly as if it were a face-to-face meeting. Make an appointment. Wear appropriate clothes and watch what else is visible or audible, especially from home. Half-dressed spouses, screaming kids, and barking dogs in the background are not positive distractions. All the interpersonal skills covered in Chapter Two, such as maintaining good eye contact, still apply. Pay attention to the window that shows yourself to make sure you are well-centered with your head and shoulders clearly visible. Don't get so close that they can see up your nose, and don't be a blur in the distance.

Employers are increasingly using video interviews as a way to do an initial screening and to save time and costs for candidates who live remotely. Get some practice by using Skype with your contacts.

2. Your resume and your social network profiles should be consistent. Let me give you some examples:

Make sure that the information on your resume and your profiles match. A discrepancy on where you worked and for how long will instantly undermine your credibility. It indicates that you are either not being truthful and can't keep your stories straight or that you lack attention to detail. Neither helps your cause.

A key recommendation in this book is to stop approaching the market with a generic resume full of nonspecific descriptions and tired, mean-ingless hyperbole. Be careful you do not do this in your social media profiles, either.

Another way people create discrepancies is by using one social media service while it is hot and then switching to others as new ones come out with cool features. The older ones are not kept updated but are still out there and often display an outdated resume. This can result in presenting three or four very different images.

3. Optimize your profiles for employer searches. This is actually a significant topic in its own right and one that continues to evolve.

Whole books have been dedicated to this area, so I recommend you do as much research as possible.

The first point to make is that the basic principles of alignment apply to social media too. Many people just start filling out profiles as they *currently* see themselves and what they have done so far. Keep the above definition of marketing in mind. *You are trying to position yourself to meet the needs of potential employers.* For example, LinkedIn has a "headline" that most people default to their current or last job. It is much better to use the headline space to position yourself for the job you want *next* because this is what employers and recruiters will search to meet their needs for that job.

Likewise, in the summary box, make sure you summarize *what you can do* in the position you are interested in, rather than *who you are* in vague buzzwords, as discussed before. This is even more critical online because search engines look for specific words and phrases.

The good news is you can *search engine optimize* (SEO) your profile in a similar way that companies do when they use websites to sell their products and services.

It requires you to understand what "keywords" employers look for with regard to the specific position you are interested in.

You can deduce what these keywords are by looking at job postings and by talking to your connections. In LinkedIn, you can do an advanced job postings search to help you home in on keywords listed for jobs of interest by employers. You can also do an advanced people search and see the keywords listed by people who already have those jobs of interest. Don't just guess, as they are often quite specific. They can include the names of skills, tools, and even industry jargon. Once you have your list of keywords, you must incorporate them into your headline, previous job descriptions, and the summary.

Have as many recommendations as possible. Try to ensure they support the keywords you have identified. If a skill using a tool or software application has been identified in the keywords, get a recommendation mentioning the skill and tool by name.

Have a photo. Many people are uncomfortable connecting to a faceless profile. Make sure that it is appropriate for the industry in which you want to work. A clear "head-and-shoulders" shot wearing the business attire commonly used in your desired industry is the safest bet. Check out the photos of the leadership and other key people working in the organization where you want to work (such as your interviewer!).

All this is simply another form of alignment, and like before, you have to know what you are aligning to. This requires deep research and constant updating.

Note: In the next chapter you will learn how to build a resume that is aligned to the jobs you want. Because resumes and profiles need to be consistent, I strongly recommend you read Chapter Four before you start building any profiles.

4. Many people advocate "building a brand" for yourself by posting opinions (blogging) on areas of your expertise. Once you have some experience to do so with credibility, I completely agree. However, if you are still studying or recently graduated, I recommend posting questions rather than opinions. I have seen a number of examples of so-called expert graduate bloggers and their blogs can appear very contrived. It takes *a lot* of time and effort to write with enough depth and quality to impress a potential employer. (It is also another reason/excuse to spend long hours safely at home behind your screen.)

This is time that would be better spent in face-to-face meetings with influential people.

Note: Not all companies are comfortable with their employees doing a lot of blogging. Some companies worry about how their brand could be affected by association. *Your blog could actually put someone off.* Once you are on board, you must check policy before you blog.

In Chapter Two, I covered the benefit of avoiding potential disagreements by *not* offering opinions when you try to connect with people. It is much safer to ask questions, as this gives you the opportunity to agree with their answers where appropriate. People like being agreed with. The exact same principles apply to digital interaction. When you post questions, you will get responses. This allows you to reply by agreeing, start a dialogue and develop a relationship. Also, look at the answers given to other people's questions. If you like a particular answer, agree, start a dialogue, and then make a connection in the same way.

5. Use a service such as LinkedIn to manage a portfolio of contacts. However:

Do not delude yourself that simply by adding a name (a "connection" in LinkedIn terminology) that you have made a worthwhile contact with the capability and desire to help you.

This is especially true if you do not add a personalized message when you invite someone to connect and do not follow up. Simply building a list of names is of little value and certainly not a substitute for talking to people, ideally meeting them, and building goodwill. Remember, your objective in professional networking is to build relationships with individuals who are in a position to provide you with useful information, influence others to hire you, or hire you themselves.

LinkedIn is a great tool to help you find potential contacts, be found by others, communicate with them, and manage your contact portfolio. Many people also make the initial contact on other social networks or through direct contact but then ask to connect on LinkedIn too as a way to consolidate all of their connections in one place.

6. Keep the use of social media for personal interaction with friends and family *completely separate* from connecting and portraying a professional image to the job market. Pick some networks for your social interaction and keep them on private settings. Then use other services to focus purely on your professional ambitions.

7. Keep *all* of your social media appropriate! A study by CareerBuilder indicated some 40% of employers will check all your social media profiles. They will reject your application for any indications of heavy drinking, drugs, racism, sexism, or religious discrimination. They also look at what you say about your current or past employers. You can easily lose your existing job this way, too.

In summary, social media has greatly impacted how we can make connections, market ourselves, find job opportunities, and communicate. However, keep in mind that it has *not* changed the three fundamentals of what employers look for, as described in Chapter One. Keep these and your alignment in mind.

PART IV

INTERNSHIPS

WHY DO THEM AND WHERE DO YOU FIND THEM?

WHAT ARE THEIR BENEFITS?

This is a popular and often rewarding strategy. The most common benefits of internships are as follows:

- Learn some industry specific and general transferable skills.
- Build some references.
- Gain a sense of what working in a specific industry or organization is like.
- Increase your network of contacts within an organization.
- Improve your chances of getting a career job with that organization.

These are genuine benefits that *good* internships can provide.

WHERE DO YOU FIND THEM?

Finding job sites for interns is easy. Simply type "best job sites for interns" into Google. I have looked at some of them, notably Internships.com, Experience.com, InternMatch.com, CollegeRecruiter.com, and InternJobs.com. Each has a different angle, and between them, they offer thousands of opportunities classified by industry. I highly recommend you at least look at the ones listed above. Many also have great articles on how to land internships and how to succeed in them. One site I like in particular is YouTern.com, founded by Mark Babbitt.

The key is to make sure you pick a worthwhile one.

Many people, after being told how important internships are, rush to land one only to find out that many come with minimal or no pay, do not last very long, and are sometimes little more than a way for organizations to get menial work done at low cost. Not all internships lead to jobs afterward, and this is certainly not automatically guaranteed. Try to find internships that are part of well-thought-out programs with commitment behind them because the employers understand the longer-term benefits to *them*. The way to do that is to ask lots of questions.

11 CRITICAL QUESTIONS YOU SHOULD ASK WHEN SELECTING A WORTHWHILE INTERNSHIP

1. What is the organization's primary objective of having an internship?

Offering internships to a number of candidates allows organizations to see what the candidates are like and then select the best. Internships can act as extended interviews (like a 90-day trial) during which employers can determine whether you have the three things they look for—can you do the job, will you do it, and will you fit in.

Internships are opportunities to give candidates some training so that they can be more productive the day they start their permanent position. They allow candidates to get some insight into the organization and its business to see whether they really want to work there. This makes them more committed when they join in a permanent role. Studies by the National Association of Colleges and Employers (NACE) show that interns who join organizations they interned with stay longer than direct recruits.

The least attractive internships are the ones where you will primarily be doing unstructured "low-cost grunt work" from which you will gain very little benefit. Constantly filing papers and fetching coffee is not value-added for your time and does not turn you into a candidate they will likely hire.

2. Is this a one-off internship or do you have a yearly internship program?

Look for companies who are thinking longer-term, who are planning recruitment for their expansion and have done this before. Implementing a successful internship program often involves some trial and error and adjustment from multiple parties within the organization. At the negative extremes, interns are sometimes left unmanaged and underutilized or treated with little to no respect as they are overloaded with menial tasks.

Note: If the program has been in place a few years or more, try to find out who the successful interns were. Ask who went on to join the organization and who are considered to be on their way up. Try to contact them to see if you can follow in their footsteps. Find out from them what would help you to land the intern position and succeed once you are in it. Ask them what they learned and how.

3. What are the specific duties and objectives of the intern position?

Landing an internship is identical to landing a job. If you do not know the objectives, you cannot position yourself as someone who can do the work. Find out how you will be measured. Interviewers realize that interns do not have prior experience and will supposedly make an allowance for this. However, being prepared in advance to talk about duties and objectives will immediately lift the quality of your conversation compared to someone who just sits there waiting for questions from the interviewer. A recent study showed that an intern candidate's performance during the interview was the most important factor in being selected—closely followed by relevant experience.

4. What is the culture, and what are the core values of the organization?

The answer to this type of question will help you position yourself to meet the "will you fit in?" question. Ask how interns are generally thought of and treated. Are you going to be "a slave making copies and coffees," as one disgruntled intern put it, or are you part of the team?

Note: Never start listing stuff you are not prepared to do! Whatever the answers are, remain positive. You want the internship offer even if you do not accept it. You will apply to many internship opportunities, and other organizations will ask you if you have had any offers so far. It will put you in a good position if you can look them confidently in the eye and say, "Yes, I have an offer from XYZ Company, but because of these reasons, I would very much prefer to intern with you."

Also, when you first start out, there ARE going to be menial jobs that you WILL have to do—especially as an intern. NEVER, even later in your career, give the impression that you are "above doing" anything.

Meg Whitman gives a great account of how, after she completed a Harvard Business School MBA and went to work for Procter and Gamble, her first job involved calculating the perfect size hole in the Ivory Shampoo bottle. She could have taken offense, but she chose to leave her ego at the door and make the absolute best of the job. This is a philosophy that took her all the way to becoming the CEO of eBay, the Republican nominee for governor of California, and the chairman, president, and CEO of Hewlett-Packard.

5. Whom will you report to?

In some organizations, interns are assigned to the lowest ranking members of staff. This can be another sign that the internship is little more than low-cost additional labor (although this is not always the case; see note below). If this is the case, you are unlikely to learn much or end up with a valuable reference at the end. Look for internships that report to a manager, ideally one who has successfully managed interns before— the definition of success being that a high percentage of the interns they previously managed got offered permanent jobs.

Note: Some companies deliberately ask young staff who could be management material to manage their interns. Remember this once you are in a job. Offering to manage interns is a great way to show you have management potential and a good way to break into management.

6. How is an intern judged to be a desirable recruit for a permanent position?

You need to know what the target looks like. Get specifics on their selection criteria. Find out how you would cross their thresholds. Ask for previous examples. Ask how many interns were offered a job afterward. Ask what causes interns to fail.

7. What could you be expected to learn during your internship?

This helps you judge whether the position will teach you any new skills to help you land a career job later. Look for specific core competencies and transferable skills that are related to the permanent job you ultimately want. If you are not going to learn any of the skills that your research has indicated employers will be looking for, then the internship is of questionable value.

Also, ask *how* such skills will be learned. Without a commitment from the organization to teach you the skills, you won't learn any unless *you* make the effort. You need to know how. This is where the advice of previously successful interns can be very helpful.

8. What kind of permanent job offers could the internship lead to?

Ask to see the job descriptions of such positions, and then ask which of the required skills the internship would help you build. *This way you really tie the benefits of the internship to a subsequent job offer.*

9. How do you get feedback?

Ask if there is a formal review. Will you have access to management to get advice if you need it? If you do well, will they give you a reference if there is no job available? How do they define *doing well?* This is important. If you do not get an offer after an internship, you at least need a very good reference to take with you to your next interviewer!

10. How long is the internship expected to last?

Other employers will not consider anything less than three weeks a real internship later. Internships typically align with college semesters and the minimum is closer to two to three months.

11. Is there any form of compensation?

Organizations committed to building a pool of talent from which to choose their new recruits will usually offer some form of compensation even if it is minimal. They know that having attractive internship programs brings in good potential candidates. Increased government regulation has also pushed for payment.

There are, however, still plenty of valuable unpaid internships out there. In my discussions with students, the most common complaint is that they don't know how to survive a period of up to two to three months without pay. Many are already incurring debt. For some, the only way they can endure it is to live with their parents.

Be careful as there are plenty of organizations just looking for cheap labor rather than investing in a program to help them improve the quality of their next intake. Go back to the benefits of internships listed at the beginning of this section and consider the following very common interview questions;

"What relevant skills did you learn during your internships?"

"What impact did your efforts as an intern have on the company?"

"Do you have a reference from your internship?"

"What day to day activities were you praised for during your internship?"

"Give an example where you showed initiative during your internship."

"Give an example of where you had to make an exceptional effort to ensure a task was completed."

"Give an example where you helped a colleague or volunteered to help outside the internship role."

"What did you learn about the industry?"

"Were you offered a job there?"

Try to understand upfront whether the internship will help you answer these types of questions. However once you are engaged in an internship, make the absolute best of it by constantly working towards building genuine examples through your efforts in the job. Keep these questions in mind at all times!

Your subsequent ability to answer these types of questions can mean the difference between spending a valuable three to six months growing toward your career goals or contemplating afterward what a waste of time it was.

WINNING THE INTERN SELECTION PROCESS

Landing an internship involves the exact same principles as winning a job. Internships posted on websites have high competition. Just sending standard resumes and cover letters to these internship postings suffers from the same limitations as sending them to permanent job postings.

It is critical that you prepare and align yourself in exactly the same way as you would for a permanent job opportunity. Build relationships and prepare prior to the interview. Then work through their thresholds during the interview to earn the offer.

All the chapters in this book are just as applicable to finding, landing, and succeeding in internships as they are to permanent positions.

SO, DO THEY WORK?

Internships are an excellent way to build relevant skills and improve your chances of getting a job offer afterward.

However, because people struggle to land them, do not know how to perform well once in them, or choose unsuitable ones, internships do not always live up to expectations.

The key is to choose wisely. When you do land one, keep in mind at all times that this is an opportunity to align yourself for a permanent job. Ask yourself every day;

- *Do they like me, am I building trust and references?*
- *Am I earning credibility by understanding their needs across the required skills, fit and drive thresholds?*
- *Am I actually learning any of the required skills, attitudes and behavior to match well to their needs later and pass the "suitable for hire" threshold?*
- *Am I learning how to provide value in any of their top priorities so I can differentiate myself and pass the "This is who we want!" threshold?*

Ask yourself every day what else you could do to help achieve the above points. This way you drive the internship. Don't just drift through it.

QUICK STORY

I was recently introduced to Isabella Johnston, the founder of Pivot Business Consulting in Orlando, Florida. She provides consulting services with a strong focus on start-up business ventures. She explained how she takes on interns from local colleges and trains them for assignments with her clients. This is a very interesting business model from all perspectives. The clients who are often short of funds in their early growth stages gain access to sharp, energetic minds filled with the latest theories and developments in their field and receive full value consulting oversight from Isabella at lower costs.

Meanwhile, the interns are in an environment that achieves ALL the above-listed internship benefits.

They gain coaching, training, and mentoring from Isabella in terms of interpersonal, analytical, and presentation skills. They also gain real experience in solving specific challenges for startup organizations to achieve their objectives. This way, interns get to work with a number of clients and develop references. It is not surprising that many of Isabella's interns are rapidly snapped up when they graduate.

This is a great environment to gain experience in working on top priority results, obstacles to success, and consequences of failure with customers.

This is an ideal way to learn how to engage any future interviewer on their priorities and challenges. Remember, in Chapter One we discussed how this is one of the fastest and most effective ways to connect and differentiate yourself.

I urge you to consider similar internship opportunities in your area.

SUMMARY

Out of all the job-finding strategies, networking is the most successful. For this strategy to work, however, you will need *a significant number of relationships.* Building and maintaining these relationships, especially with influential people, takes time, effort, and dedication—*lots of it!*

Use both physical and digital strategies to build your network. The time to start is immediately!

Network as if your life depends on it. The quality of your life most certainly will.

"The opposite of networking is *not* working!"

Source unknown

Then use your network to find and land the right internships. Many employers are increasingly reluctant to be the first to take the risk of offering you a full-time job. They will want to see evidence of the three things you must prove which we covered in Chapter One. This means you must provide convincing previous examples of how you;

- Can fit into their teams and culture

- Can do the job, including solve problems plus learn and apply new skills

- Will do the job and persevere in the face of adversity

The best way to do this is during internships while studying. This is when you build S.O.A.R. examples to cross the "Suitable for hire" and "This is who we want" thresholds for entry level jobs.

Choosing the right internships and making the most of them will give you a killer advantage over those who do not.

This should be one of your top priorities while at college.

CHAPTER FOUR

PREPARING FOR THE SELECTION PROCESS

"By failing to prepare, you are preparing to fail"

Benjamin Franklin

Based on the techniques in Chapters Two and Three, you can now successfully build a network of relationships. These connections will provide you with the information you need to help you choose and then *align* yourself to particular industries, functions, and eventually a number of "target" jobs in specific organizations.

As you do this, it is important to document your alignment in a resume and create supporting proof in the form of an achievement portfolio and references.

Nearly everyone realizes at some point that they need to prepare a resume. Most people put it off for too long and then do it in a hurry—often very generically. Very few people, however, also prepare an achievement portfolio to support their claims, or a group of relevant, impressive references who are willing to provide quotes and take reference calls. Let's go through each, as they will transform your performance in a selection process.

It won't be long before you need these for a job opening!

PART I

THE RESUME

WHAT IS IT?

A resume is a brief document that describes your *capabilities, desire, and team fit* that are *directly relevant* to achieving the top priority results in the job you wish to land.

WHAT IS ITS PURPOSE?

Traditionally, its purpose is to position you and your skills as the best fit for the job. It can help you secure an interview and can act as a guide for the interviewer during your meeting.

IS IT STILL RELEVANT?

I have encountered a growing number of people who have concluded that resumes are last century and no longer needed. They believe that their LinkedIn profile, for example, replaces it. They also point out that many organizations rely more on application forms. For some jobs in some industries, this may be true, and I do believe there is a trend in this direction. However, I urge you to still build a resume for a number of critical reasons which I will explain below.

Many of the people who make the final decision to employ you come from older generations. Most will be "Gen X" or even "Baby boomers," and plenty of them will still want to see a resume.

Here is why I think you need both social media profiles and resumes plus how I distinguish between them.

A profile should be built to score highly on searches from AS MANY employers as possible who have the type of job openings you are interested in.

Although your profile is specific to the type of job you want, it is by definition still somewhat generic because you are still looking for job opportunities.

A resume should be tailored to convince A SPECIFIC employer that you are the BEST FIT for THEIR particular job and organization.

Once you have found an opportunity and started a dialogue, your resume should differentiate you from all of the other candidates.

I do not see this as an either-or choice. Both are needed, and they should be based on thorough research as to what your target employers look for.

Your profile is a "build it and hope they will find you" strategy. Your resume is tailored to support a proactive sales approach into a specific organization.

A profile plays a larger role in the "find a job" stage of the job cycle while a resume plays a bigger role in the "winning the selection" stage.

Make sense?

What do interviewers typically look for in a resume? Let's revisit Chapter One to set some context, particularly for those who skipped ahead for urgent resume-writing guidance. At the most basic level, interviewers look for three things.

1. Will you fit in? Will coworkers enjoy working with you 8 to 10 hours a day? Will you be able to perform as part of their team? Will you take criticism and direction? Will you be disruptive? Will customers like you? Are you trustworthy, reliable, and loyal? Do you share the same values?

2. Can you do the job? Do you have the relevant skills and experience? Have you successfully done something like this before? Were the problems you solved and the results you achieved similar to what they are looking for?

3. Will you do this job? What motivates you? What are your ambitions? How will they affect your desire to do the job and stick around for a significant period of time? What is your track record of persevering when things get difficult?

In Chapter One we covered how you need to *align* yourself to meet the above three requirements.

A resume should be tailored to answer the above questions in the SPECIFIC CONTEXT of EACH job opportunity.

So far we have established that sending a standard resume based primarily on what *you assume any employer* wants is mostly a waste of time, especially if you describe yourself using mostly generic qualities. You need to build a network of connections and learn from them about particular jobs and their requirements. This will help you develop the specific capabilities they look for to help them overcome their obstacles to success and achieve their top priorities. Next, summarize them in a *tailored* resume—one that demonstrates that you provide what your targeted employer actually needs for the job in question. Each job opportunity will, therefore, require a different version of your resume. This has a *much* higher success rate. We referred to this as *aligning*.

With "alignment thinking" as a backdrop, let's look at some do's and don'ts of resume preparation.

START EARLY!

Many people do not start writing their resumes until they are actively searching for a job. Most have the good sense at that point to get some guidance. The good news is there is plenty of outstanding material available. The bad news is that despite how much you read, it is very difficult to create a compelling resume when you're writing it the same week you begin your job hunt.

No amount of hyperbole, clever writing, or design will make up for a lack of directly relevant skills and achievements.

Yet it is precisely the superficial "appearance" factors most people focus on when they decide they need a resume. Nearly everyone obsesses over format rather than *content*—in many cases because they have no other option.

Most managers have seen all the tricks before. All they want is a crystal-clear snapshot that answers the above three questions.

Once it is boiled down to this, people tend to have a bit of an "oh-my-God" moment as they realize their snapshot is not as attractive as it needs to be and that no amount of lipstick (in the form of overused, meaningless adjectives) will fix it.

So what should you do then?

Before we get into quick-fix ideas for a last-minute resume, I would like to show you how to avoid this situation in the first place.

HOW TO GENUINELY BUILD A TARGETED RESUME WITH A JOB IN MIND

Since you are hoping to provide your services to other organizations, let's learn from how *THEY* typically launch new services. We touched on this when we looked at standard marketing activities in the last chapter.

- Organizations begin by analyzing the market and developing a deep understanding of what the end customer wants.
- This information is turned into a specifications document of what the service department *must do* for a client.
- These specs then provide the focus for a plan to build and provide those capabilities.

- When they are ready to launch, they write promotional material to support the marketing and sales effort.

No successful business randomly develops a product or service. They build specific, targeted capabilities based on solid research of needs.

Successful companies do *not* decide to build services based only on what they *like* doing. They do *not* write generalized promotion material describing *themselves* instead of their services and resulting benefits. Any attempt to do business on this basis, especially without any understanding of what the potential clients actually need, would have little chance of success. Agree? Whenever I ask this question, everyone agrees.

Yet this is EXACTLY what many people do when it comes to developing their skills and marketing themselves!

Way too many people selected their studies without much thought as to the commercial need for such qualifications. They subsequently describe *themselves* using mostly meaningless generic terms, again without any regard to their relevance to a particular employer. We discussed this in Chapter One.

This is why starting to network as early as possible is so important. Networking is when you do the equivalent of an organization's market research.

In fact, there are many benefits to viewing yourself as a one-man company and applying the same processes and strategies in building, marketing, and selling your service capabilities.

Start thinking of yourself as a service provider who solves problems.

This immediately gets you thinking about showing what you can *do* rather than just presenting who you are. It helps you to make sure your services are *aligned* with what your target market wants. It makes you think about their top priority results, obstacles to success, and their consequences of failure. *It makes you look for problems you can solve.* This is the best way to provide value to a future employer.

Let me show you how to do this.

USE RESUME WRITING AS A PERSONAL DEVELOPMENT TOOL

With the above approach in mind, start by specifying the services you would be required to deliver in the types of jobs you are interested in.

Talk to successful people who are doing those jobs, plus their managers. Get detailed instruction about what top priority results they are responsible for. What are the most common challenges they have to deal with? What skills are most valuable for them to succeed? Find out what they have to be capable of doing every day. Try to see as many of their job descriptions as possible.

Find out what *their* resumes look like.

With this information, build a model "ideal" resume and get confirmation that it would thoroughly meet the needs of your desired employers. This becomes your personal target "services specification" which defines what you need to be able to live up to.

Then make a plan to build your capabilities to match it. Then execute the plan making sure to get feedback from your connections on how you are progressing.

This way, rather than scrambling to "write" a resume, you will "build" the one you need for the job you want.

Going through this process is often a wake-up call. I regularly meet people who blame everyone else—the economy and evil business leaders and politicians running the world—for their unemployment. However, they are often blind to their own shortcomings regarding the jobs they apply to. In their minds, they graduated, so they must be suitable. All they think they need is a good resume format.

I recently met a group of students who were refreshingly clear and enthusiastic about what they wanted to do after graduating. However, none of them had ever spoken to anyone from the types of organizations they wanted to join and *personally verified* that they were developing the qualities they needed!

Their hopes were based entirely on the assumptions and opinions of people who most often had absolutely no connection to the jobs they were after.

The point?

Your resume shouldn't be viewed as something you conjure up only at the last minute when looking for work. Otherwise, you may have to conjure with a lot of smoke and mirrors.

The longer you wait to start writing your resume, the more you will rely on hype to describe who you are versus the relevant results you are capable of delivering.

It will be full of buzzwords like *passionate, dedicated, results-focused, hardworking, enthusiastic, go-getter, unique, motivated*—each prefaced by *very, highly,* or *extremely.*

To have an effective resume, you need to start working on building targeted skills with specific jobs in mind—as early as possible.

This way you will build skills and achievements that will be highly valued because you verified that can apply them directly to helping an employer achieve their top priorities.

BUT I NEED A RESUME NOW!

"Well, this would have been great advice—if I had read it five years ago!

I hear you.

I covered the basic principles of targeted skills development first because if you do not adopt them, the danger is that you will find yourself in the exact same position in another five years. You can start applying this approach at any time during your career with immediate benefit. For example, this is a great way to make sure you are aligned to the needs of your current job.

Use it to build a "skills and services spec" for your current job and later for your desired promotion.

However, if you are starting from scratch with no contacts and no resume but urgently need one because you are looking for a job now, let's look at what you can do.

USING THE INTERNET FOR GUIDANCE

We can apply the same technique as when we optimize our online profile. There are many sites that can help you understand what organizations are looking for by job type. Enter "top 10 job sites" into Google and you will see what I mean. As with profiles, these can provide useful insight to help you build a more targeted resume.

Explore as many as you can. Search job titles that interest you, and look at the descriptions. Take note of keywords and priorities. Try to establish common themes. Then build your resume by using actual examples from your past that most closely match those themes. Use *their* keywords as much as possible. In this way, you can "reverse engineer" your resume to align it to the needs of the job in their language.

However, using this approach *alone* will result in a resume that is more like an online profile. (Not surprising, since we are using the same approach.) To take it to the level of a tailored resume, you should also *immediately start networking* as you look at these sites. You can take the keyword trends you observe in the job site descriptions and use them to form questions to ask people when you meet them. These will provide you with openings such as:

"I notice the requirement descriptions for jobs like this on the Internet emphasize the need for [XYZ]. Could you help me understand what that really means and why they want it? Could you give me some examples? What else do they look for?

Such a conversation will demonstrate that you are serious and have done your research—and help you target your resume.

Once you have written a resume based on the above type of research, you can also use these sites as a validation exercise. Start sending it to job postings you're interested in to see what kind of response you get.

Note: *Always* follow up every resume you send with a phone call to get feedback. (Just the fact that you called increases your chances of being asked for an interview.) If they do not want to interview you, ask what they felt was missing and what would have made a difference?

Clarify what they say down to specifics. For example, do not take "lack of experience" as an answer. Ask what kinds of tasks, responsibilities, and results they expect suitable candidates to have accomplished. The more details you can get, the better you can look for similar experiences from your past and position them as relevant.

It will also make clear the skills that you immediately need to start working on to improve your chances going forward.

WRITING YOUR RESUME: 10 TIPS ON CONTENT AND STRUCTURE

This section covers how to organize your credentials in such a way that your application jumps out of the pile. Although there are some design elements that can make your resume more attractive, I recommend you keep it simple and, above all, *aligned* with what the organization and interviewer likes. Find out beforehand!

1. Do not use a font size any smaller than 10 points. Anything smaller requires squinting and is annoying to the already under-pressure, overworked reader. Use bold headings and plenty of white space at the top to make the page attractive and user-friendly. Use a standard typeface that is easy to read. I personally never cared whether someone used first or third person. However, plenty of people believe you should use a third-person style.

2. On the very first line, after your name and contact information, state the title of the position for which you are applying. Interviewers have this position on their mind. Seeing the same words on the top of the page immediately shows that you are looking to fill *that* position. It can act as a subconscious nudge, edging you ahead of the candidates who submitted generic resumes and closer to the "select for interview" pile right away.

3. As we have stated before, you have to get the reader's attention within 5 to 10 seconds. When you meet people face to face, you have to build your likability, trust, and credibility as described in Chapter One first, before people will listen to you. You have to follow the alignment steps.

On a resume the reverse is true.

The reader has to believe you are capable of crossing the "This is who we want! threshold or they won't read any further. This means you have to start with the last Alignment step. From there you work backward through the alignment steps by then matching your strengths to their needs.

A great way to do this right up front is with a quote from a reputable reference at the top that *speaks directly* to the top priority results of the job in question. Choose a quote that emphasizes similar results or similar problems solved from a previous boss or client and put it just below where you list the position for which you are applying. ***Put it in bold to grab their attention!***

LinkedIn has made it quite acceptable for people to have quotes on their resumes. If you have researched a potential position, you will know its top priority results, the most common obstacles to success, and therefore the most important skills and strengths requirements. You will know what your future boss worries about most in terms of consequences of failure. There is nothing more powerful than a credible third party highlighting that you have the capabilities to solve relevant problems and achieve similar results, in a statement near the top. However, since there are often several top priorities and obstacles, have some additional quotes to confirm different but highly relevant capabilities further down on the resume under each position you have held.

Don't try squeezing all the required attributes into one quote, as this looks forced.

4. Provide a short paragraph summarizing why you believe you are a good fit for the position. The objective of this section is to immediately position yourself as directly relevant and whet the appetite of the reader to go through the rest of the resume to verify whether you cross the "suitable for hire" threshold. Again if this section fails to achieve its objective, the rest of your resume will not be read.

You do this by elaborating on the above quote. Use more examples of specific problems you solved and achievements that match the top priority results you know *they* are looking to achieve.

Note: If you have done thorough research and discovered what led to the position's former occupant failing, list that attribute as one of your strengths. It will immediately get the interviewer's attention. Remember, though: it has to be true!

Never, ever, EVER lie on your resume.

It will be there in black and white to haunt you for the rest of your career. People *always* find out, and word spreads.

If certain keywords or phrases were used in the job description or listing of requirements, make sure you use the same words in this paragraph and throughout your resume. This is increasingly important as I mentioned above; some larger companies will scan your resume before any human sees it.

In smaller companies, the chances are that the interviewer wrote the job requirements. Mirroring the interviewers' own words helps get you through their subconscious filters, as described in Chapter Two.

Use meaningful verbs like *built, created, increased, achieved,* and *won,* all of which emphasize your contributions. *Avoid hyperbole,* as discussed before.

5. Add a section on skills, particularly if you were able to obtain any certifications. Many skills are transferable to *any* position. These days, computer skills are the most obvious example. You can become proficient in various presentation tools, customer interaction systems, social media marketing, research, analytical and design programs, and many other types of software. You can also take courses on interpersonal skills such as sales, customer service, and verbal presentation. If the organizations you are interested in serve customers that speak different languages, start learning one of them.

Again, do your research and find out which of these are particularly important and *why.* Then highlight that you have them thereby matching to their needs. This is the section that should set any keyword search on fire!

Listing such skills helps the interviewer view you as a "PROACTIVE SELF-DEVELOPING ASSET" who can actually DO something useful immediately upon joining the organization.

This section can be particularly useful to recent graduates who feel that their section six (below) is a little light due to lack of experience.

Employers will understand that, as a recent graduate, you do not have much employment experience. What they will NOT understand is if you have failed to use your time wisely to learn any transferable skills like those mentioned above.

6. List your work experience in reverse chronological order, present position first. Begin with a clear title, the name of the organization, and the beginning and ending dates of employment. Briefly describe your *relevant* achievements in terms of *similar* top priorities you achieved and problems you solved. Do *NOT* simply describe your duties. Stating your duties at XYZ Company for three years does not tell the reader whether you did it well or poorly or gained any relevant experience. When possible, use *specific* hard evidence like amounts in dollars or percentage over achievement against agreed-upon objectives. Use the keywords you know they are looking for. This way each job in your past reinforces the impression that you are the right person.

Note: *Even though YOU may be proud of them, irrelevant achievements can position you as the wrong person. Interviewers look for measurable achievements that are very similar to the results THEY want. Anything else is a distraction.*

Put a short reference quote, ideally from your former boss, at the end of each position. Try to make sure that the quote confirms the results and highlights any particular skills you know to be relevant.

A quote from your manager from each job on your resume also implies that you left your previous jobs on good terms!

Knowing that you need this when you leave a position is another reason why it is *so* important to develop the right relationship with your boss from day one in the job. We cover this in Chapter Seven.

For recent college graduates, this section can be challenging due to limited work experience. If you are reading this early enough, do not look at temporary jobs simply as a source of income to get you through college. They can *all* help you. Even CEOs of large corporations were students once. They, too, waited tables, sold door to door, and stocked shelves at grocery stores. They can relate to your experience and will respect your efforts to build skills.

Regardless of how temporary or menial you feel the job may be, always look for opportunities to build transferable skills and add value. Get a written recommendation from EVERY employer for your achievement folder.

When you ask for recommendations, keep in mind the three areas future interviewers will want you to prove to them. Try to get these explicitly covered within such recommendations.

All this underlines the importance of being resume-conscious and starting to build it LONG before you need to start looking for a career job.

However, if you have left it late, use the reverse engineering technique previously described. Use the input from your connections and the keywords you have uncovered to guide you to find examples of relevant transferable skills you picked up at jobs you did while in college. This will also identify any new skills you are going to have to learn quickly so put in place plans to do so that you can describe during an interview. This takes us to point 7 below.

7. Put in a "Personal Goals" paragraph. Here you describe where you are driving your career. Describe your track record of achieving key milestones, including any promotions. Explain how this job fits into your plan and why you are motivated to do it. This is the section in which you address the "*Will you do the job?*" question. It's also where you can highlight how you overcame one of your most difficult challenges to showcase your perseverance and determination. Remember to keep it brief, though. Use it as a hook for further discussion in an interview.

8. Include a paragraph headed "Team Fit" in which you describe your ability to fit in. Discuss your experience joining and aligning with teams. Give prior examples. Use the knowledge you have gained through your connections inside the organization to highlight values and behavior you know are part of its culture. Finish with a quote from a previous manager that showcases your team dedication.

Note: Sections seven and eight are another opportunity for people early in their career who feel their section six is light. If you feel your ability to demonstrate experience that shows you can do the job is weak, at least make sure that you demonstrate your ability to fit in well, and that you have a strong desire to do the job.

9. List your academic degrees and accomplishments and where you got them. Indicate your major and any areas of specialization, along with any special recognition you achieved. Find a way to connect the relevance and benefit of what you studied to the job. This is quite a common question in early career interviews. Prepare for it. For readers just entering or still early in their studies, it's also a question you should be asking yourself *before you select* your courses. Don't rely solely on those *selling* you on the course for your information.

10. It is worth listing any professional associations and social interests, sports, or hobbies that will portray you in a favorable light. Managers like to know that you are active in professional associations. These often provide opportunities to take on responsibilities such as committee work and help you become well connected.

Note: Social interests are good, as potential employers also like to know that you are fit, healthy, and competitive. But don't leave the impression that your real passion will be satisfied at the expense of effort on the job. (Remember to align your drive.) Highlight sports and activities that are team-oriented rather than individual where possible. *Highlight your organizing, coaching, motivating, and leading skills.*

Don't forget winning! If you have a championship record, mention it. Employers know winning takes dedication, preparation, perseverance, and desire. These are all traits they look for. *They love winners.*

QUICK STORY

I was introduced to a brand-new member of our customer service department, and I asked why she thought we had selected her. (Knowing why you have been selected is important and something I will come back to in Chapter Seven.) She explained that when she saw the job advertisement, she reached out to some of her contacts as part of her research. They told her to be careful about joining us because we had launched a complicated software application that was frustrating our customers who, in turn, were putting tremendous strain on our customer service department. She did not back off. Instead, she emphasized her

170

experience with angry customers at the top of her resume. She also used a quote from one of her customers to back that up. This immediately got the attention of our customer services manager who could not wait to interview her.

SAMPLE TEMPLATE

As I said above, I put more emphasis on the content than the overall appearance as long as it is neat and clear.

Although there are literally hundreds of sample templates on the Internet that you can select from, my recommendation is to ask what layout your potential employer likes beforehand.

As part of your alignment activities, you should be able to get this info through your connections. Ask your contacts for samples of resumes *they* like. There will likely be differences from one industry to the next. An interior design company will have different expectations than an accounting firm. The best, of course, is to also understand the individual preference of the person making the decision to hire you. This should be part of how you build your "model resume" as discussed above.

I have included only a very simple template purely to indicate a standard type of layout to help you visualize the recommendations in the ten points above.

Applicant Name

Address
Phone
E-mail

Job Title Applying For

"Opening third party quote that speaks directly to the top priority results required for the job and your ability to deliver them."

PROFILE SUMMARY State what you can do and support this with relevant examples of problems that you have solved and priority results you have achieved.

SKILLS List the skills that you know from your research are considered important for producing the required results in the job.

WORK EXPERIENCE For each job, list the job title, the company, plus start and end dates.

Describe the achievements that most closely resemble the priority results of the job you are applying for.

"Have a quote from your manager endorsing you and highlighting another attribute you know to be relevant."

(Repeat this entire sequence for each job starting with your most recent and working backward.)

PERSONAL GOALS Describe your career plans and what you have achieved so far. Explain why this job is perfect for your career path.

TEAM FIT Explain how you have been a valuable team member in the past. List relevant examples.

"Have a quote from a manager supporting your team player claims."

EDUCATION List your education starting with your highest achievements. Include any relevant specialist subjects. State how your studies are applicable to the job.

SOCIAL INTERESTS List interests that fit with the company values. List team sports highlighting key positions such as captain or coach. List any significant achievements.

MAKE SURE YOUR RESUME IS READ

The best resume in the world will not help you if you cannot get it through to the right people and trigger them to read it. Both of these challenges are made significantly easier by good networking.

Getting your resume in front of the correct person when you have no connections inside the organization can be tricky. Even if you can get the right email address of the specific person making the hire, your email will often be discarded as junk by the system, or the recipient will delete it without reading it. Physical snail mail is expensive and just as likely to be discarded.

Your connections, however, will alert you to openings and point you to the right person. They can put in a good word for you and even make an introduction. This can sometimes result in an informal face-to-face briefing prior to a formal interview. This gives you the best opportunity to uncover the top priorities, challenges, and failure consequences they want to avoid. Another good question to ask any contacts you have is, "What is the one thing that would put a candidate significantly above the rest and why?" It is another way to ask what it will take to cross the "This is who we want!" threshold. The answer set you up to make sure your resume is on target and to make sure the recipient reads it.

Interviewers may get hundreds of resumes, so what will trigger them to read yours? This is what has traditionally been the subject of cover letters, dating back to when resumes were usually mailed. Now we mainly use email. Put the job title in the subject line so an interviewer immediately knows what the email is about. If you were able to speak with the reader before, start by referring to that conversation so that they connect this resume to you in person. Then summarize what was highlighted as the top priority result. Follow this with one *short* paragraph that shows exactly how you can deliver it. If you have identified a problem, show how *you* are the ideal solution. This is what will get readers' attention and spark their interest to read your resume for further details.

This is the only objective of your cover email: get the interviewer's attention and provide the motivation to click on your attached resume.

Do *not* make your cover email a lengthy rehash of your resume!

If you don't get the chance to meet or even call the interviewer to get this kind of information before sending a resume, get it from your other contacts and use it in the same way as above. If you have no contacts, then your only option is to rely on your research of keywords and phrases and your general knowledge of this type of job. Pick the most common keyword and write a short paragraph around it.

A good way to make your cover letter get the reader's attention quickly, (remember you only have seconds) is to use a quote containing keywords from a credible reference.

At this point, I often get a comment that this sounds exactly the same as the opening quote and summary on the actual resume. It's a fair point. I think they can be the same, especially if you are very confident that you know the one defining ability that will get their attention. To make the cover letter not seem identical to the resume, you can use a differently worded quote from another reference, but highlight the same quality you identified as being the most important.

If you don't know which quality is most important, or have identified that there is more than one, then you could play it safe and have a different one on the cover email versus the resume. The problem is you are guessing. You can see how much better it is to get real info from your contacts.

As stated before, always follow up with a phone call. When you have sent it, wait a day or two and then call to ask if the person received it and read it.

If the answer is yes, ask for feedback. With any negative comments, get specific details so you can learn. If positive, immediately ask for an appointment for the formal interview!

If the interviewer has not yet read it, ask if you can call for feedback the following day. This way you have made sure it was received, and subtly applied a bit of pressure to make sure it is *going* to be read.

The key point is that you often have to SELL THE RESUME before it can sell you!

This means getting your resume in front of the *right* people with a compelling reason for them to read it.

A QUICK STORY

Many years ago, I received an email with "THIS CUSTOMER IS REALLY HAPPY!" in the title.

Since high customer satisfaction ratings were one of my top priorities, I immediately opened it. I did not save the email, but it went something like this:

Dear Mr. Groenendyk

I hereby attach an e-mail I received from one of our customers. I have deleted all identity details for confidentiality reasons.

The bank was very upset and about to cancel their contract with our company as a result of what they thought were errors in our software. I was able to resolve the issues, which turned out to be operator errors by the bank staff. They are now delighted.

Their email (attached) says it all.

I have been following your company for some time and would really like to meet you to see if you have a role for me in your international operations. I would like to gain work experience outside the U.S. as an important part of my career plan.

I believe I could get the same kind of reaction from your international customers!

Do you have any time available next two weeks? I have attached my resume for your information.

Yours sincerely,
Mr. XYZ

The attached email, addressed to his boss, described how this individual had spent two days, *and the night between,* working nonstop on their premises solving a problem with their computer system. He also put in place a process to prevent the problem from happening again. They were clearly very relieved and grateful for the effort.

This was a direct appeal to a priority I was measured on—customer satisfaction.

He showed that he understood the importance of customer satisfaction and was prepared to go above and beyond the call of duty to achieve it. He highlighted a dreaded consequence of failure by mentioning that a customer was about to cancel a contract, and then he demonstrated that he had overcome specific challenges to avoid that happening. That was all I needed to trigger a "This is who I want !" reaction.

It made me *want* to read his resume.

HOW DO YOU STAND OUT ON AN APPLICATION FORM?

One of the biggest dangers when filling out an application form is that they are somewhat tedious and can cause you to fill them in robotically, especially once you have filled out quite a few. This can make you appear bland and undifferentiated. Those who believe resumes are no longer required, and who have not developed the practice of aligning themselves with the particular needs of a specific employer, are *very* susceptible to this danger.

Think of an application form as the employer's standardized format for the information in the TAILORED RESUME you prepared, based

on all the information you acquired from the connections you built in that organization.

Always go through the process described in this chapter to build your relevant and high-impact resume for any job you target. Then use the information in your resume to fill out an application form if requested to do so.

Try to connect every answer to the needs you uncovered.

Keep the key thresholds in mind as you answer questions. Ask yourself if you are crossing them. This way you ensure your answers are aligned with what the employer is looking for and allow you to differentiate yourself.

As you fill in an application form, always remember to address their top priority results and the problems that they worry about.

If the form does not have sections in it that allow you to describe your unique suitability, then cover these in a separate attention-grabbing cover email and also attach your resume. (If you are filling out a paper application form, enclose your resume and an attention-grabbing cover letter with it.)

Note: Be aware that some application forms have evolved to become mini paper-based or online interviews. This includes a tendency to ask behavioral questions. This makes it important to find out if the organization uses them and to discuss them with your contacts way ahead of filling in a form. Go online, or ask human resources or your contacts for a copy. Make a note of all the behavioral questions and discuss them with your connections. Find out what these questions are looking for, and then prepare your answers.

If you attempt to fill in a standard application form without any of the above prior preparation, your chances of differentiating yourself are slim to none!

If despite your research and preparation you are faced with a question you are still not sure about, remember that most questions are addressing one of the three areas: *Will you fit in? Can you do the job?* and *Will you do the job?* Always ensure your answer addresses something you know is important to the employer within one of the above areas.

The key is not to treat an application as "just another form to fill in." Every answer needs careful thought as to how it can increase your chances of being selected.

Think about what lies behind the question.

PART II

ACHIEVEMENT PORTFOLIO

WHAT IS IT AND WHY IS IT IMPORTANT?

Whether you're applying for a job, seeking a promotion, or just coming up for a performance review, you need a readily available source of *hard evidence* to support your claims.

This is where a portfolio full of your certifications, achievements and reference letters comes into play. Its purpose is to reinforce your credibility.

Even if you have achieved everything you claim on your resume, if you have no evidence to prove it, some managers and interviewers may not be convinced.

Earlier I recommended building a model or ideal resume that acts as a specification document for developing the required skills and achievements for the job you want. Your achievement folder should be filled with the results of developing yourself to meet those requirements. Your final "actual" resume should only claim what the contents of your achievement folder can support.

HOW TO STRUCTURE A PORTFOLIO THAT WILL DRIVE YOUR DEVELOPMENT AND IMPRESS ANY INTERVIEWER.

Divide your portfolio into the following three headings and subsections.

Start with a heading called;

TOP PRIORITY RESULTS AND MATCHING ACHIEVEMENTS

Target Results

In this section list and describe the top priority results you have uncovered as being highly desirable for the type of jobs you are interested in.

Matching Results

Below this heading, describe your achievements that most closely match the above target results and describe their impact to the business. Include *how* you achieved them by describing the *actions* you took.

Action Plans

In this section document your plans to achieve additional matching results. This is especially important if you do not have any relevant matching results. Talk to your connections for advice on the best way to do this.

Evidence of Matching Results

Include evidence such as thank you emails and letters of appreciation. Proactively get such evidence from your managers, colleagues, and customers.

Have another heading called;

OBSTACLES TO SUCCESS AND MATCHING EXAMPLES

Target Obstacles

List and describe the key challenges and problems anyone in your jobs of choice needs to be able to solve to achieve the priority results expected of them. (You can get this information from your connections.)

Matching Examples

Below this, describe similar problems you have overcome. Use the Achievement methodology covered in Chapter Ten to describe *how* you did so.

Action Plans

If you have no such examples, set goals and document your plans to gain the required experience along with any evidence that you are actually carrying out your plans. Think courses, volunteering, and internships for example.

Evidence of obstacles solved – Results!

Include any supporting documentation that acts as proof of the above examples.

This approach ensures you become very conscious of developing the experience you need for the jobs you want.

This is often an eye-opening exercise that highlights your shortcomings. Empty sections will drive you to proactively find ways and make plans to gain the experience you need. It will prevent you from drifting as valuable time goes by without adding to the credentials you need. Also, having plans to build missing experience along with evidence that you are carrying out these plans is a lot better than simply stating you have no relevant experience. It indicates your *desire* to align.

Note: Some people are uncomfortable asking for documentation after they have achieved something to confirm it for their portfolio. It feels too much like begging for a compliment. Part of why you build good connections and relationships is precisely so that you *can* ask. This is why I put so much emphasis on interpersonal skills in the early chapters. If you have taken the time to understand your colleagues' or managers' expectations and then exceeded them, you have helped those people exceed *their* objectives. Providing a written commendation can be the easiest way for them to thank you.

So don't hesitate to ask!

If someone expresses appreciation for your work and you would like those comments in your portfolio, ask for a letter or email *immediately*, while that person is feeling good about you.

If you wait six months until just before your next performance review or when you decide to interview for another job, the person may have forgotten what you did or left the organization.

References may also suddenly be withheld once someone knows you are looking for another job. (Or you may have botched something and upset that person since then!)

Sometimes, you can even create the evidence yourself. For example, if you excelled in a task, send a thank-you email to anyone who provided assistance, along with their manager(s). Summarize what was achieved, the help you received, and the impact. Add a sentence about something relevant that you learned in the process from those who helped you. You are very likely to get a response, which serves as verification. (Remember it *must* be genuine and not appear self-serving!) Put a copy of both your email and the response in your portfolio. You will also be building loyalty and putting goodwill in the tanks of those you thank and give credit to. You will certainly need their help again.

Have a heading called

KEY SKILLS AND QUALIFICATIONS. As above, put in subheads as follows.

Target Skills and Qualifications

List each target skill or qualification you know is required for your desired jobs and promotions.

Matching Skills and Qualifications

For each skill, document how you have acquired it and put it to use.

Skills Development Action Plans

Document how you plan to further improve such skills. If you are missing a key skill, document how you plan to acquire it.

Skills Evidence

Always get a certificate of completion if you go for specialized training. If none exists, get written proof to verify it. (When looking for any courses, check first what form of certification you will receive at the end. Also, check how well this certification is recognized and regarded by asking the employers you are interested in.) Of course, include all certificates from high school and college.

Note: As with the above heading on achievements, you are much more likely to actually develop these skills if you document your plans to achieve them. Regularly going over what your connections have advised that you need in terms of your skills and achievements will act as a mechanism for you to keep pursuing them.

These three sections above effectively define "YOUR top priority results" in your quest to get your jobs of your choice.

Your consequences of failure are clear—failure to land the jobs you want!

Have a heading called;

PREPARED ANSWERS.

Sometimes when I am with students, I will ask someone in the group how they would answer the following question;

> "How can you assure me you will persevere through difficult tasks when we are under pressure to get something important done?"

I get responses like, "Well, I am very determined!" It's an empty assurance that conveys no information, so I ask for examples. This is usually followed by a mixture of rambling, long silences, and lots of ums.

To score well on interview answers, you need to anticipate the questions and prepare specific examples of WHAT YOU DID in order to demonstrate WHAT YOU CAN DO.

A better answer would be, "Well, I have several examples of where I had to really knuckle down against tough deadlines to keep customers happy. My first example is working through three weekends in a row to finish a difficult project on time for a customer. As you can see (as you hand over a copy of an email from your achievement folder), the customer in question wrote to my boss thanking us for our efforts. As a result, they recommended us to another organization that subsequently acquired our software, too. Is this the kind of evidence you are looking for?"

You need *stories* in your portfolio showing actual behavior that indicates you have the qualities a specific employer is looking for.

You can't make up relevant examples from your memory and articulate them well under the pressure of an interview. You have to prepare for them.

This is indeed hard work, but it really pays off. Without such preparation, you will have no chance against any competing candidate who *does* prepare this way.

Make a list of the key questions you may be asked. Divide them into the three areas we have discussed before.

1. Will you fit in? Will it be a pleasure to manage you? Will you listen, take criticism and direction? Will you be able to perform as part of the team? Will other managers, colleagues and customers like you? Are you trustworthy, reliable, and loyal? Do you share the same values?

2. Can you do the job? Will you be effective? Do you have the relevant skills and experience? Have you successfully done something like this before? What were the problems you solved? Are you creative? How do you keep improving and adding to your skills? Could you do more? Are you management and leadership material?

3. Will you do this job? Will you be committed to the mission? Will you care enough never to let anyone down? What motivates you? What are your ambitions and are they aligned? Will you stick around for a significant period of time? What is your track record of persevering when things get difficult? What are your career plans and what is your progress to date? Have you been promoted?

You know me by now—I like structure. So here is another little structure that will help you **soar** above your competitors!

When you prepare your examples, use a simple structure that will make your answer concise and easy for the interviewer to listen to. To help you remember it, think of **S.O.A.R.**

Situation. Start with a brief description of the situation to provide context, a background that is relevant to the question being asked.

Objective. Describe what you were trying to accomplish in that situation. Again it should be relevant and similar to objectives in the target job.

Actions. Explain the actions you took. These should be actions which demonstrate you can do what is being asked in the target job.

Results. Describe the impact of your actions *preferably in results* and have written proof of these results available. These results should match the results you are being asked for in the job you are applying for.

At the end of the answer ALWAYS check if the interviewer is satisfied. If they are not satisfied, you can clarify why and you can try answering again until you are on target. If they like your answer, you can refer to it again later to help differentiate yourself during the negotiations.

Using the above S.O.A.R. structure start building and writing down answers to the obvious questions above. Prepare at least two or three answers that would get you over the ability, fit and drive thresholds. Do the same for the "This is who we want !" threshold. Then add to them by asking your connections which questions are most often used in interviews in their organization. In the next chapter, I will cover many of the basic questions, and I will also show you how to ask "set up" questions of your own that open opportunities for you to use S.O.A.R. as you bring up pre-prepared relevant examples of your strengths.

Do not underestimate the power of your achievement portfolio. In any selection process, all other things being equal, the candidates with tangible, relevant, well-prepared, and rehearsed evidence will win.

Some people keep hard copies while others prefer to do this electronically. I recommend both. Having something you can physically show and hand over during interviews can be very useful, particularly for more traditional interviewers.

Start filling out the sections immediately. Make it a habit. Develop a sense of pride about your folder. Review it frequently, at least once per month. Set monthly goals around skills and achievements, document them, and add them. Rehearse your prepared answers to your connections and get feedback from them. It builds confidence, motivation, and a sense of forward momentum.

This will completely transform how professional you appear when you meet your target employers. If you have never done this before and are in a job already, doing so now will completely transform how you will be regarded by your boss.

Lastly, *ALWAYS HAVE BACKUP COPIES.* Lose your portfolio and risk losing your credibility with it.

Now that you have a good resume backed by an achievement portfolio full of relevant information, it is time to talk about references.

PART III

REFERENCES

HOW TO USE THEM TO SEAL THE DEAL

Unfortunately many candidates exaggerate their abilities and performance. *(I know you would never do that!)* Nevertheless, many employers have developed a high degree of skepticism. They want measurable results they can verify with your former supervisors and human resources departments. They need the reassurance of talking to someone *other than you* about your capabilities.

Many organizations have policies in place that INSIST they talk to references.

It will, therefore, be very hard to land a job without references.

Developing a relationship that encourages anyone you work for to become a great reference should be a personal TOP PRIORITY for you.

The first opportunity to utilize your references is for those quotes on your resume to emphasize your strengths that match their key requirements. Begin by asking your best references. Reassure them their contact details will not be circulated and that they will only be contacted after you have asked their permission and only for references on "real" job opportunities.

Make it easy for them by offering to write the quote yourself.

As long as you have taken the trouble to develop the right relationship as I will show you later, you do not need to be shy about this. Say something like, "Based on my research, they are looking for [XYZ]. To make it easy for you, I can write a quote on your behalf that will play exactly into what they are looking for. Of course, I will send it to you for your approval before I use it." This saves them time and effort and ensures you get a quote that fits your needs. It also ensures you get it quickly as it is much easier for your reference to approve something than write it from scratch.

Note: It is very awkward going back to ask a reference to hurry or, even worse, having to ask them to modify a quote because it wasn't quite right.

When it comes to providing "live" references, usually by phone, make sure you get their permission as stated above and warn them first. *Your references will not appreciate a surprise call.*

Above all, BRIEF THEM in detail on the requirements of any such opportunity so that the reference they give is also ALIGNED to the needs of the job.

Give them detailed insight by describing the position's top priorities and challenges. Remind your references of relevant examples of achievements that you would like them to bring to your interviewer's attention.

Most references will be contacted after you have succeeded in an interview. Go over the questions you were asked and the answers you responded with. Your references will likely be asked the same questions. Remember, a good interviewer will dig into what you achieved and how you achieved it. They will ask about strengths and require supporting examples of your strengths in action. They will ask about weaknesses and their impact on your performance. Make sure your references are prepared and that their answers are consistent with yours.

Make sure they are capable of carrying you over the key thresholds.

Go through this with your references, ideally in person or by telephone.

Then summarize the key points by email for your references to access when they receive the call from your potential employer. Send your reference each relevant S.O.A.R. you have pre-prepared for the target job.

This is very critical.

Even your best reference may forget key points and can inadvertently position you as the WRONG candidate if you do not brief the person in detail and in writing.

However, NOTHING is more compelling to a potential employer than a credible reference such as a previous boss providing highly relevant and detailed examples (using S.O.A.R.) of how you delivered results that are similar to the top priority results required in the job you are after.

This is why building references is *SO* important.

Develop a 24x7 reference building mindset!

Whenever you are interacting with your boss, colleagues, or any internal or external customers, ask yourself how you can turn this situation into a job winning reference opportunity. This will spur you on to do your absolute best each and every time.

If you fail to do so, you will feel very naked the next time you are asked for a reference!

FOUR TIPS ON BUILDING LASTING REFERENCES

The alignment actions in Chapter One set you up perfectly to build references. Remember, you are connecting, forming relationships, understanding their objectives, and then focusing your efforts to maximize your performance to meet those objectives. However, even if you excel at this, do not rely on people to become references automatically—*just because you think you deserve them.* Managers are busy with their own pressures, and they also change jobs.

References need to be cultivated and maintained both while you are working for them—AND long afterward.

Here are some key steps:

1. Practice the alignment actions. Without them, you will not satisfy the requirements of any boss and therefore won't build any reference potential. You have built up enough goodwill in their tanks *and keep maintaining it* for them to *want* to help you.

2. Make sure any successful results you achieve are clearly documented and acknowledged by the boss immediately upon completion. Remember to use S.O.A.R. as a structure. With the right relationship in place, you can be very transparent about this. Make time for a face-to-face meeting armed with a written summary of your achievement. Go over it and ask if they agree with your summary and whether they would sign off on it. Put the documentation in your achievement folder. This process keeps your manager informed of your results, reinforces your good performance in their mind, and gives you tangible evidence at performance appraisals. It builds your track record as an achiever, which makes you easy to promote and provide a good reference for. Years later, when you want that reference to highlight a particularly relevant achievement, you can send them a copy of your summary to provide the details.

Note: If you do not do this, it is easy for a busy manager to be completely unaware of your role in an achievement. Also, the world is full of people willing to steal the credit for what you did!

3. In addition to your direct managers, identify other senior people, colleagues, and customers throughout your career and ask if you can rely on them as "anchor" references. These are the people you will turn to most often when you need a reference.

Maintain the connections through regular contact and doing things to keep their goodwill tanks filled. Do not contact them only when you need them.

Note: I meet many people who appear to rely on one major reference that they repeatedly turn to. This can dry out their goodwill tank. Also, they might not be available one day. It is a dangerous situation, usually the result of not making enough effort to satisfy *all* of their previous bosses or a failure to cultivate them as references. Interviewers will spot that you only have one and deliberately ask for more. For example, they will routinely ask for *all your previous bosses* and a list of some of your colleagues as references to get a sense of your team player skills.

4. A great way to create really good references (beyond blowing their minds with your outstanding performance) is to ask some of them to become mentors. Mentors become invested in their protégés and want to help. Mentors are also much more likely to remain good references and willing to help you long after you have stopped working for them. Likewise being a good mentor for your direct reports later in your career will ensure not only a positively developing team who perform better but a pool of subordinate references when you need them.

SUMMARY

Your objective is to convince a skeptical recruiter that you have the ability to fit into their team, accomplish challenging results, and have the drive to want to do the job. More specifically you have to show that you understand more clearly than your competitors what the top priority results are and how they will be measured. You need to understand what problems could prevent success and that you are the best candidate to deal with these problems.

To be relevant and compelling, you need to have prepared examples (using S.O.A.R) of how you solved similar problems and achieved similar results.

This will put you in great shape to be invited for an interview and soar through it!

It is possible to reverse engineer your resume to bring it on target. However:

A resume is like the tip of an iceberg. Much of what creates a good resume is the out-of-sight previous goals and targeted efforts to build an achievement portfolio bursting with relevant examples of your capabilities, supported by credible references.

Early adoption of the "targeted-skill-building" approach for the jobs you want is the best way to create a solid base to support your resume. You do this by connecting with the right people, learning what problems they have to solve, what results they have to deliver, and what skills they needed to build. You then set those skills as your personal development goals. This is how you build genuine, compelling relevance—with less need for reverse engineering and lipstick!

This requires a great deal of commitment and the words of Bud Wilkinson come to mind.

"The will to prepare is as important as the will to win."

Bud Wilkinson

CHAPTER FIVE

NAILING THE INTERVIEW

You have an interview! Everything up to now has been aimed at getting you face-to-face with an employer. This is the *pivotal moment* in the selection process, and this chapter's objective is to help you make the most of it.

Let's start by looking at this from the interviewer's perspective.

Interviewers do not look for people in a vacuum. They will be meeting you with their top priority results, obstacles to success, and consequences of failure in mind. They will have specific needs and equally specific *selection criteria*. These will be influenced by specific difficulties prevailing at the time, new initiatives they want to get started, the strengths and weaknesses of previous employees in the job, the company culture, and the personal likes and dislikes of the interviewers themselves.

They will come to the meeting with a list of questions addressing these issues. A brief introduction will be followed by formal questioning after which the interview will be closed with a "Thank you. We will let you know."

Do NOT just sit there and allow this to happen!

Many people do, perhaps because they are nervous and have always been urged to do as they are told. They are eager to please, and therefore they just go with the flow.

You must also create your own flow—one that clearly shows how ALIGNED you are with the interviewer's requirements and personality.

PART I

PRE-INTERVIEW ALIGNMENT

It is very easy to tell who has aligned prior to the interview and who has not. Two old favorite questions will do the trick every time.

Why do you want this job?

Those who have aligned talk about how through networking they learned about many different jobs, what was involved in each on a daily basis and how they decided this is what they want to do and why. They talk about whom they networked with and how they learned about what makes people successful in this role. They can describe their personal and career goals and how this role fits into them.

Why should we hire you?

Those who have aligned already know what the top priorities of the job are and why. They understand the expected results and consequences of failure. They can relate their strengths to the specific needs of the job. They have examples ready.

Hopefully, you got the interview by following the steps outlined in the previous chapters. If so you would have aligned yourself and easily be able to demonstrate how you are able to do the job, are a good cultural fit, and how everything you have done to position yourself shows your motivation, commitment, and drive.

However, *it is possible* to land an interview without going through this process. For example, if you have optimized your online profile as previously described, you may be identified through a search from an employer or a recruiter and get an invite. In this case, you must cram in some detailed research and preparation before the interview. Don't feel pressure to just accept an interview appointment time as soon as possible. Make sure you have the time to research by scheduling the interview at least a week out if you can and then really get to work! Keep asking yourself:

How are you going to compete with someone who has already spent months, even years, aligning for the same job?

So how can you find out as much as possible about the job, the department, the manager, the company, and the industry with no inside connections?

There is a great deal of information available on the Internet. You can start with the website of the company in question. You can learn a lot by reading about the leadership team, news, and events—such as new product launches and so on. Look at the management team LinkedIn profiles (including your interviewer's profile) and see what they cite as their achievements. See if you can find profiles of other people with the same job title you are applying for in their organization. See what they highlight as their achievements. See what they are blogging about. This will provide great information which you can clarify, make complementary comments on, and use to highlight common interests during the connect phase.

Go to sites such as www.CareerOneStop.org. It has information on what skills are typically required by job type (under Skills Profiler) and what the industry trends are. They also provide salary ranges and trends, such as whether they are growing or on the decline.

While sites like this are very useful, the information is bound to be somewhat generic.

Try going to your existing contacts in similar organizations to help clarify the top priorities and common challenges in similar positions there. Also, the knowledge that you have been invited for an interview elsewhere can sometimes spark an interview request in these organizations too. They'll be thinking, "John really prepares seriously. I have just looked at his profile. I am not surprised ABC Company has asked him for an interview.

Don't *we* have anything for him?" Also, find out if your contacts in similar organizations know anyone in the company that invited you for an interview. People move around within industries, so it is very likely. Ask if they could make an immediate introduction. Alternatively, ask if you can use their names while making your own introductions. The latter is sometimes better when time is short as it puts you in control.

CALL THE HUMAN RESOURCES MANAGER

Does the organization have a human resources department? Call and ask to speak to the HR manager. Explain you have been invited for an interview and want to ask some advice. Remember to use the call structure I showed you in Chapter Three on networking when speaking with the manager.

The Introduction

"Good morning, Mr. Smith. My name is John Brown."

The Opening

"I have been invited for an interview with Ms. Jones. I very much liked the job description, and I'm excited at the possibility of joining your organization."

The Request

"However, I have a few questions that could help me prepare the relevant information for Ms. Jones when we meet."

The Benefit

"I would like to make sure that Ms. Jones's time is well spent."

The Close

"Could you spare a few minutes on the phone to go over my questions? I would be happy to call back at a more convenient time if you prefer." (*Wait for the HR manager to agree or suggest another time.*)

Mention your interview in the introduction to provide immediate context. Provide a benefit statement to keep their attention. Include a compliment in the opening (it is quite possible that HR prepared the job description), then go straight to requesting a few minutes of their time. Once they agree, you're free to ask your questions. Go to their objectives, priorities and challenges!

Is this risky? I do not believe so. It is in the HR managers' interest that the interviewer's time is not wasted by an ill-prepared candidate. They will appreciate any actions that will allow the organization to make a better assessment of your abilities. Have your list of questions prepared so that you stay crisp and professional. When you are done, be sure to thank them. Get an email address so you can send a more formal thank you in writing. If the call was friendly, ask if you could stop by the HR office to say hello when you come for the interview. Arrange a time an hour before the interview. You will almost certainly be able to learn something else that can help you. In the process, you will make a friend, a contact that can start coaching you onto the inside track. As a result, the HR manager is more likely to take a greater interest in your application and ask the interviewer how you did. Afterward, you can ask the HR manager for feedback.

I believe HR managers are relatively low-risk advice contacts. They understand what you are trying to do. Just keep it totally professional.

CALL THE INTERVIEWER

It is possible that the HR manager may not be able to give you much information if the company is very large because they are not close enough to what is happening in the department you wish to join. In this case, you could ask the HR manager whether it would be advisable to speak to the interviewer direct.

This is *definitely* higher risk, and *you should* ask the HR manager for advice. Personally, if candidates called me prior to an interview to make sure they were well prepared, I would take their calls. However, not everyone feels the same way, so I advise caution.

Here is how a direct call to the interviewer could go:

The Introduction

"Good morning, Ms. Jones. My name is John Brown."

The Opening

"I have a scheduled interview with you for a position in your customer service department at 9 a.m. next Tuesday. Do you have a minute?"

(I recommend asking if now is convenient right up front because you may have called at a bad time, in which case Ms. Jones will not listen to a word you say. Better to find out right away and ask for another time. Continue if now is convenient.)

"First, thank you for inviting me. I am extremely interested in this position. I really liked the job description."

Get the compliment in early!

The Request

"I would like some information *because* I want to be fully prepared for when we meet."

Remember people respond to the word "because."

The Benefit

"Hopefully, this will ensure your time is well spent, too."

Get the benefit in.

The Close

"I basically have three questions. May I proceed?"

(Saying that you only have three questions makes you sound prepared, concise, and not likely to take up too much time.)

How risky is this? The most likely response you will get is, "What kind of questions?" This is your opening to go into your well-rehearsed list. Choose your questions carefully and remember to position them so that making an effort to answer appears to be in *the organization's* interest. Do *not* start the interview over the phone or—worse—give the person enough info to decide not to bother with the interview! *So don't start talking about yourself.* If there was a job description, do not ask questions that were already covered there. If there was no description, you have *every* reason to call the interviewer to get at least a verbal version.

Try something like this:

"It would help me greatly to know what areas you want to focus on so that I can prepare in more detail. For example, what would you say are the top three priorities in this job?" Then let the interviewer talk. A good second question to ask is, "What are the most difficult challenges this position must be capable of dealing with?" The obvious third question is "What do you see as the top skills anyone in this job must have?"

As the person describes their priorities, you have the opportunity to clarify and ask *why* they are important so that you can talk to *consequences* during the interview. This will help you to build up an arsenal of relevant examples. How many questions you actually end up being able to ask will depend on how open and friendly the interviewer is. I will talk about different personality types shortly. Certain personalities will entertain a call like this. Others, depending on their moods, may simply tell you to save it for the day of the interview. I recommend limiting your questions to the above, or you risk doing the interview over the phone or irritating the interviewer by taking up too much time.

Whatever happens, stay courteous, do not take longer than 10 minutes, thank the person if they helped you, and reconfirm the interview time. Remember the objective of this pre-interview phase is to gain information to help you prepare for the main interview, *not* to talk about yourself.

PREPARE AND PRACTICE

Practice on somebody.

Yes, I am serious. You may think you have your answers (and your questions) clear in your mind, but they will sound totally different when you try to say them out loud to somebody else. If you just rely on saying what comes to mind without any practice, you will hesitate, um and ah, and can easily get tongue-tied. This is especially true if you are nervous. Before you know it you will have lost the interviewer's attention and left a poor impression.

Knowing that you have questions and answers developed and well-rehearsed gives you a massive confidence boost that will be very apparent. How confident and articulate you are (or are not!) has a huge impact on those vital first impressions. Just a few stumbles at the beginning of the interview can cost you the job.

Sit down and spend the time brainstorming the questions you want to ask, the likely answers you'll get, and vice versa. Of course, there are literally hundreds of questions interviewers can ask; you can find plenty on the Internet. Entire books have been dedicated to the topic. I have listed a few of the most common during the section on building your achievement portfolio in Chapter Four and provided some more in Part IV of this chapter.

Ask one or two of your senior-executive contacts to help you do a practice interview.

Go into full role-play for the entire interview, and have a debriefing afterward. It is a great way to get feedback and help you hone your answers.

You may think your answers sound great, but many will sound lame to a senior executive.

Feedback and guidance can *transform* your answers. If you do not have any senior connections, it is time to make some! I cannot stress this enough. Do *NOT* go to an important interview without preparing and rehearsing first. Interviews are not easy to come by, so do not waste them—interviewers know instantly who has rehearsed and who hasn't.

Let me put it more provocatively.

Candidates with weaker skills than you will be selected instead of you if they have researched and rehearsed more than you.

Let's move on to how you make the most out of the actual interview.

PART II

HOW TO DRIVE AN INTERVIEW

This is the time where all your alignment efforts come together.

You cannot be passive and hope the interviewer will ask you questions that will allow you to highlight all your relevant strengths.

The good news is you can use the exact same alignment steps I showed you in Chapter One to drive the interview to the subjects *YOU* want to cover.

Note: I will go over these steps as if you have *NOT* pre-aligned through extensive networking before the interview. This is so you can see how the steps will help you align *during* an interview as there will be times you have to be able to do this. I will then show you the incredible advantage someone who *HAS* networked and pre-aligned will have in executing these steps.

1. CONNECT

In the very initial stage of the interview, you need to take the initiative with a warm but professional smile, lock eyes and reach forward for a confident handshake. You use your interpersonal skills to connect and start building a relationship with the interviewer. Your objective is to reach a *threshold of likeability and trust* before you attempt to go any further. Failure to do this will undermine *all your efforts* in the following steps.

Remember each step acts as a pre-requisite foundation for the next step. Each has a threshold of acceptability before you can proceed to the following step. You have to earn the right to cross over each threshold.

In Chapter Two, we discussed how people like others who appear, think, sound and behave as they do. They like people who agree with them, compliment them, and share common experiences and beliefs. Ask wide open questions to help you look for opportunities to do this. Look for an opportunity to connect using any information you learned from your contacts, LinkedIn, and Google. Look around the interviewer's office for talking points during the introductory period. This is also the phase during which you assess the interviewer's personality type. I will cover how personalities can affect an interview later in this chapter.

Remember your first impressions!

A quick review of do's and don'ts:

- Find out if the company has a dress code and adhere to it. If in doubt, go business professional.
- I should not have to say this, but hygiene matters, so smell and look clean. You would be surprised what I have experienced in interviews. On several occasions, my assistant held her nose behind candidates as she ushered them into my office. The candidate had virtually no chance after that! Do not overdo the cologne or perfume, either. It can be equally offensive or at least distracting.
- Never ever be late! Build at least an hour or more contingency into your travel plan to the interview location.
- Be in control of your face. Tense, nervous faces with averted eyes do not earn trust, confidence, or likability. Put on the confident smile you have practiced, and maintain good eye contact. Breathe deeply, *and look happy to be there!* This is the opportunity you wanted! Don't look as if you are expecting root canal work.
- Practice introducing yourself in a clear, confident voice. Nervous squeaky tones with a hesitation or a stumble right at the beginning are instant turn-offs.

2. UNDERSTAND

Once you have reached a threshold of likeability and trust, you can then ask targeted open questions to uncover their needs.

Your objective is to reassure the interviewer that you fully understand their requirements. If the interviewer does not believe you understand their needs, they will not take you or anything you say seriously. You have to reach a *credibility threshold* in the mind of the interviewer.

The information you obtain in this step enables you to link your answers to their specific needs in the next step. Your questions must cover their expectations regarding your fit into their team, your ability to do the job and your motivations to do it.

The more you can get the interviewer talking, the more needs you will find which give you opportunities to respond with a statement such as, "Oh, I have specific experience with that" which you can then elaborate on. This is why we call them "set up" questions. They set you up to be able to provide a matching strength statement.

Here are a number of questions you can use to set up your strength statements.

"How would you describe the company culture and key values?"

"What do you see as the top priority results for this position?"

"What do you see as the biggest challenges facing the individual in this role?"

"What would you say are the most important skills and experience the candidate needs to have?"

"What are the most important attitudes this role requires?

"Have others failed in this role and, if so, why?"

"How does success or failure by this person affect you and the rest of the department?"

"What are the most important criteria you are using to choose one candidate over another?"

Every question is designed to get you information that sets you up to align yourself with a follow-up answer.

As an example, consider the two different dialogues below.

Example one – passive approach

The interviewer is worrying about one of their top priority results, which is improving customer satisfaction. So as you sit passively going with their flow, they say, "Tell me about your experience handling customers."

You respond, "Oh, yes, I have had two years in customer service at my previous company. I know a lot about handling customers." You might think, *"Nailed it!"* because now they know you have two years of customer service experience.

However, neither of you have actually learned much. It is up to the interviewer whether to explore the topic further or not. If you created a good first impression and they like you, they might follow up with more questions. This is why the connect phase is so important. It increases your margin for error and still be in the game. However if they're pressed for time or just an inexperienced interviewer, they may give you a check in a box along with other candidates that have customer service experience and move on. Opportunity for high impact differentiation lost.

Example two – proactive questioning approach

You ask the interviewer a set-up question, such as "Could you tell me a little about the top priorities you see for this role?"

The interviewer responds, "I would say it is improving customer satisfaction."

You say, "I see. Would you mind elaborating a little more? What kind of satisfaction issues do you have?"

The interviewer responds with, "Our help desk has been struggling and getting a lot of criticism."

You can see how by asking questions *you* are in control of the conversation and can decide whether to dig deeper or not, depending on whether this is leading to a setup for one of your strengths. Assuming you have help desk or customer service experience, you could clarify further for specific issues. You could say, "That is interesting. I worked at help desks for several years. What kind of criticism are they getting?"

The interviewer might clarify, "Well, the people at our help desk just do not have enough expertise in our technology to help our customers."

Now you have a specific issue you can use as an opportunity. Once you have enough information, you can respond with, "Oh, yes, I am very familiar with that kind of problem. Here is how we dealt with that at my last company."

At this point, you go to step three where you match your strengths.

Can you see the difference in the two exchanges? You have gained valuable information to help you align. The interviewer comes away with a strong impression that you understand their needs and will be interested to hear what you have to say. *You just crossed their credibility threshold.*

You have also put into the interviewer's mind that you had a common experience—which, you may remember, is one of the ways you can make people feel they've connected with you.

3. MATCH

Your objective is to provide *compelling strength statements* that are *directly relevant* to the *needs uncovered* in the previous step. We refer to this as crossing the "suitable for hire" threshold.

First of all keep it short!

I've said it before, but it's that important:

Try not to talk for more than 30 seconds at a time under any circumstances. Twenty to 25 seconds is the best point to stop and ask for feedback.

Most pressured managers have short attention spans. Do not give their minds an excuse to wander. You'll also put yourself in danger of going off on the wrong track.

Nothing is less compelling than a candidate going on and on without a breath about something of little or no interest or relevance.

The second the interviewer breaks eye contact, ask for feedback to regain their attention. This way you guide yourself to stay on target. Remember questions give you control.

HAVE YOUR ANSWERS READY

As we covered in the section on building your achievement portfolio in the previous chapter, you need to give real-life accounts of what you did and back them up with evidence wherever you can. Many interviewers tend to start their questions with "Give me an example where you...." Make sure you have your examples prepared.

Let's continue with the above case where you found out there were problems at the help desk. If you could highlight some examples of how you trained the help desk staff to please upset clients, you will get the interviewer's attention. If you can speak to the *results*, such as higher customer satisfaction scores and examples of customers engaging in more business with you, then you have increased the impact significantly. If at the end you can also show documentation, such as a thank-you email from your manager or a customer, you have indeed been compelling.

You cannot risk an eye-glazing ramble at this point in the interview. So remember to use the **S.O.A.R** structure I described to you in Chapter Four.

Situation: Start by describing the situation to provide context.

Objective: Explain what the objective or challenge was and how it was similar and relevant.

Action: Describe the actions you took.

Results: Describe the impact of your actions in terms of measurable results where possible.

Keeping the 30-second rule in mind, I advise you stop after you have explained the situation and the objective, check for eye contact and ask for feedback that they agree your example is indeed relevant. This stops you going off in the wrong direction. Also, when an interviewer confirms the relevance of an example they are more likely to remember it later.

It is also critical that you ask for feedback that you have successfully made your point at the end after you have finished explaining the results. If their answer is no, then you have the opportunity to clarify why and try again. If the answer is yes, then you can move on to the next point. Make notes of what they confirm as good strength matches. You can use these notes as a way of summarizing all the good points when you want to establish that you have reached the hiring threshold toward the end of this step.

4. CLOSE

Reaching the suitable "for hire" threshold is a major achievement! However, you will nearly always have other candidates competing with you for the job. In this step, you convince them why they should be hiring *you*.

You do this by asking open questions that target the differentiation opportunities we discussed in Chapter One. Here is where you ask about what keeps them up at night. Ask about their top priorities and their most worrying challenges. Then go straight on to use **S.O.A.R** to provide examples of how you have overcome similar challenges and achieved such priorities before. Here are two examples.

"What do you consider the most difficult part of the job?" This leads you to follow-up questions such as, "What do you feel are the most important skills required to overcome such difficulties?" If you can show you can do the most difficult part, you are well on your way!

"Are there any important qualities that you have had trouble finding in the candidates you have interviewed so far?" This question can highlight something critical they have not yet found. If you can satisfy them in *that* area, you have just differentiated yourself from the rest. This can put you straight into the lead *and* give you a basis to negotiate a better deal when they make you an offer.

Your objective in step 4, is to cross the *"This is who we want!"* threshold.

See Diagram below.

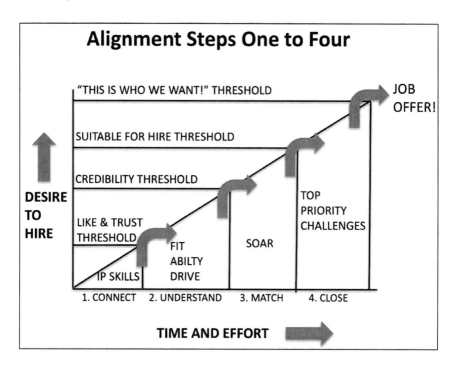

On the horizontal axis is time and effort spent with an interviewer. On the vertical axis is their increasing desire to hire you as you progress in time and effort going through the four steps. Your objective in each step is to progress upwards along the diagonal line, crossing each threshold, and earning the right to move onto the next step toward the job offer.

The benefit of this structured approach is that it guides you as to where you are in the interview and what you should be focusing on. This avoids you being tempted to talk about your strengths too early before establishing your likeability, trust and a need for your strengths. Believe me, 90% of interview candidates make this mistake. Because of this, I am often asked;

"How do you know if you have crossed a threshold?"

The key is to ask for feedback.

Many people feel it is a little awkward to ask for direct feedback regarding whether someone likes and trusts them. In Chapter Two we covered simple steps to significantly improve your likability and trust rating plus assess how you are doing. Look for sustained eye contact, forward leaning body posture and a smile. Loss of eye contact means they are not listening. If this is combined with an interest in something else, like their cell phone, a body movement away from you like leaning back in their chairs and folding their arms across their chest, the chances are you have failed to cross the like and trust threshold. At this point, it is perfectly acceptable to ask if everything is OK before you continue.

With all the other thresholds it is very easy to ask. For example;

Re: Credibility threshold,

"Based on our discussion do you feel comfortable I understand the full responsibilities and requirements of this job?"

"I think I understand all the responsibilities of this job; however, is there anything else we have not covered?"

Re: Capability threshold,

"Have I covered all the skills required for this job?"

"Are there any skills you feel I am lacking?"

Re: Fit threshold,

"Do you think I would be a fit for your team?"

"Do you think the rest of the team would accept me into the organization?"

"Do you have any concerns regarding my personality and attitudes as far as fitting into the team and culture here?"

Re: Drive threshold,

"In terms of motivation and drive do you think I have what it takes to succeed here?"

"Do you have any concerns regarding my commitment and desire to succeed here?"

Re: Suitable for hire threshold,

"Are there any remaining areas that concern you and would prevent you from hiring me?"

These are very simple *closed* questions to get a yes or no answer. If you get a positive response, you can keep going. If you get a negative response you must stop, clarify and deal with it. If it turns out you can't deal with it, such as a skill that you do not have, ask if it is a selection show-stopper or something that could be addressed once on board. In my experience, if you have passed the like and trust threshold well, you are probably going to pass the fit threshold too. If you can also get past the drive threshold, you may be able to convince the interviewer that because you are good match everywhere else it is worth taking you on and training you to cover the missing skill.

WHY A PRE-ALIGNED NETWORKER WILL WIN EVERY TIME!

At the beginning of this section, I indicated that I would cover the steps as if you had *not* previously networked into the organization. Using the four Alignment steps will certainly help you control the interview and help you work your way past the important thresholds as described above. It is the best way to systematically work your way to an offer.

HOWEVER;

Good networkers can make their way over most of the hiring thresholds long before a formal interview.

They will already have built trusted relationships that could include the interviewer.

They will have had plenty of time to build their understanding of the job requirements and therefore their credibility. Their questions start with;

"I understand from our previous discussions that the top priorities are.....is that still correct?"

The person who has not previously networked asks;

"What are the top priorities?"

This creates a very different impression to the interviewer.

Networkers will have aligned for some time through targeted skills development, including internships. They will have absorbed their culture, language and dress code to look like they already belong there.

After a sustained networking campaign, a formal interview is a conversation *near the end* of the selection process. After re-confirming their suitability for hire, all their focus is on crossing the final "This is who we want!" threshold. For the accomplished and aligned networker, the interview is a *natural conclusion.*

Meanwhile, the interview is the *first conversation* in the selection process for someone who has not networked into the organization. They are starting with step one—focusing on being liked and trusted.

If the interview is the first time you meet an employer, your chances of concluding it with a job offer are about the same as getting a marriage proposal at the end of a blind date!

So be the networker and pre-align.

However be aware of complacency.

Never ASSUME you have crossed all the thresholds.

This is another reason why I went through the four alignment steps as if you had not previously aligned.

No matter how well you think you have pre-aligned, ALWAYS go through the steps and check to make sure all your thresholds are safely crossed.

KEEPING A BALANCED INTERVIEW

So far we have revisited the alignment steps to help you understand how to take control and drive an interview through a series of increasing "desire to hire" thresholds in the mind of an interviewer.

In reality, however, most interviewers will try to retain control. They will do so by interrupting this nice structure with questions of their own. If you ignore their questions, they will turn off and some will even get angry. The challenge is to keep the thresholds in mind and at the same time create a balance of give and take during the interview. For example, I know some tough Driver personality types who may skip any nice preliminary small talk and ask you their toughest questions as soon as you sit down. They simply do not want to waste any time with you if you can't answer their top priority questions. Failure to answer them instantly usually results in game over. So you need to know how!

Do not fear questions. If you get questions, even tough ones that sound like objections, it means they are *interested*. If they don't ask any questions, it almost *always* means they are uninterested or not listening. In fact, you want to encourage questions so that an interviewer feels like they have thoroughly interviewed you. As I said in the opening of this chapter, they will be coming to the interview with issues on their mind. Your job is to get them into the discussion and deal with them. You can do this through your questions and by handling their questions.

HOW TO ANSWER ANY QUESTIONS WELL

Here is a 5 step process that many people find very helpful.

1. CLARIFY

Under pressure, it is easy to misunderstand a question and immediately begin giving the wrong answer. This can frustrate the interviewer and set yourself back. It is vital to really clarify and get to the root of what you've been asked. Unless it is blindingly obvious, even if you think you know where they are coming from, it is still a good policy to use some targeted open questions that allow the questioner to talk more. Use phrases such as "Would you mind putting this in context so I fully understand your question?" "Could you clarify why this is critical... ?" "Could you explain the consequences of ...?"

Caution: Use your judgment. Some questions really are so obvious that asking for clarification can be annoying and make you look foolish. If the question is really that simple, go right to step three.

2. SUMMARIZE

Rephrase the question in your own words to make sure you have understood it correctly. "So, just to be clear, you want to know if ...?" "To make sure I have this correct, you are concerned that ...?" These two steps give the other person confidence that you really care and that you have taken the time to listen, diagnose their question, and understand it.

Bonus: These initial two steps also buy you time to think about your answer. In fact, in many cases, the process encourages questioners to either answer their own questions or at least make the answer pretty obvious.

3. ANSWER

Now that you have clarity on the question, you should recognize whether it is open or closed. Does the questioner want you to talk and give information, or are they looking for a yes or no answer to confirm something? Make sure you answer appropriately. Short, one-word answers to open questions make you appear unresponsive and abrupt. It will not enhance the customer experience. Lengthy responses to closed questions will make you appear evasive, can undermine trust, and will immediately frustrate people, especially strong driver personalities. If it was an open question asking for information remember to use **S.O.A.R** to keep your answer relevant, compelling and succinct.

4. GAIN FEEDBACK

As soon as you have given a response, ask the person if it answered the question to their satisfaction. This is a simple closed question after which you must remain silent until you get a response. If you get a "no", go back to step one and re-build your understanding. Repeat the steps until you have confirmation that your answer was satisfactory. It is also a good idea to follow up and ask if there are any *other* questions or concerns just to be sure nothing is left unaddressed. If there are none, move ahead. If there are, you know what to do—go back to step one and clarify the additional concerns.

If the issue is important, put the agreement in writing so that the question and its resolution are documented.

5. ASK A QUESTION OF YOUR OWN

As soon as you have successfully handled a question use it as an opportunity to take back control of the interview by asking a question of your own. You have just earned the right to do so. Use one of your "set up" questions. When you receive your answer, you can then use **S.O.A.R** to provide a matching strength statement. When you have gained feedback that you indeed matched up well, hand control back to the interviewer. Say something like, "I have more questions but do you have any critical issues you want to cover first?" They will either retake control of the interview by asking you another question or give you the go ahead to ask another set-up question.

You can use these steps for handling *any* question very successful during interviews.

Steps 1 and 2 act like a homing mechanism to help you lock onto your target.

Step 3 ensures your answer is a precision missile with high impact.

Step 4 tells you whether your missile hit the target.

Step 5 helps you retake control to identify your next target.

As with any of the structures in this book you don't need to use it in its entirety every time. Build the habit and then use your judgment.

The one step I recommend you use without fail is step four—gain feedback.

Never ASSUME someone has listened, understood and agreed to anything you have just said.

Always check that your answer was on target and that the listener is satisfied. This will give you another chance if you missed the target, and it creates a positive customer experience.

Make getting feedback through direct closed questions a habit. This way you build a momentum of yes as you progress through any conversation.

The earlier you discover a "no," the more time you have to turn it into a "yes." Ask for feedback after every point you make.

217

This 5-step question handling technique will help you answer questions well *and* keep a balanced control of the interview.

AVOIDING THE "DON'T CALL US, WE'LL CALL YOU" ENDING

You can normally tell after 45 minutes to an hour that an interview is ending. Do not just let the questions fade out and allow the interviewer to close with this well-known statement. Use your own questions to bring the conversation to an agreed set of actions.

At this stage of the interview, you can ask closed questions such as:

"Are there any other areas you would like to cover?"

"Have I addressed all your questions to your satisfaction?"

"Were there any questions you felt I answered badly?"

"Do you see any issues preventing me from being selected?"

"Are you comfortable with recommending me to move to the next step?"

These are closed questions designed to elicit yes or no responses so you can clearly establish how you performed and where you stand.

Once they have acknowledged that you match up to their most difficult challenges and agreed there are no other reasons to stop them from hiring you, it is time to close the evaluation and move to the negotiation.

You do this by again by asking a simple question:

"So, could we move on to discussing the offer?"

This is not rocket science. Unfortunately, many people are too uncomfortable asking this question. However, at that point, it is perfectly natural to ask because you have earned it. You have established that you can help them with their top priorities and that there is nothing else left to stop them making an offer. You have crossed the "This is who we want!" threshold.

Note: Quite often there will be multiple interviewers of increasing seniority. Only the last most senior one will approve moving to the job offer stage. If this is the case, then your initial interview goals become not the offer but a recommendation that you be interviewed by the next person in line.

Further note: When an interviewer likes you enough to move you forward to the next step in the selection process, they have, to some degree, staked their reputation on you. If you perform badly at the next interview, you will make the initial interviewer look bad. Take advantage of this moment to get as much advice as possible. Find out who else will be interviewing you, their likes and dislikes, their favorite interview questions, and so on.

Turn this person into your coach!

Meanwhile, if the meeting has not gone well, you will have a good understanding of why, because you asked and clarified as described above. ***Never get defensive.*** Thank the interviewer for the feedback and explain that you would really like to learn from it. Stay courteous and focus on the *why*. Ask clarifying questions to get specifics. If the interviewer makes valid points, acknowledge and document them. Always ask the interviewer for advice. It starts to turn them into a coach. Then ask if you could reapply at a later date if you can demonstrate that you have improved in those areas. At the very least, you will learn from the experience and perform better in your next interviews.

If you genuinely believe the interviewer has misunderstood something, very politely ask if you could revisit that topic. Clarify the needs and try to match yourself again. Then ask whether you were able to change their perspective. As long as you are polite and do not come across as defensive or desperate, it is worth trying.

I know an executive who always *deliberately* misunderstands something to see if the interviewee is sharp enough to realize it and has the spine and desire to straighten out the mix-up. His logic is that misunderstandings happen in business all the time. If candidates do not have the alert sensitivity to spot such confusion, or the courage and drive to fix it when it could significantly impact their careers in the immediate future, then they are unlikely to do so in a situation affecting the business of the organization. He has a point.

Finally, leave with the utmost grace as you never know what can happen.

Some interviewers (such as the one above) are very tough and tell ALL the candidates they failed. They want to see how you react under pressure and how hard you clarify why you were rejected and how hard you keep trying.

PART III

ALIGNING TO THE PERSONALITY OF THE INTERVIEWER

DEALING WITH THE DIFFERENT SOCIAL STYLES AND QUESTIONS FROM THE FOUR PERSONALITY TYPES

Many people tend to forget that interviewers are not robots. And neither are you! Their decisions about you are not based on pure logic. They are people with *personalities* which greatly influence their judgment of you and *your personality*.

You may have all the right skills the job needs, but if your social style rubs the interviewer the wrong way, even slightly, you are not getting the job. You won't get through the like and trust threshold.

So let's look at the four basic social styles we covered in Chapter Two.

THE DRIVER

Drivers are aggressive, task oriented, to the point, and time-conscious. Do not waste any time with the Driver. Stay on topic with relevant examples of actions and results. A Driver will ask predominantly *closed* questions to which you must reply with short answers and rock-steady eye contact. They tend not to trust people. They trust action plans, frequent reviews, and evidence, usually in the form of numbers. Therefore do not put them in a position of having to trust you. The phrase "trust me" is a total turn off to most interviewers but especially Drivers and Analyticals.

Drivers will be interested primarily in the *evidence* of what you have *actually done* and how that proves *you can do* what *they want done*.

Language they hate: I think I can do that, I should be able to, I would like the opportunity to try to do that, etc.

Language they love: I know I can do that because I have successfully done that before with the following results. Here is the evidence.

Questions you might get from Drivers:

How were you measured? What were your targets? What were your results?

They are looking for concise, number-oriented answers that closely match how the position is measured and targeted. Make sure you have this prepared ahead of time so you can answer *instantly*. Any hesitation or vagueness will turn a Driver off.

What was the most difficult aspect of your last job?

They want to assess your level of capability and to know that you have the perseverance and drive to overcome difficulties. Have examples ready that are relevant and equivalent to the role in question.

It is critical you use S.O.A.R with a driver.

Did you ever fail to achieve any of your targets? If so, what happened?

Everybody has experienced some failures unless they have always avoided risks and never stretched beyond their comfort zone. Drivers do not like "safe" types, so do not say you never failed. Pick an example, preferably one that is *NOT* relevant to the role. Explain what actions you took, how close you came and, above all, explain what you learned and did differently to nail the target next time.

How do I know you will succeed at this job?

Explain that you have researched this job very thoroughly. It is the job you have targeted as part of your overall professional plans. You have been coached by your contacts in terms of the skills and experience necessary to succeed in this job. You have set yourself goals to build targeted skills and achieved them to prepare yourself accordingly. You have the proof in your achievement folder. Explain that success in this job is critical to your overall career strategy and that you are therefore highly driven. Finish with an example that demonstrated a "failure is not an option" attitude and how you will do whatever it takes to get the job done.

Give me an example of where you showed initiative.

Drivers want to know that their staff will not just stop in the face of obstacles. They want employees who will take the initiative to get the job done. They are also assessing your judgment so that when you do take initiative you are not putting the company at risk. Again—prepare a relevant example.

How do you manage deadlines?

Drivers are very deadline-oriented. Explain that you get things done because you believe all objectives need to be broken down into smaller deadline-driven tasks. Explain that without deadlines, you feel there is no commitment. They will readily agree with you!

Have you ever felt that the demands put upon you were unreasonable?

They want to know that you are not going to resent extra work when they need a final push to succeed in something critical. Explain how you trust that when management demands effort, there are good reasons for doing so. Explain that you have stayed through the night or come in on weekends to help ensure deadlines are met. To illustrate, have an example and explain that you see such instances as opportunities to build great relationships and put some goodwill in people's tanks.

Use their types of words and phrases when you respond to their questions. Keep it under 25 seconds, and then ask if your answers met what they were looking for. In fact, you should do this with all interviewers. It gets them in the habit of saying "yes" which is important for your final question, which is to ask if they feel you are suitable for the job. Drivers like a direct approach.

Other common Driver questions include:

"What drives you?"

"What sacrifices are you prepared to make for the success of the company?"

"Why do you want to quit your current job?"

"How many hours do you normally work?"

"Give me an example of a new idea you contributed."

THE ANALYTICAL

Stick to the facts. Avoid hyperbole. For example, do not tell an Analytical personality type that you are a *great* salesperson. It will turn them off. Instead, say, "I made 127% of my target last year, and I have been the highest-achieving sales executive over the last three years at my present company." They will ask the same types of questions as the Driver. However, they tend to want more facts and details to support your answers. Their "what" questions are usually followed by "how" questions. So they may include follow-ups such as:

Explain to me your process for getting important tasks done.

They are looking for detailed confirmation that you personally got the results you claimed. Have an example that would be relevant to this job and describe *how* you got it done. In Chapter Nine, I cover an achievement methodology on how to get challenging tasks completed which you should master prior to any interview. Always make sure you have your numbers correct regarding measurements and results. Analyticals have a habit of asking additional questions to crosscheck that your story adds up.

What percentage of time do you spend on your various responsibilities?

They want to know that you have thought about priorities and have organized accordingly. They want to know that you don't just spend all your time responding to situations, or doing the one or two things you like doing best at the expense of other harder tasks.

How do you typically make an important decision?

They want to know that you make objective, fact-based decisions and not impulsive, emotion-driven ones. Give some examples of decisions you made that could occur in the job you are interviewing for. I cover a decision-making process in Chapter Ten. Use it as a structure to describe *how* you made your decisions.

How do you solve problems?

They want to know that you approach problems and deal with them effectively and that you do not let them fester and cause stress. Give relevant examples of problems you were able to resolve and include the positive impact on the business. I also cover a problem-solving process in Chapter Ten. Again, use that structure to describe *how* you solved your problems.

Other common questions from Analyticals include;

"How do you keep yourself organized? Do you use any tools?"

"How do you keep up to date? What information sources do you subscribe to?"

"What new skills have you learned recently?"

"Give me some examples where you used structured thinking."

THE EXPRESSIVE

Expressives like to use hyperbole themselves. In an interview with an Expressive, say, "I am a *great* salesperson because I have consistently exceeded my targets. I was at 127% last year and have been the top achiever at my present company for three years." In other words, use a combination of fact *and* hyperbole. Expressives want to feel that energy and excitement! They tend to ask the following types of questions:

What is your greatest achievement?

Use an example that would be relevant to the role you are applying to. Describe how you achieved it and the impact it had on the business. Be proud. Try to pick an achievement that involved winning or beating the competition.

What is your greatest strength?

Based on the research you have done on the position, you will know the key strengths the interviewer is looking for. Pick one and show, with an example, why you believe that to be your biggest strength.

What gets you excited?

Pick something like being part of a *successful* team and the feeling of *winning*. This is what Expressive personalities relate to. They are often in sales and marketing, where their entire focus is about beating the competition. If you are not highly competitive, you will not enjoy working for this personality style.

How creative are you?

Explain how you have a systematic process for coming up with new ideas and how to solve problems. This is also a good area to highlight as something that gets you excited. Expressive types like this. Give an example that closely relates to the open job. I cover a creative process in Chapter Ten.

What are your goals? How would you describe success in one, three, and five years' time?

Expressive types are all about achievement. They want to know that you are motivated to succeed. Explain that you want to start with success in *this* role, and then take on more responsibilities and achieve your long-term career goals. Explain these goals and what you have achieved so far. Show off your achievement folder; Expressive types love them!

Why should I hire you rather than the other candidates?

They want some hyperbole here. They want to feel your passion and desire. Show that you have the best understanding of the top priorities and consequences of failure. State that you have the most closely matching experience in dealing with similar obstacles to success and have produced the most closely matching results. Show evidence from your achievement folder in terms of references to back you up. Keep eye contact with a twinkle and a smile as you go through this.

Other common Expressive type questions include;

"Do you have a personal mission statement?"

"Give me an example of an important goal you have achieved."

"How competitive are you?"

"What sports do you play?"

"What does success really mean to you?"

"How do you judge your own performance?"

THE AMIABLE

Amiable types care about people and want to be sure you do too. Continuing the above example, to the Amiable you would say, "I helped the department and my boss reach our targets by exceeding mine by 127%."

Beware of the Amiables because while they make you *feel* the most comfortable during interviews, they often ask the hardest and most subjective questions. They can quickly interpret your answers in ways that will cost you the job. Do not be lulled into letting your guard down by these "nice" types as they make you feel relaxed. If you start admitting weaknesses they will smile and show their appreciation for your openness; however, your resume will be in their shredder before you have left the building!

Describe your relationships with your previous managers. Are they all referenceable?

Any form of criticism is instant death! Talk about how you view managers as your most valuable customers. Explain how you try to align to their requirements and deliver the results they expect. Consequently, you have built valuable relationships and now consider many past supervisors as coaches, mentors, and great references. Give examples from your achievement folder. I explain how to build the right relationship with your boss in Chapters Seven and Eight.

How do you like to work with others?

Explain how you understand that almost everything in an organization is achieved through teamwork. Therefore, emphasize that you enjoy being part of a team with examples to support it. Explain how you like to be part of something bigger than just yourself. Bring up your pre-prepared examples of where you have helped team members and how you focus on team goals as well as your own. Talk about team sports if you have participated in any.

How do you handle colleagues you dislike?

Again, this is a trap question you must avoid. Explain that you make a great deal of effort to use your interpersonal skills to get along with everyone so you can focus on getting the job done. If it appears that someone has taken a dislike to you, you immediately try to clarify and fix the situation. Describe your belief that team spirit is vital to success and that there is no room for petty squabbles.

How do you handle internal or external customers you feel are making unreasonable demands from you?

State that your starting position is always to clarify any issues and understand where customers are coming from, regardless of whether they are external or internal. If you genuinely feel you cannot satisfy their demands, you raise it with your manager to get help assessing whether the demands are reasonable, and for advice on finding a way to move forward.

How do you handle a disagreement with your manager?

Make it clear that you have always been able to earn the right to bring up your concerns in a constructive manner, and that sometimes your previous managers accepted your point of view while at other times there were bigger-picture reasons for why you were overruled. When that happens, you always support the decision out of loyalty to your boss, and because you always try to make sure you understand the bigger picture.

What are your biggest failings?

Do not volunteer too much! Avoid anything that could impact your ability to deliver the results expected from the role you are applying for. Pick something that could actually be a strength. For example, explain that you can sometimes be a perfectionist and a little intolerant of anything less than top-quality work from your colleagues.

What is the worst mistake you have made or failure you have experienced?

Again, pick something that is *not relevant* to the open position. Show how you fixed the mistake, and then emphasize what you learned from it to the extent that it *created a strength*. Do not just say you cannot think of any. Everyone has made blunders in their career. Have something prepared.

Here are some more examples of their questions.

Amiable types are masters at asking the disguised question. Many people argue that questions such as "give me an example of XYZ" clearly flags to the interviewee what the interviewer wants to hear. Amiable types often do not make it quite so obvious.

"Who was your worst boss?"

You will not score well if you rip into a previous boss! You have to interpret the question as;

"Give me an example of how you handled what you thought was an unreasonable request from a manager in a constructive and positive way."

Here are some more common ones.

"Describe the last time you were angry at work."

"What was your most boring job?"

"When did you last feel overwhelmed in your job?"

"Does anyone care about your job?"

"How would one of your colleagues who dislikes you describe you?"

"What kind of person would you refuse to work with?"

"Do you socialize with colleagues?"

"List the top three weaknesses your manager has identified."

"Give me an example where your manager criticized you".

DO NOT just answer any of these questions at face value. Ask yourself which of the three categories (will you fit in, can you and will you) is being explored. Use the five steps to answer a question described in Part II of this chapter.

Here are some sample answers. Each one should be accompanied by an example.

"I do not tend to get angry and focus on understanding what is going on so that situations can be made better. In fact, my manager has complimented my diffusion skills particularly with angry customers."

"I tend not to find jobs boring because I enjoy the challenge of trying to do it better, and I focus on the results and why those results are needed."

"Rather than feeling overwhelmed, if I feel I cannot deliver the results expected from me I discuss ways to get help with my manager. I make a point of helping other people when they need it, so I rarely have trouble getting help when I need it."

"I don't believe there are any colleagues who really dislike me. In fact, my manager would rate my team work as one of my biggest strengths."

"I have never refused to work with anyone. I have to trust that my manager is building a team that can work together. Sometimes we all have to make adjustments."

Note: The key is to remember that the interviewer does not want to hear about bad bosses, your anger, your most boring job, etc.

They want to hear what you did to turn a negative situation around.

Again this may all sound obvious, but you would be astonished at how many people (at least 50% in my experience) will happily describe negative situations without adding any information about how they resolved it, learned from it or avoided it in the first place.

HOW THE PERSONALITY TYPES LOOK AT THE THREE THINGS YOU MUST PROVE.

Although all four personalities will be looking into the three basic questions we covered in Chapter One and can ask any question about anything, each personality type tends to emphasize one or two areas.

The Driver is results-oriented and will primarily want you to prove that you **can and will** do the job. They want to reach a conclusion as fast as possible because they are so busy.

The Analytical is similarly focused to a Driver, but will want more supporting evidence particularly around **how** you will do it. They will take the time to dig for details that either support or undermine your claims.

The Expressive sees being able to do the job as a basic requirement but really wants you to prove that you **will** do it. They want to know where your energy and desire to succeed and win comes from. They will dig into your motivators.

The Amiable also sees being able to do the job as a basic requirement but really wants you to prove that you **will fit in**. They also want to be sure that you do not disrupt the team spirit and negatively affect others. The Amiable believes that if you can do the job and fit in well, chances are you will be happy and will **want** to do the job.

SUMMARY

The interview is where all your previous alignment efforts come together in one critical moment.

Research, prepare, *practice!*

Use the alignment steps to:

- Connect and adapt to the personality to be liked and trusted.
- Uncover the needs.
- Use **S.O.A.R** to tell your stories to show you match up to those needs.

- Focus on top priority results and challenges and show how you can help them to differentiate you and win the selection.

Use questions to control and direct the conversation in a give and take manner.

Establish how you did in the interview and close by asking to move on to the offer (or on specific follow-up actions if they are not the decision maker).

KEY MESSAGE

Doing research, preparing, and rehearsing is something that anyone can do. There is no excuse for not doing it. It provides the foundation for your performance in the interview.

An interviewer can instantly tell whether you have done so or not.

They believe that if you cannot be bothered to make the effort for your own future, then it is very unlikely you will make any effort for the organization.

Not only will your overall performance in the interview suffer greatly, but you will also ENTIRELY FAIL the "will you do the job" test.

This is another one of those "say it with me" moments. Repeat the five "P"s after me.

Proper preparation prevents poor performance!

Never forget that there will be good networkers competing with you who don't just prepare well, they will have crossed all but the last "This is who we want!" threshold long before the interview through a sustained networking campaign over months.

Be one of those networkers.

As a student, you should be starting these campaigns while at college and not wait until after you graduate.

The same applies if you are in a job and want to be promoted. Start your alignment through internal networking long before a formal interview for a promotion opportunity arises. Much more on that in Chapter Eleven.

FINAL POINT - ALWAYS WRITE BACK

Always write an email to each of your interviewers thanking them for their time and summarizing the meeting. If it went well, highlight the top three discussion points on which you got feedback that you hit the bull's eye. These should be about how you can add value toward achieving their top priority results.

This reconfirms your suitability in the mind of the interviewers when they read your email. The email will also go into your file and will be there when they discuss all the candidates to make their final decision. It is a way to keep their positive memory of you detailed and fresh.

Failure to write back can easily cost you the job to an equal candidate that did write back.

Then go on to summarize the agreed next steps.

If it did not go well, proceed as follows:

Start by highlighting the areas on which you did get feedback that you were on target, as above. It is important that they remember positive points about you first. Then go on to cover the area where you got feedback that you were lacking. Repeat back the specific issues and any advice they gave you on how to rectify them. Meanwhile, talk to your contacts and also ask them for advice. Summarize this information into a plan on how you will fix the issues as a top priority. Thank them for the feedback.

Finally, reconfirm your strong interest in joining and ask if you can reapply once you have completed the above plan and are in a position to demonstrate that you have the gaps filled.

This leaves a positive and professional impression that you are serious, persistent, and coachable.

The process also ensures that you learn from the experience and develop a plan to improve. Depending on what those issues were, in a few months' time you will be able to contact your interviewer and say:

"My name is John Brown. You interviewed me back in March and highlighted that I needed to work on XYZ to be a more suitable candidate. I took your advice, and I have completed your recommended actions. I believe I now have them covered. I wanted to thank you for the recommendations you made and would really like to come and see you to assess whether I could reapply. Do you have any time next week?"

Even if the answer is no, the entire process is still worth it because what that interviewer saw as gaps will likely be seen the same way by others. This way you get the gaps filled and improve your chances for the next opportunity.

CHAPTER SIX

NEGOTIATING THE BEST DEAL

**"In life you don't get what you deserve—
you get what you negotiate."**

Krishna Sagar

Some people seem to have a knack for getting what they want while others whine about how unfair this world is. Generally, those who can get what they want *through mutual agreement and without causing resentment* are good at negotiating.

Good negotiating skills will transform your life!

PART I

THE BASICS

Congratulations. Interviews are drawing to a close, you have crossed the "This is who we want!" threshold, and they are making you an offer!

This is what you may hear:

"We are delighted to offer you $40,000 to come onboard. It is *WAY* over what we normally pay for that position and will give finance a heart attack since it's also over budget, but we think you are worth it. When can you start?"

Unfortunately, you were hoping for $50,000. Based on your research, *you know* this is a low-ball offer.

Statistically, it may have taken you up to two years to get this offer; meanwhile, you've been waiting tables to survive. You want this job. You've worked damn hard to get it. At last, a ticket out of your parents' house is within your grasp!

Who, at this point, has the courage to negotiate and potentially jeopardize the opportunity?

So, you leap across the interviewer's desk, hug them, try not to cry, ask where you need to sign, and say you will start that afternoon.

No one would fault you for it. However, later the same day, your interviewer will be boasting how he just saved the company $10,000 that can now go into the Christmas party fund!

So, let's examine some alternatives.

The worst thing that can happen is that the employer asks who the hell you think you are trying to get a higher salary, and withdraws the offer. It's possible, *but is it likely?*

Remember, they have gone through a fairly lengthy and expensive process to select you and make an offer. They almost certainly had to get prior approval, which means they have already "sold" you as the right person to their superiors. There is no guarantee that the next-best candidate will accept a low-ball offer either.

All things considered, the chances are that as long as you are *courteous and reasonable*, you will be able to at least have a discussion. Here's another thing: in many organizations they *expect* you to negotiate, especially if you are applying for a role that deals with customers or suppliers where negotiation skills are key.

They WANT to see whether you have the ability and backbone to do so.

WHAT A SUCCESSFUL NEGOTIATION CAN BE WORTH

The financial impact is often bigger than many people realize. If you accept $40,000 when they could have gone to $50,000, you have lost $10,000. That's obvious. Let's say next year you get a 5% raise. At $40,000, this comes out to $2,000. Had you negotiated $50,000, that raise would have amounted to $2,500. Each year, this 5% increase results in a greater difference. After five annual pay reviews, not only will you be $12,763 behind the market in your annual salary but you'll have missed out on over $55,000! That's a down payment on a house!

Experienced interviewers will explain they cannot go over budget: it's beyond their authority; they have mandatory salary bands and that the job is not worth more to them. They might also tell you that they need an immediate decision because there is another candidate if you are not interested.

This is undoubtedly intimidating. *It is meant to be.* Regardless, this does *not* mean you should simply accept their offer.

Remember the adage I have already mentioned.

"If you *never* ask, the answer is *always no!*"

I repeat it because so many people talk themselves out of asking for anything.

So, let's go for it!

WHEN TO NEGOTIATE

Most people understand that early on in the interview process is *not* the time to start negotiating employment terms. However, as part of the screening process, to eliminate those they either cannot afford or whose experience is insufficient, interviewers generally ask what your salary expectations are.

Do *NOT* give a number out at this point.

If you do, you have played your hand, and you risk elimination. *There is no upside.* Their starting position will *always* be less than your number. When you get this question, answer by saying that at this early stage all you want is a fair market value for the services you are expected to provide. Right now, you're much more interested in discussing *what you can do for them* and that you trust them to make a fair offer. This sets the right tone.

The only time you engage in a discussion about the terms of your employment is AFTER they have made an offer.

At this point, *they* have decided they want *you.* All your alignment efforts have paid off. This is the point in time their "desire to hire" you is at its highest because you just crossed the "This is who we want!" threshold. (remember diagram three in the previous chapter). *They want YOU, more than anyone else!* They may even be under pressure to get you started quickly. The balance of power shifts from them to you.

This is a fleeting moment; you must take full advantage of it!

HOW TO DEVELOP YOUR NEGOTIATING POWER

Contrary to popular belief, negotiating power does not come from "tricks" or some intrinsic talent. The truth is very simple:

In any negotiation, the power lies with the side that has the best alternatives if negotiations fail.

For example, your negotiating power is high if you genuinely have other job offers *that you are willing to accept* should this negotiation fall apart *and* if you know the organization you wish to join has no alternative candidates who come close to your ability to match the requirements of the job.

If you have no other job offers and are running out of money, and if there is minimal difference between you and the next candidate, then your power is clearly low.

The interviewers may not know what other offers you have, and so their perception and belief that you have options could determine the result. Likewise, you probably do not know how strong the next-best candidate is, and, therefore, *your perception* also comes into play.

Their job is to make you believe they can't pay you more and that there are plenty of candidates just as good as you who will accept their terms in a heartbeat. Your job is to differentiate yourself throughout the selection process and make them believe they could lose you to alternative better offers.

Now that you know where this power comes from, think ahead and plan to have as many alternatives available as possible. Throughout the selection process, try to differentiate yourself from the other candidates. Get feedback on where you stand versus your competing candidates whenever possible so that you can address perceived weaknesses and leverage perceived strengths. So, although the timing of the actual negotiation dialogue is only after you've been made an offer, you have to be *very* proactive and lay the groundwork way in advance.

A good candidate is interviewing to win the selection process. A well-paid candidate also interviews with the negotiation in mind!

You might be thinking, "Are you kidding? It took two years to find one job opportunity! I can't just conjure up several more to use for negotiating leverage! Plus, there were hundreds of applicants! How can I possibly know how close the next-best person is?"

This is an understandable reaction, but it comes mainly from those who didn't rely on networking-based strategies to land an interview. If you have truly:

- networked to build a large number of connections within your industries of choice,
- targeted and researched the requirements of specific job functions in a significant number of organizations within those industries,
- used targeted skills development to align with your jobs of interest,
- developed your online profile using keywords to optimize it for searches,
- tailored your resume to meet the specific needs of each opportunity,
- Prepared and rehearsed compelling examples that match the top priority results of the job opportunity,
- and applied your new and improved interviewing skills,

then your chances of having more than one offer will be considerably higher. Your competition will have decreased because you are in the *unpublished* job market. Meanwhile, most of your competitors are still fishing the overcrowded waters of the published job market with generic resumes.

GETTING MULTIPLE OFFERS

The great benefit of genuinely having multiple offers is that you can use another offer as a reason for asking how you are doing in a selection process—the implication being that you need to know whether to accept the other offer or not. If you are the favorite, the process will speed up and their opening offer will nearly always be higher. It is also a pretty clear indication of where you stand if mentioning the fact that you have other offers has *no* impact.

Note: *NEVER* fake alternative offers. It only takes one or two questions from a good interviewer to spot a lie. It's not worth damaging your reputation and your chances of winning the selection along with it. *Do the real work to build alternatives.*

A common mistake people make is to stop all further job-search activity once they land an interview. Their rationale is to focus and concentrate on the job that is within their grasp—a bird in the hand. *Don't! In fact, do the opposite.*

The second you get an invitation for an interview, STEP UP your efforts to get other interviews elsewhere.

Use that confidence boost and enthusiasm to chase other opportunities. Call *every* contact you have in the other organizations you have been pursuing. The world changes fast. People resign, get fired, relocate, or get promoted. They leave gaps that need to be filled. Organizations grow and reorganize which also creates openings. As soon as you get an invitation for an interview, maximize your efforts to find any new gaps in the other organizations you have been talking to. Do everything you can to get into *their* selection processes as well.

As I have said before, always give yourself some extra time by not agreeing to do an interview immediately. Invitations often come with a proposed date and time, sometimes with minimum notice. Explain politely that you already have a meeting with another organization at that time and ask if they could make it a few days later or early the following week.

This will rarely be an issue, and it immediately signals that you may have alternatives. It also gives you time to get yourself prepared for the interview and to call contacts in other organizations to see if there are any other similar opportunities available.

Without other activity, you are at a serious disadvantage, so get some meetings set up. This way, if the interviewer asks, you can honestly, without hesitation and with good, direct eye contact, say that you *are* talking to a number of organizations. Do not underestimate the power of this! It's a strange quirk of human nature that we want something more if we fear we can't have it. Interviewers are not immune. The opening offer will instantly start to creep up!

Make a habit of developing alternative plans as a way of life. They are the foundation for dealing with any negotiation—and unexpected setbacks.

Note: Always let your alternative options down gently, and stay in touch. You never know when you might need them!

KNOWLEDGE IS POWER

Be sure you know the market rate for any given position. Recruiters, along with your contacts within these organizations, will be able to give you an indication. There are also websites (JobStar.org, Glassdoor.com, Salary.com, and others) that cover salary ranges by job type. Armed with this knowledge, you can confidently play the "I only want the fair market rate" card.

This research is not optional if you want to be able to negotiate.

I am constantly surprised at how many people admit to *NOT* doing it. If they were buying or selling a car, they absolutely would have done it. In many cases this is because they do not have the contacts, they are afraid to ask, they don't know about the job sites, or it just doesn't occur to them.

Knowing what the market salary range is for the jobs you want is fundamental; in fact, it is the foundation for your negotiation.

Without it, you are very vulnerable.

TACTICS AND BEHAVIOR TO EXPECT DURING NEGOTIATION

Up to now, we have talked about what you can do to prepare yourself. Now let's go to the moment of truth.

The actual experience will, to a large degree, depend on the personalities or social types of the interviewer and how well they have been trained to manage your expectations. Let's look at how the four personality types described in Chapter Five might behave during negotiations.

Drivers can be abrupt and intimidating.

If a Driver makes a below-expectations offer, repeat that you are very excited to join the team but disappointed in the terms. Come straight to the point with good, steady eye contact. State that you have done your research and know from national data, your connections, and discussions you are having with other organizations that this offer is below fair market rate. Then stay quiet.

Strong Drivers, who believe they have the power, are very likely to respond with something like this:

"Look, I'm sorry, but I don't have the time to discuss this. The offer is what it is, take it or leave it!"

Keep calm and remind yourself that *they* want *you*. Do not succumb to fear; maintain your enthusiasm. Explain that the process has already taken considerable time and effort on both sides, and you still very much want to join but need two or three days to consider it.

This gives you time to contact connections within the organization and ask for advice. It also allows you to talk to people in your other selection processes to find out how close you are. Explain that you have been made an offer and ask for feedback on where you stand. If they can't or will not tell you, assume it is unlikely you are their frontrunner. If you were, they would tell you. If they say that you are still in the running, try to clarify. Ask if there is a short list, and if so, how many others are on it. Ask for an indication of the salary range they were planning to offer the winner. If they tell you a number that is higher than your offer you can use that in your negotiation. Ask if there is a timeframe for their decision. All this information will help you establish the strength of your alternatives.

Meanwhile, asking for a few days to consider the offer while you do the above research gives a strong signal to the first interviewer that you are serious about your number and gives them time to regroup and perhaps improve the offer. Usually, you will be granted consideration time because it is a reasonable request.

However, a really hard-nosed Driver may respond with, "No, I need an answer right now, or I will withdraw this offer and contact the next candidate because I have neither time nor flexibility." In this case, I advise you to accept it unless you already have a better offer you'd be happy to take instead.

Accepting the offer at least gives you the option to make the absolute best of it, as I will show you in the next chapters. You can work hard to gain above-average salary increases that will bring you up to fair market value. However, be aware that this could take *years*. That's why you should always at least *try* to negotiate first.

Taking the job does not prevent you from completing the selection process in another organization if you feel you are close to getting a better offer. Employers will not thank me for saying this, but it is the risk they take by forcing employees to take below-market salaries.

If the interviewer in the above example is your future boss and is prepared to treat you that way before you have even joined, chances are you will have quite a challenge working for them. You have to ask yourself whether such a boss will ever let you catch up to market rates. Many people would advise you to reject the offer in such circumstances—and if you have alternatives, that is fine. Otherwise, take the view that you will regularly have to deal with difficult Drivers. The sooner you learn, the better, so you might as well start now. Then keep up your networking discipline to find other opportunities. In the meantime, you are gaining experience and getting paid.

Alternatively, a Driver might immediately throw the ball in your court by responding with, "What were you expecting?" Do not just blurt out the number you were hoping for. A strong Driver will likely dismiss your request as ridiculous and insist on the original number or come up a *very* small percentage and say it's the absolute best they can do.

Instead, have a prepared, rehearsed argument that summarizes the facts from your connections and public data that support your view of a fair market salary for the job. I will show you exactly how to do this in the "How to Negotiate" section below. Bear with me for now.

Analytical types are less likely to be intimidating and will respond better to facts and figures from websites and alternative offers. They will not respond to "promises" of how hard you will work or how much value you will bring. Only a facts-based logical argument will win them over.

Expressives will respond to value examples from your past, particularly if you can provide specific examples of how much your previous boss and team benefited from your achievements. They will respond to some degree of hype and promise as they want to feel the energy. They want to win (not lose you to the competition) and will respond to the fact that you have alternative offers. Be aware that the Expressive personality types can get heated and appear intimidating, too.

Amiable types will respond to how much the *team* benefited from your past achievements. They like to hear that *all* you are looking for is a *fair* deal, and just like Analytical types, will want data from recognized sites to support your view of a fair salary. Amiable types do not tend to intimidate because they value the relationship and tend to dislike confrontations.

Regardless of the personality in front of you, stay calm. At this late stage, do not give the interviewer any reason to question whether you will fit in. Always present your arguments as *reasonable* and *NEVER* as an ultimatum. State your desired number and then stay quiet. Drivers and Expressives may rant and try to intimidate you into bringing your number down. Analyticals will bring their own set of facts and logic but are usually calm in the process. Amiable types are liable just to stay quiet and let the silence drive you to start lowering your own offer!

PART II

HOW TO NEGOTIATE

HOW TO MAKE A DETAILED NEGOTIATION PLAN

Negotiation is a process. Never go into one without a well-researched and thought out plan.

Let's go through a negotiating process using basic salary as an example. Basic salary is the component of your pay that is *guaranteed* provided you are not terminated. This means employers want to keep it as low as possible. In fact, many employers have salary bands to provide constraints on how much money their managers can offer to prevent overall costs from escalating.

Of course, because it is guaranteed, *you* want it to be as *high* as possible. Follow me through the next steps. I advise reading this section a few times.

A. Decide on your bottom-line **reject** number. As the name describes, offers below this line will be rejected. Build a budget on a spreadsheet (practice that skill while you're at it) where you have itemized all your living expenses at the lowest level you could handle. Do not forget to deduct your taxes and include costs such as travel to and from work and medical insurance. It is always worth having someone else check your calculations to make sure you have not forgotten anything that would make your baseline unsustainable. Then add another 10% for unforeseen expenses.

This exercise is very important. It will give you clarity and conviction about why you cannot accept an offer below a certain point. Should you walk away, you'll know you did so for the right reasons. If you do not do this, there is a chance you will accept the job on terms you cannot live on. This results in stress, rapid performance deterioration, followed by an exit, invariably with no references.

NOTE: *You do NOT disclose your reject number. EVER.* If it is not reached during the offer or negotiation process, you simply ask for more or walk away.

B. Have the *acceptable* number you would like clear in your mind. This should be based on a second budget that includes additional expenses at a higher standard of living. Include a level of monthly savings, continued personal development and training, gym membership, a better vehicle, better apartment, a vacation involving travel, etc.

NOTE: *Do NOT disclose your acceptable number either.*

C. Create your *asking* number. This is the salary you "ask" for and the starting point from which you'll negotiate. Do not refer to this as the "asking" number when talking to your potential employer or you signal that it's a negotiable number. Merely position it as the salary you feel is *fair.*

You create this by getting information on what the market rate for the job is. As I said above, you do this by getting firsthand information from contacts inside the organization and contacts in similar organizations, talking to headhunters, and getting information from reputable websites. What you will end up with is a range.

Let's use an example. (*Note*: These are numbers plucked out of the air and not meant to indicate any real or current rates for any job).

Remember the above example where you were offered $40,000 but wanted $50,000? Let's say your research uncovered a range of $45,000 to $55,000 for similar jobs. You could, for example, set $45,000 as your reject number, below which you walk away, $50,000 as your acceptable number, and $52,500 as your asking number.

The conversation may go along the following lines:

The interviewer will say, "I am happy to offer you $40,000 as your base salary."

You respond with something like, "As you know, while targeting jobs like this one I made many connections within this organization and others to find an opening and make sure I had the ideal skills and experience to win it. I have also checked with job sites and recruitment companies. In that process, I found out that the market rate is between $45,000 and $55,000 per year. I would like to earn $52,500 and believe that my skills, my previous achievements, and the value I will bring justifies that. This positions me as just above the middle of the range, which I believe is fair. The feedback I have received throughout this selection process is that I am an above-average candidate."

Note the following carefully:

The **ONLY** numbers you communicate are the ***top and bottom of the range*** and your ***asking*** number. I repeat, ***NEVER*** *disclose your acceptable number or, even worse, your bottom line reject number, as that is all you will get—at best.* If you disclose your genuine acceptable number, your best-case scenario is that this is where the negotiations will **start.** The offers will only ever go ***down*** from there. In fact, many interviewers will ignore your acceptable number and deliberately lowball to find your reject number. Meanwhile, if you tell them your reject number, they will believe it is your acceptable number and treat it as such by still offering you less! Confused?

Your objective is to convince the interviewer that your asking salary is appropriately positioned within the market range given your experience and the value you will bring.

If you have compelling examples of matching high priority results backed by great reference letters and testimonials, you could consider starting with a higher asking number nearer the top of the range. It's a judgment call you will need to make. Very early in your career when you are applying for entry level positions this may be difficult. I advocate positioning yourself halfway between the middle of the range and the top. You can justify this by saying the feedback you received supports this: You were *not* selected because you were average, and you are not so bigheaded that you think you are the best; you therefore picked the 75th percentile. This makes you sound reasonable.

Experienced interviewers will try to manage your expectations by making a low offer and either sticking to it or coming up in *very* small increments. They want you to focus on numbers near their low offer. Ignore that and keep focusing on numbers near *your* asking number. Do *NOT* come down in large jumps just because they are staying near theirs.

Why have a middle number? Why not just an asking number and a reject number? It's a question I hear a lot. If you do not have a middle number, people under pressure tend to drop way too quickly to the reject number. Good negotiators will keep the pressure on *until they feel genuine resistance.*

Negotiation is about coming down in small increments from your asking number to your acceptable number, NOT to your reject number.

You want the interviewer to believe that your acceptable number is your reject number by creating resistance at that point. Here's how:

Just to recap, you were offered $40,000. Through your research, you found a range of $45,000 to $55,000. You decided that $50,000 was your acceptable number, which you kept to yourself. You asked for $52,500. You positioned your asking number as *reasonable* because it is half way between the middle of the range and the top. ($45,000 is your reject or "walk away" number which you never disclose.)

As you come down from your "asking" number and reach $50,000, request a break in the discussion. Remain enthusiastic about joining, but indicate their offer is still not what you were hoping for. Explain that, based on your research; you believe the offer is below a fair market rate for you. Say that you need a day or two to think about the offer, as it will require you to revisit your living expenses and consider your options.

This is a strong signal to make the interviewer believe that your reject number has been reached when it is in fact your acceptable number.

It also gives you a breather to assess your chances of a better offer by talking to your connections and start planning which other components of the compensation package you might now also start negotiating. When you return to the discussion, there will basically be only three scenarios. Beware of the first one!

1. Extreme negotiators who sense they have the power may **drop** their offer in an attempt to scare you away from focusing on a higher number and get you scrambling to retain the first (unacceptable) offer. They might say they discussed it with their superiors and were told that they had offered too much, that their previous offer was out of line with other existing staff, and that it is now $38,500. Be wary of these tactics. Clearly, this is not what you want to hear, but do not be intimidated! This technique has worked for employers, especially with unprepared, first-time job seekers in today's tough market. It is also a good way for them to test your backbone, so be ready!
2. They may just hold firm and reiterate that the offer cannot be changed.
3. They may make an improvement toward your desired number which will vary in size depending on their perception of their negotiating power versus yours and what they genuinely believe to be a fair market rate.

Unless you are offered what you last asked for, in **all** cases, I recommend at least one more attempt to justify a higher number. Use the break in the discussion to talk to your connections and come up with more reasons to defend a higher number. Remember, some employers are just waiting to see if you have what it takes to fight for your case.

WATCH OUT FOR "LET'S SPLIT THE DIFFERENCE"

This is a common technique, especially for lazy negotiators. It is justified on the basis that it *seems* fair. Knowing that this is a possibility, make sure that the halfway point between your target salary and their offer is higher than your reject number. Ideally, it should be at least equal to or higher than your acceptable number. Unfortunately, you cannot always do this within the constraints of the real market salary ranges. In the above example, the midway point between the offer of $40,000 and your asking salary of $52,500 is $46,250. This is just above your walk away number, but not by much. If you get feedback that this is how your interviewer negotiates, you might want to increase your target salary to about $54,000 so that when you split the difference you are a bit closer to your acceptable number.

The key, however, is only to go with the flow on this negotiating tactic if it is acceptable to you. Otherwise simply explain that splitting the difference on a below market offer is *not* a fair way forward.

This example demonstrates another principle I have found to be true:

The HIGHER the asking number when you START the negotiation, the HIGHER the END number will be when you FINISH the negotiation.

Therefore, you need to put a lot of thought into your asking number and how you justify it. Do not be shy about this or you will be giving away money before you even start negotiating.

DEFUSING THE ANGRY INTERVIEWER

You may make a strong Driver or Expressive type angry. It's unlikely if you have been logical, reasonable, and courteous, but it may happen. I know several senior executives who will quickly get angry for effect. They have learned it is a shortcut to get what they want! Do not panic. Simply explain that you did not mean to offend, but that you have to fight for what you believe is right. Explain that you are planning to work a long time at this organization; therefore, the numbers need to be the best you can make them. Look the person in the eye and say something like, "I presume you would expect me to fight hard for the company's interests once on board. One of the reasons I believe I am worth the salary is because I will easily earn it back for you in negotiations with suppliers and customers."

NOTE: When you reach a conclusion that you absolutely cannot get any higher on the base salary, pause, ***do not accept it.*** Instead, move the discussion to other areas such as those described below.

GET MORE BY INCREASING THE RESPONSIBILITIES

Basic salary is usually determined by the *responsibilities* of the role. When you have reached a point at which you really believe you cannot increase their offer any further for the responsibilities as *originally* defined, try to explore whether there are ways to increase or add to the responsibilities and use that to increase the offer.

You have to set up your ability to do this by asking the interviewer and your connections inside the organization about additional challenges they are facing, particularly challenges that are associated or adjacent to your presumed role. The better you understand these challenges, the better your chances of identifying areas where you could provide additional value to justify a higher base salary.

This means changing your approach from simply asking for higher pay to asking how could you EARN more by DOING more.

This is often much more acceptable and can give the interviewer more justification for getting around internal salary constraints.

A QUICK STORY

A good example of someone who used this approach is a computer programmer who applied to work for us on our core banking computer system. Prior to securing an interview, he learned from his connections that we were worried about the impact of cloud computing on our future. He had studied cloud computing while earning his computer science degree. Upon discovering our concerns, he researched cloud computing in the context of banking systems and brought this "expertise" into the negotiations. We increased the scope of his job by adding him to the team responsible for researching our initial path into cloud computing, which earned him an increase to his base salary.

The key here is to think this through well in advance of the negotiations. This is hard to pull off in the moment, under pressure.

WHAT ELSE YOU SHOULD NEGOTIATE

There is more to compensation than salary, so let's talk about some of the other key components that you might negotiate.

PERFORMANCE BONUSES

These are extra payments dependent on overachieving against agreed goals. The organization is happy the targets have been achieved and therefore prepared to pay more for more. Because bonuses are not paid if goals are not met, they are sometimes referred to as the "at risk" component of a compensation package. Many employers are more open to negotiating here.

Once you've reached your base salary ceiling, it is worth switching the discussion to see if they will consider a bonus for exceeding certain goals. If you have done your homework, you will have questioned and understood what your interviewer needs you to deliver, i.e. the top priority results. We have previously stressed the importance of being able to define this in measurable terms, so there is no uncertainty about whether you are succeeding. Measurable terms allow you to set goals. If you can establish the value you bring in exceeding those goals by a certain percentage, you can sometimes get employers to pay you extra. It makes sense for them to offer incentives to figure out how to deliver more as they pay extra only if *they gain* extra, it is "win-win" for both sides.

Again notice how this discussion is dependent on laying groundwork before and during the interview in terms of understanding requirements in *measurable* terms. It is very difficult to define this in the middle of a negotiation. The best way to ensure that you do this is to constantly utilize the four alignment actions from Chapter One. Without them, you will end up with minimal power to negotiate any performance bonus unless the concept already exists within the organization for this position.

TRIAL PAY

If you have reached a point where the employer has exceeded your reject number but is clearly not going to reach your acceptable pay level you can try another approach. Assuming you really like the job and can see the long-term potential, then offer to do the job at their rate with a salary review after six months. If by then you have proven that you added the value you believe you can deliver, the deal is that they will increase your salary to your acceptable number. This, in effect, shows you are willing to "walk the walk" before they give you your desired number.

There are several variations of this approach, but again, *do not* bring them up until you feel you have reached their ceiling, or you could be giving away money. Make sure the terms for gaining the extra salary are measurable and achievable and that the six-month pay raise does *not* affect your annual raise due in another six months. It is a popular trick!

They'll say, "Well, you just *had* a pay raise, so the next review will be a year out from your six-month raise." Get that clear up front by understanding how and when annual raises are calculated. Get a written statement that this initial payment structure will not affect your first anniversary salary review. Otherwise, you will simply fall behind again the following year.

COMMISSION

Commission is a form of performance bonus that generally applies to people in sales roles. The employer will pay a small percentage of each sale on top of a base salary to incentivize maximum sales efforts. In sales, base salary is often low, in some cases even zero. The employer expects salespeople to be entirely dependent on their own efforts. In most cases, the organization will have established commission rates, which makes it more difficult to negotiate. However, in many organizations, these percentages are driven by the volume of sales.

For example, you may be paid 2% for the first 100 units, 2.5% for the next 100 units, and 3% for the next 100 units. Sometimes it is possible to negotiate the volumes at which the commission percentages go up. You might be able to negotiate 2% for the first 75 units, 2.5% for the next 75 units, and 3% from there on. This means that from 150 units on (as opposed to 200) you will be paid a higher percentage. This can vary greatly from organization to organization and industry to industry and is, therefore, worth exploring.

Note: Make sure you have done your homework, check with connections about how many units other salespeople have been selling so you get a sense of what is realistic. I have seen many instances where individuals were delighted with the terms of an offer in sales only to find that no salespeople had achieved their targets or made decent commissions for years because the boss always set unrealistic targets.

SHARES AND OPTIONS

There are many types of shares and options packages. In general, these involve you being granted shares based on performance or tenure and seniority in the organization. They are a great way for an organization to align the interests of its employees with its own. If the company does well, shares or options become more valuable, and all shareholders benefit. These are usually a long-term form of compensation, as it will take years for them to accumulate and grow in value. Eventually, however, they can be worth a fortune and are well worth shooting for as part of a deal. The bad news is that they are rarely offered to employees in their first few jobs. *It's always worth asking, though.* Find out if and when they could be available. Sometimes there are schemes where you can buy into stock options at a discount.

Even if there are no such corporate schemes available, if you are joining a public company, try to buy some stock on the open market.

Then get into the habit of discussing the price movement of the stock with your manager.

It not only demonstrates your commitment to the company but also means that you will get more in tune with what is good for the business and what drives the stock price up. It also subconsciously increases your commitment now that you have invested *your money* into the company. Add to your stock as you can afford it. It creates a good impression and can be a *great* way to make money as the company does well. (Make sure you understand the laws of insider trading. Depending on your knowledge of the business there may be times when you are not allowed to trade.)

TRAINING

This area is often overlooked. Many people come into the workplace expecting the organization to take care of their training needs only to be disappointed. I have met many individuals who complain that they have worked for an organization for years and had absolutely no formal training in anything! In their minds, this is the organization's fault, but *you own your future.* You must have your own goals, and a critical element of reaching them will be training. Your connections will help you identify what types will be most useful. Negotiating up front for specific training can be very worthwhile.

Training is also not something you just throw out during the negotiation. You need to lay the groundwork by previously agreeing with your interviewer that a specific type of training is not just valuable to you but also to the *organization.* If you have established this before the negotiations, there is a good chance an employer will agree to invest in such training for you as part of your package.

SUMMARY

1. *IT IS WORTH NEGOTIATING YOUR PAY!* You can add hundreds of thousands of dollars over the life of a career. As long as you are courteous and reasonable, you need not fear jeopardizing the offer.

2. The time to prepare and lay the groundwork for the negotiations is *EARLY*. Research typical market salaries for the job you want and build a range. Research what you are expected to deliver and how it is measured. Research what other challenges the interviewer is facing to see if there are areas you can add to the responsibilities and scope of the role. Research what other components of your compensation package could be negotiable.

3. The *ONLY* time to *actually* negotiate is when you are made an offer. This is the time their desire to have *YOU* join their organization is at its highest.

4. Focus on basic salary negotiation by building a market range of pay for the job and determining where you fit in that range to create your asking number. The range and the asking salary are the only numbers you reveal. Behind the scenes and *NEVER COMMUNICATED*, decide on your acceptable number and your "walk-away" or reject number. Defend your asking number and in small increments negotiate back to your acceptable number.

Remember—the higher your starting number, the higher your ending number!

5. When you feel you have reached the end of productive discussions around your base salary, move to other components, such as adding additional objectives, performance bonuses, and training.

6. Your ability to negotiate will depend on the balance of power between you and the potential employer.

The power lies with the person who has the best alternatives and the most knowledge.

If you have differentiated yourself well from other candidates, if the employer does not have the time to find any more candidates due to pressure to fill the position, and if they perceive that *you do* have alternatives, then the balance is in your favor.

With enough forethought, preparation, and effort, your differentiation, your alternatives and your knowledge of the market are all elements you CAN control to your advantage!

CHAPTER SEVEN

JOINING THE TEAM

THE RIGHT WAY TO START

Congratulations. You have accepted an offer and are stepping on board.

Now you need to live up to the expectations you set during the selection process!

However, in the excitement and bewilderment of starting a job, it is very easy to make mistakes. This is not surprising since you are trying to absorb so much and everything feels totally unfamiliar. This often leads you to focus on becoming accepted by your peers because that is where you feel you should belong.

Meanwhile, the most important people for your future are your bosses, and they are watching every move you make!

Managers want to be instantly reassured. They want to see the same characteristics and behavior they observed when they selected you—and entrusted you with the responsibilities of the job.

Remember, a lot is at stake, not just *your* future. Your managers may have spent a considerable amount of time, effort and money choosing you over many others. Their judgment is on the line. If you let them down, it is a reflection of their ability to do their jobs, too. Your success, in terms of the actual results you produce, could impact many people around you, including the end customers. Therefore, your managers will be scrutinizing you with the exact same criteria they had in mind during the interview process.

Everything you do, from the minute you first walk in the front door, needs to confirm the impressions you made to earn that job offer.

Treat everything about your first days and weeks as if you are *still* in the selection process. During this period, many of the people you meet will be getting their first impressions of you. Remember, first impressions act like filters and only allow information through that confirms those initial feelings about you. A poor start can hinder your progress for a *long* time.

Use the interpersonal skills we covered in Chapter Two to connect well with everyone you meet.

As you navigate those first few weeks, be aware of two potentially opposing forces.

On the one hand, you will be granted a *"honeymoon period"* when everyone, especially your boss, will help you get your bearings. For example, it will be relatively easy for you to get face-to-face time with your boss. Make sure you take advantage of this to strengthen the connection you made during the selection process.

Unfortunately, this is something many people fail to do. They are slightly nervous and keep their distance, preferring to settle in with their new peers. Yes, it is important to start making an effort to connect to the rest of the team on day one, but *reconnecting* with the boss should come *first*. I go into more detail on just how important that is below.

You must also keep in mind that the honeymoon period is a *probationary* period, too. Everyone *wants* you to succeed and will help you as part of the honeymoon period. However, at the same time, they are also deciding whether you are a "keeper."

Therefore, you ARE still in a selection process.

Many organizations have an official probationary period during which time it is legally much easier for them to terminate you and cut their losses. With the job offer signed and safely tucked away at home, plus everyone being friendly and helpful, it is easy to forget you are also in a trial period. Do not drop your guard, become overfamiliar, waste time chatting, or admit to any weaknesses that could hurt you. Be especially careful during your first few after-work social drinks! Under no circumstances should you complain or criticize anything! Stay alert and keep asking your manager, "Am I doing all that is expected of me?" Get in the habit of asking for feedback early.

Treat everybody as though your boss is going to ask them whether you were a good hire—there's a good chance they will ask!

KNOW WHY YOU WERE SELECTED

When I ask individuals why they were selected over their competition, 9 times out of 10 they don't know. They have some ideas, but they never specifically asked, either because it did not occur to them or because it felt awkward.

It is very likely that at some point your boss was asked by their superiors, and perhaps even by your colleagues, *why you* were selected. Your boss's answer will have set expectations about you.

You *MUST* know these expectations and very deliberately make sure you live up to them, or you risk immediately disappointing people—particularly your boss! You can start off on the wrong foot without even realizing it. The first and most important thing you must do is reconnect with your manager and revisit the key reasons why you were selected. If you

265

cannot say why you were hired with certainty, it is perfectly acceptable for you to ask now. Say something like this:

"I want to make sure I live up to your expectations and validate your decision to hire me. Would you mind telling me the key reasons you picked me and just go over what you expect from me in the next few days, weeks, and months?"

The most common reason people fail in their jobs is not because of a lack of inherent talent but because of a "disconnect" from their managers' expectations.

If you do not know what is expected, you are embarking on a journey with no map, no compass, and no clear destination. The only way you will reach the destination your manager wants is through repeated *corrective* direction giving from your manager.

This constant critical feedback results in disappointment on both sides, which often creates a tense relationship that can quickly deteriorate. This is a sure way to trigger in your boss that *"I recruited the wrong person"* emotion I referred to in the introduction.

Before you know it, instead of loving your job you are dreading it because of constant criticism and micromanagement which make you feel inadequate. Soon you'll be thinking, "This is not what I signed up for," and before long you'll start looking around for another job.

In your mind, it will be entirely the fault of your psycho manager.

WHAT DOES IT TAKE TO START RIGHT?

There are many actions you could consider, such as the following:

Ask for a meeting on your first day to reconfirm objectives, priorities, and expectations. Ask what will make them view the first week as a success. Make another appointment at the end of the first week to show your boss that it was. (Even if you have to work 18 hours a day, *MAKE SURE* that the first week exceeds expectations.) Touch base briefly, every day if you can, to confirm progress. A good time to do this is early morning before everyone else gets in. Be the first into the office and the last to leave. Smile. Be extremely courteous to everyone and appear delighted to be there. Volunteer to help wherever you can. When your end-of-week meeting is an outstanding success, define objectives for the following weeks.

This way you build a series of relevant victories that cements an image of you succeeding and reconfirms their wisdom in hiring you. It will also build your confidence and enjoyment.

This book's objective is to provide you with a structure: something you can follow systematically, use as a checklist, and keep repeating. It will work if you are starting a new job or if you are in one that is not going as well as you would like. At any point in time, it will clarify your destination and act as both map and compass. Your journey starts with your boss.

DEVELOP A PROFESSIONAL RELATIONSHIP WITH YOUR BOSS

One of the most critical factors in determining your performance and professional happiness is the quality of your relationship with your manager.

Use your alignment skills here—right from day one. This will result in immediate positive feedback, which encourages you to perform even better, thus starting a positive self-fulfilling cycle.

There are two specific types of employee-manager relationships you should strive for.

FIRST, MAKE THE BOSS YOUR MOST VALUED CUSTOMER

My purpose here is to help *you* to become more customer service oriented with *everyone*, especially the boss.

Remember there are two kinds of customers. *External* customers buy goods and services produced by the organization. *Internal* customers manage or receive work from other employees as part of a supply chain to the external customer. In your case, the internal customers are your boss and any coworkers who receive your work.

Always treat your internal customers with the exact same care and urgency you would show to external customers.

If you deliver late or poor-quality work to the person in the next stage of the supply chain, they may be unable to meet their top priority results, which could include meeting the external customer's expectations. If you do this to your boss, you may put them in the position of being unable to meet *their* boss' expectations. This *WILL* earn you a severe reprimand.

While most people recognize that a service attitude is important to external customers, there are many who fail to act with the right attitude internally.

In particular, many people fail to treat their bosses as customers. Instead, they prefer to keep them at a "safe" distance because they are afraid they might ask difficult questions, assign additional tasks, or reprimand them for something.

Always remember, fair or not, your boss' opinion of you can have greater consequences for your immediate future than almost anything else.

They can also have a huge impact on your long-term future when you need a reference. We discussed their importance in Chapter Four. You can use their quotes containing keywords to enhance your resume and online profile. You will need them to support your claims during your next interviews. Without good references, you will struggle to land the jobs of your choice. Promotions will be *very* unlikely.

Too many people fail to develop the right relationship with their boss and then try to kiss up later when they need something.

From day one, your boss is clearly worth paying close attention to. So what does treating your manager as your most valued customer mean in practice? Two things:

It means *maximizing the customer experience* in your interactions and developing a deep *understanding of their top priority results, obstacles to success, and consequences of failure.* You already know how to do this. It simply requires you to keep following the alignment steps in Chapter One that got you the job in the first place.

MAXIMIZING THE CUSTOMER EXPERIENCE

Make sure every interaction with your manager (your customer) is an utterly positive experience! If you disappear when you are most needed, appear tired or grumpy, or resentfully accept extra work, complain and criticize, you will create a very negative customer experience for your manager. Even if you end up doing a reasonably good job, behavior like this will seriously affect satisfaction and the relationship. Whatever you have achieved will be taken for granted as part of what you "should have done under your responsibilities anyway" and soon be forgotten.

Your attitude, however, will always be remembered!

Always greet your supervisor enthusiastically, with a genuine smile and a sparkle in your eye. Each interaction is an opportunity to reinforce the impression you wish to make. Listen attentively with good eye contact and empathy. Ask clarifying questions and be ready to take immediate action with *visible* energy. One of the most effective ways to maximize the customer experience is to always approach your boss with a can-do attitude. Communicate regularly to make sure that priorities don't change without you realizing. Give clear and honest progress updates, volunteer to do more, and get frequent feedback to make sure your boss is satisfied.

Imagine your boss has to complete a feedback survey after each inter-action and send it to the president or owner of the company.

Behave in a way that would score five stars every time! You will find that you will also enjoy the experience and, in the process, turn your boss into a raving reference.

A critical part of maximizing the customer experience is building trust. This means being reliable in how you behave, showing up on time, and delivering what was asked of you on time. A can-do attitude will not help you for long if you continually let the boss down by missing deadlines.

It also means being loyal. Nothing kills a good customer experience faster than the boss finding out that someone has been critical behind their back. Of course, it means being ethical and honest, too. It is extremely embarrassing for managers if one of their recruits turns out to be untrustworthy for any of the above reasons. It will very likely get you fired.

Part of building trust is that you provide the exact same service attitude to others, too. Your boss needs to be able to count on you to also take care of any other internal (and external) customers. Otherwise, guess whom those people will complain to? This will earn you a reputation for being two-faced and then nobody will trust you anymore.

Ask yourself continuously, "Have I done everything I can to satisfy my most valued clients? Is the boss delighted with me? Is the boss getting good feedback about me?"

BLOW THE LIGHTS OUT ON THE FIRST TASKS!

The results you deliver at the beginning will either confirm the employer's decision to hire you or make them question it indefinitely. As stated above, even if you need to work 18 hours per day to deliver beyond expectations, do it! *This is your opportunity to confirm that you are the person they wanted and prevent early onset of any thoughts of having made a mistake in recruiting you.*

The key is to understand the expectations.

In most cases, you will be given at least some tasks and objectives when you join the organization. Make sure you understand them—particularly the expected results, how they are measured, and the deadlines. *If you have any uncertainty, you must clarify.*

Remember, you may be on a probationary period and cannot afford to start off on the wrong foot. Fail to deliver during that time and you may not be given a second chance.

WHAT IF YOU DO SCREW UP?

Imagine your boss asked you to do something important and set a deadline for the end of the month. You agreed. It is now the first of the following month, and you are enduring a severe reprimand for failing to deliver. Your boss is beside himself yelling;

"How could you let me down like this?"

"The customer is furious!"

"Our chairman is furious!"

"You have embarrassed the entire department!"

"Do you understand how much this has cost the company?"

"How can I ever trust you again?"

This can easily happen, especially early in the job when you do not fully understand everything. I have felt the searing pain of several such rants as a result of my failings and witnessed others receive similar beatings. I have seen employees get defensive and blame others. I have seen people slink away and hide hoping things will blow over. I have seen people lose confidence and never quite recover. I have seen grown men cry.

These can be pivotal moments in your relationship with your boss, your colleagues and indeed your career.

So if it happens to you - sorry that should read – if YOU LET this happen to you, what should you do?

SIX STEPS TO RECOVERY!

I am a great believer in structured thinking. When you are really under pressure, such as in the above situation, it is difficult to control your emotions. This, in turn, makes it hard to think clearly and take constructive actions. Controlling your emotions are critical. Therefore, I recommend the following six steps.

1. Acknowledge and apologize for your failure.

Until your boss sees that you are genuinely sorry, he or she will remain in a high state of anger during which nothing constructive can be agreed. The worst thing you can do is argue, deny it, get defensive or throw someone else under the bus.

Even if you do not think it is entirely your fault, your objective in step one is to get emotions calmed down. Do not try to defend yourself in any way until the facts have been established in Step 2 below.

2. Analyze what happened.

Once tempers have cooled, ask if you can go over the events that led to the failure for advice on what went wrong and what you should do differently to fix the situation as quickly as possible. Obviously, each situation is different. If you simply forgot to do something important then take your beating and go straight to Step 4 and promise to work through the night, through the weekend, whatever it takes to get the job done. If there genuinely were some mitigating circumstances, then this is where you carefully bring them to your manager's attention, not as a way to divert blame, but to make sure there is a complete solution going forward. Your point will still be made.

3. Summarize lessons learned.

At the end of Step 2 take the time to summarize the mistakes made and the lessons learned. Doing so helps you learn and not forget. It also gives your manager confidence that you have really taken the lessons on board. It confirms that you are genuinely sorry and that you are taking this very seriously.

4. Make a detailed action plan to correct the failing.

Agree and document a plan that very specifically details what you are going to do and by when to deliver what you were supposed to. This is your opportunity to redeem yourself. *You must convey a sense of the utmost urgency.* The actions need to start the minute you walk out of your manager's office. Ideally, there should be some immediate tangible results coming out of the plan to reassure your boss that quick progress will be made.

Managing your manager's attitude towards you is as important as managing your own attitude. It is very hard to be constructive and do the right things to recover the situation if your boss treats you in a way that makes it clear they think you are a lazy and stupid liability.

Take the time to look your boss in the eye at the end of this step and ask if you have their support to execute the plan. Without it, you are likely to fail again. This is a critical component to successfully recovering a bad situation you caused.

5. Set up frequent progress reports.

The more serious the failure, the more frequent the updates should be. A good manager will insist on this, but a good manager could also have seen that you were failing in the first place and stepped in earlier to help you. Remember one of the mantras of this book. You own your own future. Be proactive and make giving your boss frequent updates

273

your normal way of working with them, even if they do not ask for it. It is part of their "customer experience" with you and will help give them confidence in you. You will sense this, which will make you feel better too. Do not delay for one second if anything goes wrong to alert your boss and get help.

6. Set up a closure meeting.

When you do finally get the job done, go back to your boss and ask for a meeting to:

- Once again apologize for the initial failure
- Make sure they are now satisfied with the result
- Thank them for the opportunity to put things right
- Highlight the lesson learned and assure them it will never happen again

By focusing on these six steps, you will avoid that fight or flight urge when your boss is really angry with you. Either reaction can leave you with permanent career damage. Face the music and go through the steps. It won't be easy. It won't go smoothly. But you can come out of the process having learned from your mistake and proven your grit.

Sometimes this can result in a better relationship with your manager than before. They know everyone will screw up. What they don't know is how everyone will react to fix it.

PREVENTATIVE TIP

Throughout my career, I have screwed up myself and had to deal with other people's screw ups more times than I care to admit. Sure there were instances of laziness and stupidity, but that is always the conclusion in the heat of the moment. With the benefit of hindsight the most common themes were in fact:

- Lack of understanding of management's expectations in a measurable way

- Conflicting workloads and not understanding priorities
- Not fully understanding other people's dependencies on the result
- Not understanding the consequences of failure

Just taking the time up front to really understand these factors in any important task will dramatically reduce your likely hood of failure. So let's look at this in more detail.

UNDERSTAND YOUR BOSS' TOP-PRIORITY RESULTS AND THE CONSEQUENCES OF FAILURE

In Chapter One, I described how the organization's high-level objectives are shared across all the different functions with each manager breaking their share into smaller tasks and delegating them across their teams. In this way, objectives are delegated all the way down the organization's structure. Each job will end up with top priority results that must be achieved. We discussed how understanding these, plus any obstacles to success, and consequences of failure, was how you differentiate yourself to win the selection.

Once you have joined the organization, you need to spend more time with your boss to revisit these objectives and priorities to deepen your knowledge and stay up to date because things change, sometimes very quickly.

After excelling in your first tasks and filling their goodwill tanks, start expanding your knowledge a small amount at a time. Do not to take up too much time with your boss trying to gain all the information at once.

Start by making sure you understand how your tasks come together with your co-workers' tasks to meet your manager's objectives. This will identify the top priorities *you* have to deliver and how you may have to coordinate with colleagues to satisfy your boss. Discuss the challenges so that you can anticipate and prepare for any obstacles.

To fully grasp the consequences of your performance, you need to understand the knock-on impact up the chain—in other words, how your success or failure could affect not just your manager but also their manager and anyone else.

To understand this, ask your manager to start at the top and work down the chain. Revisit in detail the following types of questions:

- What are the high-level missions of the organization? What value does it strive to provide its customers? What problems does it solve for the customer? What happens if it fails to solve those problems?
- Why do external customers buy from this organization versus competitors? What are the top priority results the customers expect from the organization? What satisfies clients and what tends to upset them?
- How does the organization make money? What measurements do its leaders pay most attention to and why?

For example: In addition to obvious measurements such as profit, every organization worries about the cash flow coming into the business to pay the bills, including your salary. This will *absolutely* be one of the measurements management pays attention to. Getting satisfied customers to pay their bills on time will be one of the corporate top priority results that everybody should know about. You need to understand how your job could directly or indirectly impact this. Any positive improvement you can make to cash flow will get you instant recognition. The opposite gets you an instant and often severe reprimand.

Ask what the key objectives of your manager's boss are. What are that person's priorities and why? How are they measured? What are the consequences of failure at that level?

What is your boss' role in helping their manager achieve the above objectives, and how does this translate into what your boss' objectives, priorities, and key measurements are? Is anyone else affected by your boss' results?

Then bring it all back and connect the dots in terms of reconfirming how your role impacts your boss and anyone else. Specifically, make sure you understand what actions from you will improve or deteriorate how your boss or anyone else is measured.

All this information will make you highly aware of consequences, which, as we discussed in Chapter One, has a direct impact on your motivation. It will give you great insight and allow you to add more value, make better decisions, and prevent blunders.

A mistake early on because "you didn't understand," "you didn't know" or "nobody told you" can be the start of a downward spiral in your relationship with your manager that can be *very* hard to recover from.

It's YOUR responsibility to find out how everything works around you.

Managers immediately realize which employees make the effort to do this and which ones don't. It's the ones that do who rapidly move up.

Such understanding will have a huge impact on your sense of being involved and part of something bigger. It will give you a visible sense of purpose, which will positively impact how your boss and other senior executives regard you.

As your understanding of who does what and why grows, you will also develop a sense of direction as to which jobs you would like to target as you move up.

Another key benefit of this approach is that you build the knowledge to expand your responsibilities without being officially promoted. You will be able to spot opportunities to volunteer for additional tasks to add more value. Over time, your job will have greater significance and become even more fulfilling. This is a great way to get excellent performance reviews, pay raises, and the experience you need for the higher positions of your choice.

Note: You do not have to get all this information directly from your boss. Remember, you also need to build your internal network. Talk to people in sales and customer service about customers. Talk to people in accounting and internal audit about processes and measurements. This way you get different perspectives, you avoid overburdening your boss with too many questions, and you continue to build connections who can help you get things done and help you get promoted in the future.

Gaining this understanding is part of your alignment. Doing it better than your colleagues differentiates you as promotion material in exactly the same way it helped you differentiate yourself to win the selection process.

It triggers the "This employee really 'gets' our business!" reaction. Add good communication skills and a reputation for getting the job done (which I cover in the next two chapters), and you will soon be on the fast track.

SECOND, TURN YOUR BOSS INTO A MENTOR

All the information you need will be much easier to obtain if you have a mentor relationship in place. For one thing, it will give you much more face time with your manager. If you focus your interactions on how you can better meet your manager's needs, you have given them an incentive to mentor you. This is the key to asking your manager to be your mentor. You can paraphrase it as *"Help me to help you."*

Once you have demonstrated that you listen, learn, and actually *do* perform better, and help your managers achieve their objectives, you can broaden your discussion topics. For example, you can get advice on the skills you need to develop to take on more responsibilities and begin lining yourself up for a promotion.

Managers with strong mentoring relationships develop a sense of pride in their mentees. You will transition from employee to protégé.

This is a huge benefit. Micro-managing tendencies will soften, trust will increase, and your managers will develop pride in your success. As they rise in the ranks, you are in a good position to rise with them.

FIVE TIPS ON BEING A GOOD MENTEE

1. Start by being clear that the focus is on improving your performance to better support your manager.

Make the initial conversations primarily about how your objectives impact your manager.

Then discuss your perceived strengths and weaknesses in relation to your ability to achieve those objectives.

Create goals and action plans to strengthen the necessary skills. A great structure to follow for your mentoring goals are the Alignment steps in Chapter One.

2. Never get defensive. Listen, take notes, and make plans to revisit their criticism after taking the agreed-upon actions to improve.

Your managers' perception is their reality. It is your job to manage that perception.

The way you do that is to listen, act, and come back with better results as proof. It is the *only* way. Any defensiveness is a turnoff to managers. It makes them think they cannot improve you, and, as a result, they will no longer want to mentor you. It can even lead to your exit.

So, even if you think your manager's perception is wrong, unless you have immediate and very compelling evidence at your fingertips, *do not argue!* At best you may persuade them to some degree; at worst you will annoy them. Do not let your pride get in the way here. Use this type of situation as an opportunity to make *them* feel good about coaching you.

Come back with improved results and give your mentor the credit.

Seeing improved results that stem from their advice will make the mentor feel that they are doing something worthwhile and cement you as their protégé.

3. Have a mix of scheduled and unscheduled meetings. I recommend one formally scheduled 30-minute meeting every month. This provides a background *discipline* to keep the mentoring relationship going.

It provides deadlines to force you to take action on weaknesses and come back with improved results.

Be prepared for these meetings with agendas, material, and objectives. Document key conclusions, actions, and results. Some of it may be achievement folder-worthy as you accomplish agreed-upon tasks, and it will certainly prove useful at annual reviews or pre-promotion discussions.

You should also have impromptu meetings, coffee, or lunch to discuss something very specific. Once you have established yourself as a protégé, you will be able to get advice whenever you need it.

Note: A good mentor is likely to be a successful and busy person. Do not expect them to drive the relationship. *You own your future, so the onus is on you to organize it and keep the momentum going.*

4. If the mentoring relationship is progressing well, ask for opportunities you would not otherwise have to gain exposure to situations and people.

For example, ask to be in on a customer call or help on a presentation your manager is putting together. If your work affects another department or requires their cooperation, ask if your boss can set up a meeting with the manager of that department for feedback. Your boss is a great source of contacts so ask for introductions. When the mentoring relationship has clearly produced results, you can bring up your aspirations. Talk about your ideal next job and how best to get you groomed for it.

5. You should also discuss who might make a good secondary mentor, perhaps for a particular project because this person has done it successfully many times before. Or you might want someone for a particular skill. Always discuss this with your manager so that they are aware and not in any way concerned. Most mentors develop a sense of ownership over their protégés, which is generally very good. This can, however, make them concerned if their protégés approach people they see as competitors, people they have difficulty working with, or people who might poach their protégés from their team. Be sensitive to this.

Also, make sure you understand how well your boss is regarded and their potential upward mobility to move up. If they look good, then hanging on to their coattails can be a smart strategy. However, if your boss is not well regarded, you may need to choose someone else as a mentor too, especially for your career plans. Take careful stock of the situation before making that choice.

SOME DOS AND DON'TS

Do look for something you can teach your manager. It makes it more interesting for the manager if you bring something to the table that they could benefit from too. Older managers sometimes struggle with the latest technology. Perhaps you could help them. Learn their self-perceived weaknesses and make those your strengths so that you can become a source of expertise to them. It adds credibility to your "help me to help you" attitude. This can start positioning you as a *trusted advisor* as well as a protégé.

Remember at all times that this is your boss! Always be respectful and never overfamiliar. Be sensible about what you confide. Avoid talking about personal habits such as how much you can party, opinions about others you work with or whom you find attractive—even if your boss brings up any of these subjects. It could be a test! It is best you keep anything that could hurt your reputation to yourself. Do not waste valuable mentoring appointments by discussing day-to-day issues or just complaining.

Final note: *ALWAYS have a mentor!*

All top athletes have them and owe them a *HUGE* part of their success. The earlier you start, even in high school, the better. While in college try to find successful people in the industries and jobs you are interested in and get them to mentor you. Continue this practice throughout all levels of your career.

Cherish and nurture any mentoring relationships you have by treating your mentors' time with the utmost professionalism and always try to provide some value in return.

SUMMARY

Joining an organization does not mean just showing up and waiting for instructions.

Interpret the word "join" in the job cycle as proactively making the effort to really integrate and participate as part of a team. Start with the team's captain.

Use your aligning skills to start in the best way possible by understanding and then exceeding all initial expectations. Use every opportunity to maximize your manager's customer experience with you and develop a comprehensive understanding of their needs. In the process, develop a mentoring relationship that turns you into their protégé and trusted advisor.

This approach will not only transform your performance, but the positive reinforcement you will receive will also ensure you enjoy your work and develop a passion for it.

Lastly, never forget that one of the most likely questions your next interviewer will ask is;

"When I contact your previous managers, how will they rate your performance?"

Always be thinking about what actions you should be taking every day and during every interaction with your bosses so that you look forward to that question instead of dreading it.

CHAPTER EIGHT

KEY COMMUNICATION SKILLS

WHY ARE COMMUNICATION SKILLS SO IMPORTANT?

An organization cannot achieve its goals without a great deal of communication down the chain of command to give direction, back up it to report progress, and across it to coordinate activities.

As an individual, you will not survive in this environment without an ability to proactively get information, clarify it, and convey it in a manner that is effective and creates an enjoyable customer experience.

Communication skills are the FOUNDATION for your ability to work with your managers, colleagues, and customers.

Management will be looking for this ability during the selection process *AND* once you come on board. So it's worth taking a look at how you become good at communicating.

THE SIX STEPS OF EFFECTIVE COMMUNICATION

So what is effective communication? You may have said something or written an email or even given a presentation, but does that mean you have conveyed anything successfully? Just because you used logic that made sense to *you* does not mean it made sense to others. Being eloquent or entertaining does not guarantee your message was received either.

All communication has an objective. The only measure of its effectiveness is the extent to which the objective is met.

The objective could be to make your audience understand something, be convinced of something, or be moved to take a specific action. To help your communication achieve an objective, there is a simple structure you can follow, whether it is done in conversation, in a presentation, or in writing.

1. DEFINE YOUR OBJECTIVE

Do not begin any *important* conversation, presentation, or email before clearly defining your desired outcome.

Decide what you expect to happen when the conversation is over.

Is it just agreement with your opinion? (If so, why is that important?)

Are you providing an update on progress? Looking to reassure the boss all is well? (What would please the boss?)

Do you need to alert people that help may be needed? (What would get their attention?)

Is your objective to gain approval for something? (On what basis would it be granted?)

Do you want the other party to take or refrain from a certain action? (Why would they do this?)

There are many such objectives.

Make sure the objective is clear to YOU before you attempt to make it clear to other people.

This will help you structure your information and logic. You won't make it clear to others if it's not clear to you first.

2. GET ATTENTION

Do not reveal the critical part of the message until your audience is receptive and ready to listen. They may be distracted by something urgent or bad news they have just received. They may be hungry, tired, or just not mentally present. Get their attention first with something you know is of interest to them.

In a conversation, it may be as simple as asking, "May I have your attention? I have something important I wish to discuss," with good eye contact. We have covered this before, watch for this—*lack of eye contact nearly always means not listening.* Consider starting the conversation with a startling, attention-grabbing fact. This is a common strategy used to open presentations and draw everyone into the moment. Describing an urgent problem can be a good way to do this.

The important thing is to make sure you have their attention, and they have clearly indicated they are listening. Never *assume* they are listening. Keep checking throughout the conversation or presentation.

3. BUILD DESIRE TO TAKE ACTION

Keep in mind that in today's stressful, competitive world, it is likely that the people you communicate with are likely to be preoccupied with THEIR challenges, not yours.

Any desired outcome that requires effort from the audience means you need to think about *what is in it for them* and communicate those benefits quickly before you lose their attention.

Use your AUDIENCE'S logic concerning benefits to THEM, not your logic concerning benefits to you.

Remember to consider the personalities of those you are addressing. Play to their social style. Use *their* language about topics that are important to them. Anticipate any objections they might raise and be ready to deal with them.

4. MAKE THE REQUEST

When your audience is paying attention and interested enough to hear your message or request, provide it in clear, simple and direct terms. There should be no room for any doubt or confusion.

If your message or call to action is not clear, you will have immediately failed in your objective.

Think this through beforehand. Rehearse it for very important situations.

5. GET FEEDBACK

We have covered this before. *Never assume* listeners have understood and are still following you. Ask them regularly and do not move on until they tell you they have understood and are in agreement. This means regularly asking things like, "Do you follow this logic? Do you agree?" These questions ensure you do not lose listeners at an early stage without realizing. Get the listeners in the habit of nodding "yes" throughout the conversation. This makes the final yes feel natural and almost automatic. This is much easier than going for the big yes at the end of the conversation and backtracking to find where you lost them if the answer is no.

6. CLOSE

Once you're sure your listeners are onboard, ask for *agreement or commitment.* Use a closed yes or no question to confirm it. Then, very deliberately close the conversation by asking if you can consider the matter finalized. This prevents any argument later that it was not. On important matters, document agreed-upon actions, start and end dates, how you will monitor progress, and when you will meet to review it.

CREATE A GOOD LISTENER EXPERIENCE

It's not just what you say, but how you say it!

It also has to be a positive experience because negative experiences, particularly if they are consistently negative, undermine your objectives. Remember, you will have to communicate with the same people repeatedly—especially your boss—often multiple times a day. You will not be able to communicate successfully for long if you become disliked in the process.

Using the above six steps will already create a professional experience. You can add to this with your interpersonal skills. Control your face, your tone, and your body language. Also, take note of the other people's word choices and their personality types and align with them. Always be courteous as any form of disrespect, frustration, patronization, or intimidation will ruin the customer experience. Refresh yourself on Chapter Two if necessary.

Note: I strongly discourage you from communicating anything important via letter or email. How your written words are interpreted can vary enormously. You are not present to clarify any misunderstandings. Finally, you put all the power regarding when they might respond, or whether they will, in *their* hands. Be aware that there will be many times when your manager will ask whether you have communicated something to someone else. If you respond by saying you sent an email and consider that email the extent of the communication effort required, your boss will not be pleased. You will have no idea whether the recipients understood it, how they reacted, or if they even read it! Leaving voicemail suffers from the same flaws.

The rule is that you have not communicated anything until the recipient confirms they have heard and understood. You have not communicated SUCCESSFULLY until the recipient confirms their willingness to meet your objective.

Generally, it is much better to have the conversation in person first, and then confirm the agreement (or disagreement) by email. Unfortunately, many people hide behind the written word because of nerves or just laziness. It is less scary and takes less effort to tap the keyboard than it is to go and see someone or make a phone call. Even worse, people say things in emails they would never say face-to-face, which does *NOT* make for a good customer experience and can be very counterproductive to achieving their objectives. This can easily cause long-term damage to relationships.

Nervousness about the possible outcome is all the more reason to use the best form of communication. This is ALWAYS face to face.

Like many of the structures in this book, these steps may initially seem difficult or even excessive. However, just keeping them in mind will improve the clarity and effectiveness of your communication skills in all situations. It will get you in the habit of thinking through why you want to say something, what you are going to say, and how. Forethought helps you prepare the best approach to succeed. Taking the listeners' point of view *into account* will make sure you have their attention and greatly increase your chances of gaining their agreement.

In particular, this approach will greatly help you when dealing with your boss—especially when they are under pressure with low tolerance for unstructured rambling or emotional conversations.

DEALING WITH ANGRY PEOPLE—INCLUDING YOUR BOSS

At times, you will meet emotionally charged, angry, or upset people, such as unsatisfied customers. At some point, this will include your boss. It is inevitable. Your ability to defuse and resolve issues with angry people, especially your manager, is vital—not only to your success but to your very survival.

To do this, follow the same simple steps we covered in Chapter Five on answering questions. This time, we add a new first step which is to empathize.

1. *Empathize* by indicating that you understand why the person is upset.

Many people simply will not hear or "take in" a word you say until their emotions have calmed down.

Say things like, "I am sorry this has upset you" and "I can see you have a problem." This takes the emotional charge down without admitting any liability that could be used against you later.

In this litigious world, it can be dangerous to admit liability. So don't say, "Oh, I see our delivery department really screwed this one up didn't they!" You would be surprised what some people say when they do not believe they were personally at fault!

This is a critical first step in which you make it clear you are *not* going to be defensive and are there to *help*.

2. *Clarify* the situation. Make sure you understand the causes *and* the impact or consequences of the grievance on their top priorities. Find out the what, where, when, by whom, etc. Only by diagnosing causes and effects can you recommend a solution that achieves their desired outcome. It seems obvious but is easily forgotten in the stress of the moment, especially when you feel under attack. Before you know it you can find yourself defending rather than diagnosing.

Throughout all this, be very sincere. Use lots of eye contact. Nod your head to indicate you understand and take notes.

3. *Rephrase* their grievance in your own words when you feel you have a good understanding. "Just to make certain I have this completely correct, what you are saying is…"

You must clearly signal that you understand, care, and want to resolve the issue as fast as possible.

4. *Provide a solution* which must include *an action* that takes care of the issue upsetting the individual. The action must be clear in terms of what it is, the expected outcome, who will do it, and by when.

5. *Get Feedback* from the upset person to make certain the action meets expectations. If yes, move to step six; if not, loop back to step two and start again. Clarify until you understand why your suggested action was not acceptable and can modify it until it is acceptable. Then check again. Don't forget to ask if there are any other issues.

6. *Close* the conversation if you were able to resolve the issue with your solution, and there were no other concerns. Specifically, ask if the issue can be considered a closed matter. If yes, summarize the actions, and agree on a follow-up time to talk and assess progress in the resolution. If not, go back to step two and start clarifying. Keep looping until you reach closure.

No matter how rough things get, a structure like this can be very useful in helping you maintain composure and professionalism when others around you start becoming emotional and intimidating.

Turning unhappy people around can be incredibly rewarding in its own right. On top of that, it can be a powerful way to develop relationships.

Once you have successfully resolved an issue that was important enough for someone to get angry about you can make lifelong connections and gain some of the best references.

So remember, don't join the others in hiding when angry people are around, especially if they are the boss or any other internal or external customers. Step up to the plate, use the six-step process and turn them around.

View angry people as opportunities. You will increase your confidence and build compelling stories for your portfolio.

Remember, at some point you will encounter your boss in an angry mood. It may be because of something you did or failed to do. It may be because of something entirely unrelated to you. How you handle your boss in these circumstances can have a lasting impact on your relationship.

An ability to maintain your tact, defuse a situation, accurately assess the causes, and suggest a viable way forward will create a very good customer experience.

It will provide a positive and productive basis for you and the customer or your boss to continue working together. If you let your own emotions escalate, things can be said from which the relationship cannot recover. Distancing yourself from your boss under such circumstances does not work either. It will inevitably lead to feelings of fear and resentment that will undermine your performance and the relationship. Staying calm and using a process to manage the situation can actually strengthen the relationship considerably. When your boss has calmed down, they will see you in a new light.

It is how you earn the reputation of having a "cool head under pressure."

SUMMARY

Achieving anything in most working environments involves a great deal of communication. Organizations cannot operate without it.

You will not become an effective participant in an organization without good communication skills.

Use a structured approach to help you plan what to say. Be conscious of how you say it, plus how to clarify and answer questions, especially in a volatile situation.

There are few things that will have a greater impact on how you are regarded and your effectiveness than your communication skills

These skills are also a fundamental prerequisite for mastering the Achievement Methodology to accomplish great things, which is the subject of the next chapter.

CHAPTER NINE

GETTING THE JOB DONE!

Following the Job Cycle chronologically in this book, you now know how to create a customer experience for your boss that will make for a productive professional relationship. You are clear on what it is you have to do, by when, and why.

Now it's time to deliver. You have to be able to actually get things done!

This chapter will show you how.

PART I

TAKE ACTION

JUST DO IT!

Taking the step to actually **DO** something is *the* fundamental require-ment for **ANY** success. You cannot achieve anything of significance with-out action. You won't even get started. Nothing in this book is of any value unless you make a move.

"You cannot plow a field by turning it over in your mind."

Gordon B. Hinckley

Many of you will be groaning at this because it's *SO* obvious! However, the world is full of well-intentioned people who do *NOT* take action. Many people are happy to discuss what is wrong and what needs to be done, and complain about what *should* have been done. Few people will actually *do* something.

Fewer still will take ownership and persist in their actions, especially in the face of difficulty and criticism, until the job is completed.

These are the people management looks for.

Sure, it is important to consider alternatives and the consequences of your actions, but do not let analysis turn into paralysis! Spontaneous people, those who rush in with little planning, may fail. But with a bit of common sense, quick reactions, good guidance, and luck, they may achieve something. And if they do fail, at least they can learn from their mistakes. They *will* get closer next time.

Those who debate everything tend to achieve nothing!

Contemplative people often sound sensible and seem like the cautionary voice of reason. In fact, this is often caused by fear and an "I can't" attitude. Some are just lazy and are only providing reasons to justify not making any effort.

Most managers believe it is easier to teach risk takers to become more analytical than it is to turn the fearful or lazy into action takers.

Also, keep in mind what others have called the **law of diminishing intentions.** This states that the likelihood you will take action diminishes as time goes by. Procrastination is a habit, and it is deadly to your productivity. Get into the practice of taking immediate action instead.

"You can't build a reputation on what you are *going* to do."

Henry Ford

One thing all managers have in common is distaste for people who are unresponsive or slow to take action. It is the same feeling parents get when they ask their teenagers to take out the trash. First, there is no response, then, after the request is repeated, there is a sigh, then an excuse, followed by an "I will do it later." Finally, under duress, the teenager gets it done. Managers have absolutely *NO* tolerance for this type of behavior and want to see an *instant* response.

Remember, your boss is your most valued client. Inaction does not maximize the customer experience. Immediate, enthusiastic action does!

SEVEN TIPS ON BECOMING HIGHLY ACTION ORIENTED

1. Ask yourself every evening as you prepare for the following workday, "What *actions* will I take?" "What will I *get done?*"

Make a list and have the discipline to follow it.

Review the list at the end of each day and prepare for the next. At the end of the week, summarize your accomplishments. For repetitive tasks, set daily and weekly targets. Make a point of beating them and increasing your goals. It is very satisfying, and you will be surprised by how much more you accomplish.

Ask yourself whether you would be proud to send that list to your boss, or whether it is embarrassingly light.

By the way, I know many managers who ask for such info in weekly reports, so you might as well develop the habit now.

2. Make it your personal discipline not to let any conversation go by without asking yourself and, if appropriate, the participants, *what is the desired result, what actions should be taken, by whom and by when.*

3. Become a "now" person. Get into the habit of using phrases like "Let's do it now!" "Can we start on it right away?" "Is there anything to prevent us from getting on with it right now?"

4. Use phrases like "consider it done!" when your boss asks you to do something. It creates a great customer experience. Then make *SURE* it gets done! This will soon position you as someone your boss relies on.

5. Volunteer whenever and wherever you can. If possible, lead actions. It is a great way to visibly demonstrate that you are action-oriented, put goodwill in those relationship tanks, and to practice using your Achievement Methodology which is covered in the next section.

6. Whenever you get recognition for achieving a task, use the moment to reinforce your brand for action and getting the job done still further. Respond with, "Thank you! I like to get things done—whatever it takes!" "Is there anything else you would like me to take care of?"

7. Document significant actions and put them in your Achievement Portfolio. Regularly review and assess whether your portfolio shows that you are an action taker. *Is it full of things YOU got done?*

PART II

ACHIEVEMENT METHODOLOGY

A 10 STEP PROCESS FOR ACHIEVING SIGNIFICANT TASKS

The world is full of dreamers who talk a great game. They are always *about to do* something great, but never actually achieve anything. In some cases, they didn't take any or enough action. In others, they try to take action but are simply ineffective.

Becoming an EFFECTIVE action taker is the subject of this section.

As any high achiever will tell you, the key is following a *proven process*.

Such processes will help you clearly define your objectives, make plans, and execute them with consistent results. They help you build energy and drive and also prepare you to anticipate and deal with difficulties quickly before you lose momentum. They will transform your ability to achieve your top priority results and overcome any obstacles to success.

The Achievement Methodology is a process that will both guide you to success *and* enable you to explain, succinctly, how you got it done or how you will. A clear description of the steps you followed or are following will inspire confidence and trust.

Meanwhile, an inability to do so will instantly undermine your credibility.

> *"If you cannot describe your actions as part of a process then you probably don't know what you are doing!"*
>
> *W. Edwards*

Cautionary note: This section is so important to your success it should become part of how you operate—*like achievement DNA.* Absorbing it is not easy. I urge you to read it at least twice. From time to time read it again and refresh.

The following 10-step process will become your foundation for achieving your top priorities and solving obstacles. It also provides a structure for making sound decisions, plus knowing when to lead and when to manage.

I have made this section comprehensive enough to help you understand the principles of tackling major initiatives in the workplace. You can use it with equal effect on personal objectives. However, that does not mean you *have* to use it in its *entirety* for *everything.* This could grind you to a halt on the small stuff.

Stay with me on this, as it *WILL* dramatically improve your effectiveness!

KEY STEPS

1. DEFINE YOUR OBJECTIVE

The root cause of many failed initiatives, including people failing in jobs, is a lack of clearly documented objectives, as we discussed in Chapter One.

Write down a description of the desired results (such as one of your top priorities) and how it will be measured.

This vital first step acts as the foundation upon which the rest of the process is built. You have to get this crystal clear before you do anything else.

To help you define an objective, try applying the principles of a useful acronym—**SMART**—which says that an objective should be Simple, Measurable, Achievable, Rewarding, and completed by a defined Time.

Simple. If the objective or goal is too complex, break it down into something simpler. You should be able to state a goal in one sentence. Too much complexity can create confusion and misdirected effort.

Measurable. If you cannot measure the goal, it's probably too vague. Find a way to restate it in such a way that you can ask, "How many?" "How much?" "How often?" "By what percent?" "By when?" and so on. Measurement is required in order to agree on expectations and assess progress. This safeguards you from failing to meet expectations that were never understood or agreed upon at the start.

Achievable. Goals perceived as impossible are doomed from the outset. The flip side is that many people fail at tasks they believed were achievable, but in reality had no chance of succeeding. This was either because the goal was unrealistic or because they had no clue how to go about achieving it. This is where an achievement process is so helpful. It will guide you through the actions you will need to take, the risks involved, and the necessary time and effort required. The steps are detailed enough to help you realize what is achievable and how.

Rewarding. The goal must have a purpose, a good reason in the form of a measurable benefit to justify making the effort. This is what fuels your motivation to succeed. Without it, you will not. This point will be expanded in step two below.

Timeline. Objectives need deadlines. Otherwise, it is not a *commitment* but an indication of something you would like to do someday.

Without deadlines, most endeavors, especially big complex ones, never reach completion. This is because of another important law in the working environment:

> *"Any task that has no deadline will lose*
> *priority to tasks that do have one."*

Each of your top priorities must have deadlines. Also, remember this law when you are relying on someone else to complete a task that is vital to you in order to achieve one of your top priorities. If you do not set a deadline for what you need, the chances are high that you *will* be let down.

2. BUILD THE CASE

You must be able to state clearly and motivationally WHY you are doing it and why NOW.

Fear of change, fear of failing, unwillingness to incur costs, other priorities, and sheer laziness are just a few of the forces that will prevent you from even getting *started*, let alone reach completion. In this step, you articulate in very clear terms the rewarding aspect of your objective. Sometimes this is called the "business case," especially if it is defined in revenue, costs, and profits. The purpose is to motivate you, and anyone else involved, to overcome this inertia.

Without a strong case, a new initiative can be hard to get started. Even if you do, the moment you feel tired, hit an obstacle, or get distracted by something else, the initiative will peter out.

No amount of hope or positive attitude will overcome this principle!

It can be helpful to create an impact statement describing the impact of success in terms of benefits to the organization, its customers, your manager, yourself, and all participating individuals. In business, these are often referred to as the stakeholders.

Speak to both their corporate and personal top priority objectives. This avoids you trying to build the case only around what *you* care about. This is always a good practice, and for any corporate initiatives, a good manager will require that you demonstrate how you took all the stakeholders into account. Corporate results are usually anything that increases revenue and customer satisfaction and decreases costs, therefore increasing profit. Personal ones could be learning valuable new skills and gaining greater recognition, more money, promotions, and so on. If you understand and take their top priority objectives into consideration, you won't go far wrong.

Paint a picture of what success looks like in the most vivid way possible so you and anyone else involved can *imagine* it. All involved must be able to *see it, smell it, and believe it!* Make sure that the consequences of failure are painted equally vividly.

> **"If you are working on something exciting that you really care about you don't have to be pushed. The vision pulls you."**
>
> **Steve Jobs**

Document this step for easy reference. Use it to build your motivation and to rekindle dwindling energy in the face of any problems.

3. DEFINE THE SHORTFALL

Compare the present results with the desired future results. The difference is the shortfall or gap. Bridging it is going to become your focus, often referred to as the *scope* of your task.

In cases where you may be trying to increase something, such as sales or production, the difference between today's actual and the desired future is the gap. If it is a new initiative, then present reality could be zero. The entire desired outcome would be the shortfall in this case.

Note: Shortfall thinking can apply to anything, including skills development when you are aligning yourself to a future job opportunity. We referred to this in Chapter Four when identifying your shortfall for the skills needed for a job and using targeted skills development to bridge the gap.

4. DEFINE THE CAUSES OF THE SHORTFALL

In situations where you are trying to alter existing results, once the shortfall has been identified keep asking "why do we have" or "what causes" today's results. Ask "what prevents" tomorrow's desired results. Dig deep until you are sure you are dealing with root causes for the shortfall and not just addressing symptoms. It is often said that after asking "why?"

five times in a row, you will probably have reached a root cause. You will also have annoyed the heck out of those around you!

If this is a completely new initiative with no existing results, then this step is less important. I recommend moving straight to step five.

5. DEFINE ACTIONS THAT BRIDGE THE SHORTFALL

Brainstorm a list of actions that could bring the present situation to the desired future. Look for expertise to help you suggest actions. There may be a whole range of possibilities. Don't stifle any creativity by judging the pros and cons of any idea too early.

Likewise don't give up if you feel you are not coming up with any workable ideas. When you are faced with solving a difficult problem, this is the step that requires creativity, resourcefulness, and determination. This is where you start earning your reputation. This is so important that I will go into more detail in the next chapter on problem-solving.

6. EVALUATE, SELECT, VERIFY, AND PRIORITIZE THE PROPOSED ACTIONS

Once you have a list of ideas from step five, evaluate and pick the best. Some will be low-impact or impractical; others will have potentially negative side effects, and a few might be unacceptable to one or more of the stakeholders. Narrow the list down to options that appear to have the most impact and put the rest aside. Look for ways to verify your decision. Ask people with relevant experience.

The course of action you choose will finalize the scope and, by definition, the *boundaries*, of what you plan on doing. *Anything else is deemed out of scope.* This step is absolutely vital.

Without scope, and the discipline to stay within it, any significant initiative is doomed to inefficiency, delays, and usually failure.

7. CREATE AN EXECUTION PLAN

This is where you turn your selected actions into a workable plan. Estimate the time and effort required (in hours, days, weeks, and months) for all the activities and schedule them on the calendar with a start and end date for each task.

The mere act of scheduling tasks in your calendar doubles the chances of you doing them. Without a schedule, other low-priority, low-impact busy work will fill your day.

Prioritize your selected list of actions according to their impact, and plan to execute them in that order whenever possible. This way, you are likely to make significant progress and build momentum early. This is important for boosting not only your own confidence but also management's.

Note: this is not always possible; basic groundwork that does not yield visible results may need to be in place first, in which case you should manage expectations accordingly to avoid any loss of confidence.

Throughout this process, it is always useful to find others who have successfully achieved your objective, and learn from them. Get a sense of how they approached things and how long particular tasks took. Do not be afraid to ask to see their plans and ask where the actual initiative went off course. Find out what went wrong, why, and what they would do differently. This can be a tremendous time-saver and help develop a realistic sense of achievability, manage expectations better, and avoid previously known pitfalls.

8. DO A RISK ANALYSIS

Ask what can go wrong. You have now envisioned the result you want and how to make it happen and created a plan to execute.

Good preparation also involves anticipating and having backup plans for things that do not go well.

As a manager I often insisted on a thorough **SWOT** analysis:

Strengths: Why do you think you can achieve this goal? What are the required strengths to achieve it—things such as skills, time, funds, and management support? List them. How well do your strengths match up to these?

Weaknesses: What weaknesses could prevent you from achieving the goal? This could include dependencies on others. What will you need to do to compensate? List them and create compensating risk-mitigation plans.

Opportunities: What opportunities are there, such as current market trends, timing, large availability of staff, or a particular skill set? What must you do to take advantage of them?

Threats: What could threaten to derail the initiative? Possibilities might include holiday interruptions, sickness, resignations, loss of management support, change in market conditions, sudden increased workloads, and other crises. List all reasonably likely challenges and how you will respond.

Another approach that I sometimes combined with a SWOT Analysis was a **Critical Success Factor Analysis.** This asks, "What is critical to the success of this initiative?" "Which variables are *absolutely necessary* for this to succeed?" This will highlight potential weaknesses or issues with the plan. It helps focus your actions on those critical tasks.

Employ SWOT and Critical Success Factors anytime you have something important to do. Anticipating potential problems will keep you from being caught unprepared. However, no matter how well you plan, unforeseen issues will arise, so allow even more time for contingency plans on top of your SWOT analysis if you can. If everything goes as planned, you will finish ahead of schedule and beat expectations.

9. MAKE A FORMAL DECISION

Going through the previous steps will put you in a very good position to decide whether you can achieve the objective based on sound analysis and information.

Sometimes, you will simply be *ordered* to take on a task. In this case, the achievement process helps you put together a credible plan of how and when you can achieve the task. If a formal commitment to proceed was not made at the beginning, you have up until the completion of the risk analysis to recommend a more achievable objective.

However, there must be a point at which you officially decide and communicate the decision to move forward.

Three months later, when things get tough, it is easier to back out if you did not formally commit. If the initiative involves other people, they might start questioning whether this task was officially decided on and whether they really have to continue helping.

At this point, it makes sense to have your boss review the plans, plus your risk analysis, and approve a decision to move forward. Now the higher-ups are well-informed, their expectations are managed, and by approving it, they have made themselves accountable as well! When you need them, they will be more likely to help.

10. EXECUTE THE PLAN

Get Started: It is often said that the first step is the most difficult. *It is not.* Just do it! Keep the vision in mind and the energy and desire to get started will be there.

Follow the plan. Do not just view it as a handy guide for the occasional referral when needed.

Your plan is how you are going to live up to the commitment you made to get something important and worthwhile done by a certain date.

There needs to be a damn good reason to deviate from the plan *AND* a way to make up for any time lost before you allow it. Become highly disciplined. This is a key aspect that separates the completers from the dreamers.

Here is yet another one of those repeat-after-me statements:

Plan your work and work to your plan!

You live and die by it. The difference in achievement levels between those who discipline themselves to do this compared to those who don't will amaze you. It is often this discipline rather than any natural talent that defines the winners.

Manage expectations: In your eagerness to please, it is easy to sign up for impossible deadlines. Ask for some time (not a lot!) to go through the above process and come back with a deadline you know you can meet. If a deadline is imposed, work backward from that date and plan how to deliver ahead of it.

The process will help you identify any risks so that you can clearly communicate them up front, along with your actions to mitigate those risks. If the Achievement Methodology demonstrates that it's visibly impossible, alert your boss immediately. The sooner they know, the better. This gives you a logical, well-presented, and well-thought-out basis to discuss whether something can be done on time or not.

Without using the Achievement Methodology, you will come across as a whining foot-dragger when you try to warn of delays up front or a worthless failure if you say nothing but don't make the deadline later.

Break it down: The key to handling large initiatives is to break them down into smaller, more manageable tasks, all of which are deadline-driven. Do not hang your success on achieving one deadline right at the end. Multiple deadlines keep the intensity of your focus throughout the process. Too many people procrastinate, relying on a Herculean effort right at the end. Hit an obstacle with no time to resolve it and failure is inevitable. Achieving deadlines along the way will give both you and your manager confidence that progress is being made. You will gain that sense of *momentum* that management is always looking for.

Progress reports: A documented, comprehensive plan will let you know how far you have come at any time. Management wants regular updates. They do not want surprises at the very end when they have already assured their own superiors that things are going well. Managers will not be angry to learn you have encountered obstacles. They have all had personal experience with the well-known fundamental law that something will always go wrong. However, they do expect to be informed quickly of problems and what you are doing about them. If the problems are serious enough, management will need sufficient information and time to manage the expectations of *their* superiors, especially if they need to extend deadlines or delivery dates.

Note: Although managers expect problems, do not just go running back to your managers with a problem *every* time you encounter one. Use your judgment, and don't just dump the problem in their laps:

Go to management with the problem AND your suggested solution.

Report frequently. In the absence of progress reports, people form their own, often uninformed opinions of how well things are going. If their perspectives are negative, those uninformed opinions could call your initiative and your reputation into question. The workplace is full of sound bites, many of which are politically motivated by personal agendas. Remember the law of vacuums: they always get filled.

Do not leave an information vacuum, or someone else will fill it for you and you may not like the contents!

Even if you are working solo, documenting your progress tells *you* how you are doing. It can reassure you that you are on track, or help you recognize areas that may need rethinking, intensified effort, or assistance.

Document and review: If you follow the steps, you will have documented comprehensively from the beginning. This documentation is important for your achievement portfolio, particularly if you are accomplishing something significant on time, under budget, and with measurable impact. Have your manager sign off at each stage, including your initial objectives, the business case, the vision, the methodology applied, the plan, the risk analysis, and the final results. Your progress reports are also part of your documentation. Keep it all in a well-organized binder so that you can easily demonstrate how you hit the objectives. This is what people will most want to see when you come up for promotion or pursue a new job.

This documentation is the HARD EVIDENCE of your ability to achieve your top priority results.

After you have hit a significant milestone in the project, and especially at the very end, *hold a feedback session* to review what went well and what could have been done better so you can learn from successes and failures along the way. Document these sessions, too.

This will enable you to support others undertaking similar initiatives in the future, positioning you as a source of expertise and a potential manager.

ALWAYS THANK EVERYONE AND BE GENEROUS WITH PRAISE.

Very rarely will you achieve anything important without help from others.

WITHOUT FAIL, be sure to thank everyone involved.

Make sure you give credit where credit is due. Those who helped you will not do so again if you bask in the glory of a job well done based on *their* hard work. Send them a note highlighting the contributions they made. Look for something specific to compliment them on.

People appreciate the recognition, and it puts goodwill in their tanks.

In particular, those who helped you will want to know that their managers know how hard they worked and what they achieved. This is especially true if they do not report to the same person you do. Send a copy of your thank you note to both *their* managers and yours.

Do not wait until the end of the task to do this. Recognize and thank people immediately when they do something to help you, as you may need their help again later, especially on longer initiatives.

Your gratitude must be genuine, not fabricated. But there is a side benefit in that your appreciation will gain your colleagues' loyalty—and management will notice. It positions you for promotions into leadership roles.

QUICK STORY

I have recently had the privilege of working with James Bissett, President and CEO of Pathfinder Professional Solutions, Inc. His company partners with both fortune 500 companies as well as the Department of Defense on service contracts covering IT and engineering, growth management, and research and development.

James is a decorated combat veteran with multiple awards to include the Purple Heart, Bronze Star with V Device (for Valor), and the Meritorious Service Medal.

Upon completing his tours, James founded the Warriors Pathfinder Program, an organization dedicated to helping the men and women who served in the US Armed forces adapt and succeed in civilian life.

Based on his role managing and supervising combat operations James knows all too well the importance of getting the job done—and failure not being an option! As I pointed out in Chapter One, many people think this level of commitment only applies to the military because lives are clearly at stake. However, James will tell you based on direct experience with senior executives in the commercial world that the ability to get the job done is what is valued most.

*"If you cannot deliver the expected results,
you are of no value. It's as simple as that!"*

James explains that the military achieves consistent results by using processes, often referred to as "standard operating procedures" and that this type of thinking also applies to the business world.

> **"In the face of obstacles, it is the combination of using processes to guide you combined with resourcefulness and determination that gets results."**

Everything James does is driven by this philosophy, whether it is helping veterans, running his own organizations or supporting his clients.

SUMMARY

I have seen people trying to accomplish things with no clarity on what success looked like and no real plans. When expectations went unmet in the work environment, even high-potential individuals lost credibility; managers lost confidence in them, and negative cycles began. The next big initiative was passed to someone else. People even lost their jobs.

Note: Nothing will guarantee detailed and unpleasant feedback from your manager more quickly than if you are unable to clearly describe what you are doing or how and why you are spending company time, money, and resources in the process.

You may not be able to follow these key steps on *every* task. Use your judgment. In fact, just turning the steps into questions provides a good start and a way to structure your thinking. On anything important, ask yourself the following:

Is there a clear description of the goals and objectives? What are the required results and how are they measured?

Is there a good, logical case for *why* we should be doing this—and why now? How is success defined? What are the benefits and are they measurable too?

What are the consequences of not doing it?

How does this relate to or impact other top priority results?

Has a viable approach been identified? What processes can be used? What alternatives were considered?

Can we learn from someone who has done this previously?

How can we practice and rehearse the execution of any new skills that are needed?

What dependencies on other people are there?

Have we considered what could go wrong and built in contingency plans?

Has a clear decision been made to do this?

Do we have a plan with deadlines? Who is in charge of executing the plan?

Are we progressing in line with the plan? Are deadlines being met? Is there momentum?

To get into good habits, begin to view any assignment, no matter how small, as a mini-project and check whether the Achievement Methodology steps *are* or *should* be in place. Make it a part of how you operate. Developing these thought processes will be vital in how you approach anything that is important to you or the organization.

You will also notice that these are ideal questions to systematically understand what is going on around you so you can optimize your alignment.

Volunteer to help with (or lead) the next initiative that arises and apply this structure. The more you do so, the more you'll stretch the boundaries of your comfort zone, develop confidence, and display to management that you are the type that gets it done!

Those who regularly apply this structure are unimaginably more productive and successful than those who do not.

As I described in Chapter Two when discussing the four personality types, as people move up they develop Driver tendencies. This includes becoming very action oriented. This is no coincidence as without an ability to take decisive action you are not promotable.

This also means there is a good chance your interviewer will have Driver tendencies. Describing *HOW* you got such impressive, relevant and high-impact results using the Achievement Methodology is also one of the most powerful ways to *DIFFERENTIATE* yourself in an interview for a new job or promotion.

CHAPTER TEN

DEALING WITH PROBLEMS, BEING CREATIVE, AND MAKING SOUND DECISIONS

PART I

HOW TO BECOME A PROBLEM KILLER

Every major initiative you undertake will face obstacles.

It is one of those fundamental laws in life. In fact, some people believe jobs are *mainly* about solving problems. Most job descriptions, such as the advertisement in Chapter One, will specifically highlight your ability to solve problems as a selection requirement.

So do not fear problems.

Some people react as though the sky is falling every time there is one, which only adds stress to the situation. This type of reaction will instantly compromise your ability (and that of those around you) to think clearly and creatively.

As unresolved challenges grow, you can even develop health issues. Under enough pressure, many people also begin pointing fingers and blaming others, which leads to loss of trust and alienation.

This is not the behavior managers are looking for.

To manage your thoughts, call problems "opportunities" and develop a reputation for wanting the chance to take care of them.

Look at problems as situations in which you can learn, show leadership, and add tremendous value to your employer. It is incredibly satisfying and will do wonders for your upward mobility. In Chapter Twelve on attitudes, we will go over the importance of controlling your thoughts, emotions, and consequent behavior, as a way to help you.

First, I want to show you how the 10 steps from the Achievement Methodology will allow you to focus on *tangible actions* to move forward. You *have* to have these steps in place *first*.

A positive attitude will soon fade away if it is not backed by real capability.

USING THE ACHIEVEMENT METHODOLOGY TO SOLVE ANY PROBLEM

1. DEFINE THE OBJECTIVE

Problems usually prevent or interfere with a desired result, such as a top priority. Start with a clear description of the desired result in question. If you are using the Achievement Methodology, go back to the documentation and use the description from step one as your starting point for solving your problem.

However, most day-to-day issues do not always have such clarity. In this case, begin by identifying or defining the specific outcome the problem is preventing.

This immediately provides clarity and a focus on how to achieve the positive outcome instead of being overwhelmed by negative emotions. Finally, it will also act as the compass for any suggested solutions as a test to see whether they will achieve the desired result.

2. BUILD THE CASE

The outcome being threatened by the problem must have clear benefits, or there will not be any motivation to fix the problem. Again, if this is a problem in one of your big Achievement Methodology-driven initiatives, go back to step two in the documentation.

If it's a day-to-day issue, first clarify what outcome is being jeopardized, as per Step One, and then identify its benefits, ideally in measurable terms.

This step brings into focus the importance of the desired outcome, and therefore the potential seriousness of the problem.

3. DEFINE THE SHORTFALL (IMPACT)

By comparing the actual results while the problem is still unsolved against the *desired* results, and documenting where and how they fall short, you define the *impact.*

These first three steps are simply a very structured way to assess your problem on a scale ranging from a small impact on results with minor consequences to high impact on results with major consequences. This way of looking at problems allows you to either calm yourself and others down or bring urgency to the situation using objective and measurable terms. You will not always have the luxury of dealing with only one problem at a time. This approach also helps you take the emotion out of the situation and prioritize problems.

In most cases this will just be a series of quick questions in your head as you ask yourself:

> *"What is being impacted, by how much,*
> *and what are the consequences?"*

4. DEFINE THE CAUSES

Once you are clear on the effects, you can start identifying causes. Keep asking why to get to the root cause.

5. DEFINE ACTIONS THAT SOLVE THE PROBLEM AND ACHIEVE THE OBJECTIVE

There are different opinions on how far you should go to develop solutions. Some people advocate moving on as soon as you find one that works. They believe speed in solving a problem is more important than trying to find a better solution. Others believe *more* ideas will bring you to the *best* solution. I recommend a middle-of-the-road method. Come up with one or two solutions per cause then go to Step Six to evaluate them. This will reveal pros and cons, allowing you to come up with solutions based on your knowledge of what works and what does not. No sense in wasting time straining to produce lots of ideas that don't work. This is the step that usually involves the most creativity, which I cover in more detail below.

6. EVALUATE, SELECT, AND PRIORITIZE YOUR PROPOSED ACTIONS

How well does each different idea solve the problem? Look at the cost, effort, time scales, and payback of each. More ideas will come during this process, and often hybrid ideas emerge. Document the pros and cons of each solution.

Some solutions will have a much greater effect than others. This is why it is so important to be clear in Step One. It helps you avoid getting sucked into proposed actions that may satisfy one of the stakeholders but do not really affect the desired outcome for the majority of stakeholders.

7. CREATE AN EXECUTION PLAN

I have seen many seemingly great ideas fail when it came to the realities of trying to implement them. You cannot fully assess a solution until you have really thought through its execution plan. Everyone involved should have a firm understanding of what their responsibilities are and when they are due. Otherwise, it is just an academic exercise.

8. DO A RISK ANALYSIS

When you have selected the most effective action and created a plan to execute it, ask what could go wrong. What would prevent the problem being solved? Use the SWOT analysis and Critical Success Factors from Chapter Ten to guide your thinking. Depending on what the risk analysis turns up, either adjust the solution or the plans or build in some contingency.

9. MAKE A FORMAL DECISION

Once a clear, winning solution emerges with an agreed action plan, document the reasons it was selected. Documentation is vital. Get the boss to sign off on it, especially if you are dealing with an extensive problem on a top priority result with a high consequence of failure. You do not want to find yourself justifying your decisions with no documentation to support you if others question you later. This often happens, particularly when things do not go as planned. You may even start second-guessing yourself. A pressured boss may throw you under the bus, or a rival colleague might see an opportunity to score some points! Good documentation helps you to stay calm and to keep everyone objective.

10. EXECUTE

Use the same headings as in the Achievement Methodology.

Get started: Problems steal time. The quicker you get started, the better. In addition to the fundamental law that something always goes wrong, there is another:

The longer a problem remains unresolved, the more damage it does and the more effort it takes to fix.

Follow the plan: The above steps led you to create a plan to resolve a problem. Follow it!

If the problem was part of a larger initiative, your impact analysis in Step Three should include looking at the *entire* plan of the larger initiative to see which tasks may have been impacted by time loss. Look for ways to bring it back and get on schedule again. Remember, your reputation is at stake.

Be deadline-driven: Create several very short deadlines to get you back on track. This works well when a problem is preventing you from reaching a goal that impacts another deadline.

Report on progress: The bigger the problem's impact, the more frequent the updates need to be. This allows for faster adjustment of actions if the plan is not working and a quicker rebuilding of confidence if the plan is working.

Document: Comprehensive documentation will help you to learn and to teach others about the problem so that it can both be fixed and prevented. Put it in your achievement folder. It is great evidence of your problem-solving abilities!

Thank everyone: Make sure you thank everyone involved, or they may not be so quick to help you next time. *There will be a next time; you can count on it!*

Problems are everywhere. If you look at them as situations in which you can learn, shine, and build goodwill, you will come to realize you are surrounded by opportunity!

PROBLEM SUMMARY

1. Practice. Take a problem and put it through the process, documenting as you go. It will feel awkward at first but becomes second nature once you get the hang of it. You do not have to rigorously apply every step to every problem. Do, however, make a habit of applying this thought process to all kinds of problems, even if it's only a brief mental checklist.

2. Volunteer. Offer to help others with their problems. Helping others gives you great experience and recognition as a problem solver. It also puts goodwill in their tanks in case you need their help or references.

PART II

HOW TO BECOME CREATIVE

"There is a way to do it better—find it!"

Thomas Edison

Organizations exist in intensely competitive and ever-evolving environments. To thrive, they must constantly explore new ways to satisfy their customers. Your ability to find creative solutions can make you *highly* sought after.

CREATIVITY DOWNERS

Self-Perception

With the exception of artists and musicians, many people just do not see themselves as creative. They put way too much emphasis on having something exceptional, unique, and original appearing to them in a moment of inspiration—precisely when they need it! When people are under pressure and urgently need new ideas, this is often the exact moment they draw a blank. Consequently, they declare themselves uncreative and purely on this basis, they are correct.

Fear of Change

Many people are uncomfortable with change. They hang onto processes for decades. Those who have become comfortably set in their ways are unlikely to challenge their existing methods. Many will also actively discourage others from doing so too. They have the "If it's not broken, don't fix it" attitude.

> **"Creativity involves breaking out of established patterns
> in order to look at things in a different way."**
>
> **Edward De Bono**

Being creative requires a certain degree of courage to challenge the status quo, *and* to risk being wrong! Some company cultures encourage you to question and make suggestions; others do not. Some managers will give you the "I don't pay you to think, just do your job" attitude.

However, in a situation where a clear problem has emerged, people are more likely to accept that creativity is needed. Albert Einstein put it very well:

> **"We cannot solve our problems with the same thinking
> we used when we created them."**
>
> **Albert Einstein**

This means it can be very useful to the creative process to define something as a problem first.

You can then use the steps of the Achievement Methodology to not only come up with ideas to solve the problem, but also to implement them. An idea has no value until it is implemented with a measurable impact on results.

In this way, you are not relying on sudden, out-of-the-blue inspiration, but on a repeatable process of structured thinking.

FOUR IDEAS FOR THINKING OUTSIDE THE BOX

Even with the use of a structure, you will still hit walls. There will be times when you cannot come up with a solution. Read up on creativity. There are many suggestions for stimulating new ideas. Here are a few:

1. Problem shifting: Imagine a scenario where you have run out of ideas. Everything you come up with will not work for some reason.

Believe me, I have sat through countless meetings where for every idea we raised there was an individual with a reason to shoot it down. Go through what seemed like the most promising ideas and ask, "Can we fix the reasons we killed it?" In other words, shift your focus from the original problem to see if you can solve the issues created by the new solution. Use the same 10-step process.

Quite often you will find that the new problem is way lower in the consequences scale than the original one and that there are ways to get around it.

Make sure you look at people and processes as you look for root causes.

Many problems only exist because a particular person is involved, certain attitudes are present, or an old process is getting in the way.

Considering changing people, their attitudes, and their processes should be part of your creative thinking. You can't always solve everything within the existing circumstances.

2. Assumption testing: Make a list of every assumption associated with the required solution. Start as many sentences as you can with "It must..." To do this comprehensively, make these statements under a series of headings or questions. For example:

It must do ... what? It must meet the needs of ... whom? It must be in place by ... when? We must do this because ... why? It must be done by ... whom? It must be done for ... how much? And so on.

Then write as many sentences as you can that start with "It must not..." This defines your assumed limitations.

Then challenge each of these statements. See if any of them can be changed or eliminated to find a new way forward. Quite often, certain assumptions stem from one individual somewhere in the organization that no one has challenged.

3. Idea association: Creativity is sometimes described as taking unrelated items or ideas and coming up with something new. For example, when you are drawing a blank it can sometimes help to stimulate ideas by looking at sports or military analogies. Pick some moves from different sports or military maneuvers and ask what the equivalent in your scenario would be.

Alternatively, you can ask what "XYZ" character from a movie would do in this situation. What do different industries do? The issue when you are blank is getting started. Once you are on a roll it will trigger workable ideas.

4. Reverse thinking: List everything that could make the situation worse. Then, by considering doing the opposite, you may find a way to make something better. For instance, going back to our customer satisfaction examples, you could brainstorm everything that really annoys your customers. Get some customers involved to contribute. Many of these problems will already be on the company's radar with processes and policies in place to avoid them. However, if you do this long enough, you will find something new that you could do something about to improve your customer satisfaction even further.

CREATIVITY SUMMARY

Developing your creativity can open the door to breakthrough thinking that can bring huge value to the organization and credibility to your name. The "creative" label is specifically sought out by management. Hence you are very likely to face a "give me an example of your creativity" question during any interview. Claiming that you are creative without any evidence is not likely to impress anyone.

So look for opportunities to exercise the above creative approach. Use situation, objective, action and result (S.O.A.R) to describe your creative achievements.

The ability to clearly explain your creative process—with documented relevant and high-impact examples—will take you straight to the top of the short list for being hired and promoted!

PART III

HOW TO MAKE BETTER DECISIONS

HOW TO USE THE ACHIEVEMENT METHODOLOGY AS A DECISION-MAKING PROCESS

Decisions have consequences. Your future will be determined by the decisions you make from here on. They will define the pathways and opportunities that will be available to you.

Clearly decision-making is worth getting good at!

Many people think of decision-making as having an ability to choose the right action from different options *in the moment.* It is similar to the idea that creative inspiration comes to you in the moment you most need it. This only works for very few people.

To make important decisions wisely you need a process that enables you to get COMPLETE and CORRECT information about CAUSES and CONSEQUENCES in any given situation.

Understanding this process and becoming good at executing it, is what this section is about.

HOW WE MAKE DECISIONS

We make hundreds of decisions each day. Almost everything we think, say, or do involves a choice. We make most without much reflection. This is fine when the decisions are on low-impact issues with minor consequences, and when we have sufficient information and experience. But for some high-impact or high-consequence decisions, we need a process to ensure that all relevant factors are considered and that bias, strong emotions, and inaccurate or incomplete information do not lead us to make a mistake.

A poor, impulsive judgment or an ill-considered action can lead to the loss of a major client, your job, or even an entire business. Meanwhile, an inability to make any decisions will earn you just as unfavorable a reputation.

Beware, indecision is often disguised as patience!

The best decisions are reached through a disciplined process. The quality of thinking and activity at each step determine the quality of the end result. If the process is completed thoroughly, the final decision can become obvious. In other words:

Decision-making skills lie more in the process than in the final moment of choice.

The Achievement Methodology is designed perfectly for this!

Although there is only one major step labeled "make a decision," the fact is that you could not complete that step effectively if you did not properly complete all the steps leading up to it. In a high-impact situation, it would be dangerous to try.

For example, if you do not have a clearly defined objective (as per Step One) how can you evaluate any suggestions? Without clearly defining the difference between the present situation and the desired results, understanding the causes for the shortfall, evaluating and prioritizing actions to overcome its causes, testing them in an implementation plan, and doing a risk analysis, you *cannot* make a reliable decision.

Therefore, the Achievement Methodology is also a decision-making process.

Obviously, you will only use the entire set of steps for major decisions. Many other decisions can be made instinctively once you have a good understanding of your business, its customers, and all other stakeholders.

But you should have this method embedded in your mind so that you can apply it as needed, even if only at lightning speed in your head.

Framing the steps as questions, as we did in the previous chapter, is a great way to test a recommendation prior to making a decision:

Which of my (or my boss's) top priority results does this issue affect, and how? What benefits are at risk? Can I quantify them to objectively assess impact? Have I got down to the root causes? What solutions are there? What are the pros and cons of each? What are the practical and logistical considerations? What could go wrong? Who is involved and how will they execute the plan?

DECISION SUMMARY

This process can help protect you from situations where seemingly knowledgeable or powerful people try to use emotions or bullying tactics to get you to make a fast decision to support their agenda. Believe me, this will occur regularly! Also, note that those who emotionally push or bully you into a decision will also be the first to distance themselves from it when things take a turn for the worse. Going through the steps is the best way to filter out emotions, personal agendas, sales pressure, and politics so you can arrive at what is best for all stakeholders.

It also provides you with a logical, documented explanation for your reasons afterward.

Using the process is invaluable if a decision turns out to be wrong. It allows you to go through the steps to find out where the logic and information on causes and effects was flawed. This allows you to learn and correct the mistake more easily and quickly. Otherwise, you could easily make another mistake because you have no logical basis to choose a different course of action. When things go wrong and pressure mounts, it is very easy to make an emotionally based second mistake.

Most interviewers will have questions on your decision-making abilities. They specifically look for individuals who can consistently make timely and well-informed decisions—especially under pressure.

You can now explain during an interview how you make decisions using the Achievement Methodology as a process.

Without this ability, many jobs—and pretty much ALL promotions—will be out of reach.

Let's talk about getting promoted next.

CHAPTER ELEVEN

GETTING THE PROMOTION!

PART I

COMMIT TO A PLAN TO MOVE UP!

WHY?

It seems like a reasonable question. If you like your job, why stress yourself with trying to get a better one? Apart from better pay, higher status, and feelings of accomplishment, there are two key reasons.

1. Promotions look *GREAT* when you are applying for a job.

Employers look for people who have a track record of being promoted. They particularly like candidates who have moved up more than once in the same organization. The fact that other employers thought you were worthy of greater responsibilities, and that you lived up to their expectations to the point that you were promoted *again,* puts you at the top of their must-interview list.

2. Seeking promotions makes you more likely to succeed in a job.

In today's competitive world, unless you are doing your absolute best and are driven by a desire to be promoted, chances are you will underperform compared to those who ARE chasing the next job up.

Even if you start with the best intentions, it's likely that at some point you will slow down. Complacency will creep in, and your performance will deteriorate.

This can even put your survival at risk, especially at times when management has to cut costs during economic downturns. Furthermore, once you have been passed over a few times in favor of more motivated colleagues, other managers will take note. Your lack of upward mobility will be one more issue you will have to deal with should you ever need another job, particularly as you get older.

It pays to join with promotion in mind.

That stated, it is quite ironic that employers often say things like "Keep your head down, stay out of trouble, and just do your job well. The promotions will come when you have served your time."

Most people go along with this because they believe that promotions are tenure or reward-driven. They assume that after X number of years they will automatically move up because that's how the system works and how the organization will reward them for past efforts.

Unfortunately, this is *not* the case.

For employers to promote you, they have to believe that you will bring MORE VALUE in the higher role than you do in your present role.

It is that simple.

QUICK STORY

In one of my business units, we employed an exceptional consultant whom I shall refer to as George. He was very knowledgeable in both banking and how to get the best results from our software. He had been with us since the beginning, and all our customers knew and loved him. Many of our staff looked up to him and relied heavily on his expertise. George had a great personality and was the secret weapon of our sales staff to help convince prospects that our software would meet their needs.

When his boss, the head of customer services in that business unit, moved to another location, George *assumed* he would be promoted to that position.

When it did not happen, George appeared in my office, furious and threatening to resign. He was enraged that the business unit president had given the position to someone else without even discussing it with him.

I immediately called the head of the business unit and asked him to join us. He had no idea George was interested. George had never raised the subject with him before. If he had, he would have advised George that there was a whole range of new skills he needed to develop to be a viable candidate. Head of customer services included responsibility for custom software development, 24/7 customer help desk support, making sure multi-million dollar projects were completed on time and within budget and that customers were invoiced and chased to make sure that they also paid on time. George knew our software inside out but had no experience in any of these areas.

Had George been promoted into that position, we would have lost a super consultant and gained a severely under-experienced head of operations with potentially very negative consequences.

We advised George that it was too big a move up to make in one jump. But, now that we knew this was his career goal, we would help him develop targeted skills and experience by putting him in a series of training courses and exposing him to different responsibilities so that he would be the perfect candidate in two years' time.

Moral of the story?

The fact that you perform well in your current job, even if you have done so for years, does not necessarily mean you are a good match for a higher-level position.

Those who expect an automatic promotion after a certain time period, or who work hard and think they *deserve* a promotion as a reward, will *very likely* experience disappointment.

People who think this way often resent seeing colleagues get promotions, especially if they end up reporting to them. As a result, negative attitudes and relationship issues develop, prompting good people to look for jobs elsewhere rather than strategizing to get more responsibility. They can easily end up in the dreaded downward spiral. Had George resigned it is not likely a competitor would have given him a Head of Customer

Services position for the exact same reasons we did not. He would probably have been offered the equivalent of his current position with us. Only he would have had to rebuild all his knowledge of a new software system, work hard to prove his abilities, *and* gain the trust of colleagues and customers. It would most likely be a one or two year step back.

The best way to make sure this does not happen to you is to PROACTIVELY pursue specific promotion opportunities.

The key is to have a target promotion in mind and go after it as though you are applying for a new job—just as you did when you were looking for the job you have now.

It is the beginning of a new Job Cycle. Treat it as such.

Everything we covered when we were looking for a job in the larger market—making connections, doing the key requirements research, building targeted skills, growing your achievement folder, collecting appropriate references, and polishing your interviewing skills—*all* apply in your efforts to get a promotion. The managers making the selection will have the exact same three criteria in their minds: *Can you do the job, will you do the job*, and *will you fit in* at the *HIGHER* level? They will have top priority results, obstacles to success, and consequences of failure that they worry about—*ones that you need to know about well in advance.*

FIRST SUCCEED IN YOUR CURRENT ROLE

Although I have made it clear that it is not enough just to do your job well, it *is a prerequisite* for promotion. No one wants to promote a poor performer.

This means you need to have aligned, connected with your manager and colleagues, and delivered the top priority results with an excellent customer experience.

You should have proof of those results in your achievement folder, and you need your manager to be your mentor and reference. To do all this takes time. Therefore, you need to align from *day one* on the job as no one will entertain any thoughts about promoting you until you are clearly performing beyond their expectations.

Don't wait to get into gear in your current job until you actually see a promotion opportunity you like. By then it will be way too late!

THE IMPORTANCE OF INTERNAL CONNECTIONS

In Chapter Three, we discussed making connections and developing relationships as the best way to find your job. It is very important to *keep* doing this, even after you have landed one.

Set targets to meet people *inside* the organization where you work. They can help you understand the business better and get difficult tasks done. They will be invaluable in alerting you to promotion opportunities and providing you with inside knowledge in exactly the same way your connections were critical while you were looking for a job in the larger market. (See Chapter Three.)

THREE PROMOTION STRATEGIES

You should have the following three strategies in play at all times in regards to making and maintaining connections in your pursuit of getting promoted:

STRATEGY ONE

REPLACING YOUR BOSS

Your boss is your *BEST* connection. If you are following the alignment principles, you will have *earned* the opportunity to ask your boss to become your mentor. This ensures you'll get guidance on what you need in terms of skills and experience to position yourself as your boss' replacement when *they* get promoted.

It gives you the opportunity to prepare yourself to prove *you* can do the boss' job. It also shows that you *want* to do the job. If you have maximized your boss' customer experience in dealing and interacting with you, they already know you will fit! This way you have all three bases covered. As long as you do this better than anyone else in the department, you will be the prime candidate to replace your boss when they are promoted.

By aligning well with your bosses, you will know and understand the roles *they* wish to be promoted into and what top priority results are necessary for that to happen. You can actively help your boss achieve their ambitions, knowing that it will open a promotion opportunity for you, too. This will also give you additional knowledge and experience to help you succeed in your boss' footsteps.

Note: Whatever you do, **NEVER** undermine your boss to **anyone,** such as their boss, in an effort to get that job. Management sticks together. Your boss will likely be told and will then regard you as disloyal and untrustworthy. They will take the first opportunity to get you off the team. No other manager will want you after that either. This story generally ends with you looking for another job and a bad reference in your wake.

Do, however, make sure you gain positive exposure to your boss' direct supervisor. If your boss is promoted, chances are that you will need to be positioned as suitable to take over. This is a lot easier if you have already made a positive impression at that level. It is particularly important if your boss moves to a different department, as you would then report directly to their former supervisor if you got promoted. In this case, it is your boss' boss who will make the decision.

Always make sure you are also the natural choice for promotion in the eyes of your boss' boss.

STRATEGY TWO

LOOK FOR PROMOTION OUTSIDE YOUR DEPARTMENT

As I stated above, you must build a wide network of connections throughout your organization. However, just as when you were networking before, *NEVER* ask to meet people for job or promotion requests. This will get back to your manager with very bad consequences!

Position your meetings as a way to understand the business. Start with people in areas that either supply or receive work from your department. It is often easier to justify meetings with adjacent departments in the supply chain. You can truthfully position such meetings to genuinely help you understand your job. It is also easier to put goodwill in their tanks by offering to do things that make their lives easier and get you on their radar for future opportunities.

Expand your contacts from there. Eat lunch with people in the accounting department. First, they can further explain how things are measured, including your department and even your job. Vital information! They can help you understand other areas of the organization such as how they are measured, how they are performing, and which departments are most likely to be expanding or cutting back. They can give you insight on what obstacles to success they are struggling with and what the consequences are in monetary terms. This will allow you to prepare yourself to engage the managers of these departments on their biggest worries. See where we're going with this?

You also might focus on internal auditors. They review the entire organization and can be very knowledgeable about who does what and where. Historically, this department is viewed negatively and even feared. Many believe it is some form of corporate internal affairs that writes nasty reports about specific employees or departments. In fact, they regularly do.

This is all the more reason to connect and learn from them. Much of their work is confidential so do not try to pry into sensitive information, or they will shut the connection down. *Focus on learning about the good and bad things they look for.* Internal auditors are very process-oriented; they know how things are supposed to be done *and* who does them well. They can introduce you to these people. At some point, they will audit your department. Having a relationship that facilitates your understanding of what they look for will be very helpful in ensuring a good review. *Bad reviews from auditors do not help your promotion prospects!*

Of course, target senior people as well, such as managers of departments you might be interested in joining. Connect with people who report to such managers to get a sense of what their supervisors look for and what they are like to work for.

Your objective here is to gain the information you need in order to unearth jobs of interest, and then develop and position yourself as the best possible candidate if the position opens. As I advised when looking for a job in general, try to find problems or issues that people are struggling with and are worrying about.

At the beginning of this section, I stated that employers will promote you if they can clearly see that you can provide greater value in a higher role.

If you can position yourself as having the skills to solve obstacles to success in a higher position that have a greater positive impact or consequence of failure than those of your current role, then you have a good chance of convincing someone you can provide more value in that higher-level job.

STRATEGY THREE

LOOK FOR PROMOTION OUTSIDE YOUR ORGANIZATION

As I have stated before, future employers *will* look at how many organizations you worked for, how long you stayed at each, and whether you were promoted within the same company. They like people who stay long enough to get promoted, preferably multiple times.

However, you cannot bet your career on the boss moving up, or on finding promotion opportunities elsewhere in the organization. You need to have a backup strategy if nothing materializes or if you are passed over. Getting an internal promotion is great, but getting a promotion by moving to another organization is better than staying in one position for too long.

Food for thought: A solid job offer for a higher position at another company can sometimes prompt your existing organization to make a similar offer. If you are that good, and they do not want to lose you, they may reorganize to find a way to give you more responsibility. Continue making at least one new contact per week outside your organization. (It is also vital that you do this just in case your organization has layoffs.)

However, *NEVER* play this card unless you would be genuinely happy to accept the external job offer. Your current boss may simply accept your resignation.

GO FOR THE PROMOTION INSTEAD OF LEAVING WHEN YOU ARE UNHAPPY IN A JOB

This sounds very counter intuitive, doesn't it. However, remember that employers filter out people who constantly switch jobs because they want to get away from problems.

I recommend that whatever job you are in, no matter how low-status or unpleasant, AIM TO GET A PROMOTION before deciding to leave.

Doing so will totally change your attitude, your success, and your enjoyment in the job. It will arm you with new skills, achievements, and references. Winning that promotion will make your profile much more desirable for a better position. At best, walking away will allow you to find another job at the same level, but is in fact often the beginning of that dreaded downward spiral. The same problems will be waiting for you in the next role. Better to learn to deal with them and earn a promotion in the process.

This is particularly relevant to students and recent graduates in non-career jobs. These jobs are often viewed as just temporary ways to get funding while studying. Most are menial and not particularly rewarding. Rather than drifting through many of these, try to find a way to solve a problem, take an initiative, and get a promotion and a reference. This will provide valuable examples to support your answers when interviewing for a career job. I recently saw a resume from a finance graduate who had a headline that read "I have been promoted in every job I have had." It got my attention and made me read it.

Don't move out, move up!

In summary, always keep all three strategies active. It is the only way to line up a promotion of choice. You never know. It may also result in several possibilities arising simultaneously, which will be very important when it comes to negotiation.

WIN THE SELECTION PROCESS

RESUMES AND ACHIEVEMENT FOLDERS

Let's say your efforts to build a comprehensive network both within and outside your organization have paid off. You have found positions you would like to target as promotion opportunities. By talking to people currently in those positions, you have learned what they do, their challenges, and the necessary skills and ideal experience a candidate needs to qualify. If you talk to enough people *around* those individuals, you will also learn who is most likely to move up in the near future, leaving an opening for you to target.

By talking to these contacts, you can build the model resume for the promotion you want. The next step is to actively build your actual resume to match the necessary experience and skills in the model resume by volunteering for extra assignments and training. (This is what we called *targeted skills development* in Chapter Four.) Then start filling your achievement folder to back up your resume. When a position comes up, you will be tailor-made for it!

Note: Do not make the mistake of thinking that because you have a job that you do not need a resume. This is a very common mistake. As described above;

A resume is also a tool to help you compare your present skills profile with the one you need to get the job you want.

It helps you identify and plan to build such skills.

Note: A common example of a skill often required by a first-time manager is budgeting. Once you are in charge of a department, you need to know how much money you have to generate per month, or how much is allocated to you and how much you can spend to achieve your objectives. Simple Excel-based budgeting skills are something you can easily learn ahead of time and can bring up during promotion discussions. Senior managers love people who know their numbers and are not likely to promote those who don't.

Additionally, although a promotion is an internal move, many organizations will run a full search, *including external* candidates. This will bring in competitors who will have a closely matching, well-tailored resume! Do not let the external candidate outshine you!

You should also be aware that when you are promoted some people within your organization may worry about employees who were passed over, claiming that they worked harder and were more deserving of the job than you. To avoid legal issues, management will want to be able to demonstrate why you were selected. Your resume and achievement folder will be part of that process.

Always keep developing your resume and achievement folder with specific promotions in mind.

INTERVIEW SKILLS

Keep your interview skills sharp. Continuing to meet people and building your connections will help. However, prior to any meeting for a promotion, revisit Chapter Five on interviewing. Think through the likely questions you'll get and prepare your answers with supporting examples. Work out how you will cross their four important thresholds.

Make sure you have *your* questions for *them* prepared. Some people think that a meeting to talk about an internal promotion is just an informal discussion. They treat it as a chat with people they already know. Consequently, they do not bring their "A" game and don't compete well with external candidates who do.

Don't make this mistake.

As soon as you sense you are close to securing a meeting to discuss a promotion, go into full preparation mode as if an outside company had formally invited you for an interview.

REFERENCES

If you are primarily focused on replacing your boss, make sure this person will act as a great reference as they move up. If you have aligned and performed well, then this is likely to happen. However, in the process, you can become indispensable to your boss. If you then apply for a higher position *outside* of your department, they may decide *not* to give you a reference. It's not fair, but it does happen.

In fact, a supervisor may actively try to block you because your move is detrimental to achieving their own top priority results. This can get nasty, so you *MUST* have other references available. Ideally, you want to develop another reference within your department to counteract your boss' lack of support. You also want a reference within the department you are targeting. This is where filling goodwill tanks wherever you can pays off. Going above and beyond the call of duty for external customers can generate very compelling references, too.

In any case, it is never a good idea to rely 100% on your boss as a reference. Any number of things could go wrong. They could leave suddenly or even be fired!

Build a wide range of references from the moment you start your job.

NEGOTIATE!

Many companies will emphasize the prestige of the internal promotion while minimizing the salary raise that should come with it.

People get caught up in the excitement of the recognition and feel-good vibe of a promotion. As a result, they completely forget to negotiate. Revisit Chapter Six and refresh yourself on how and when to maximize your negotiation power. Do your homework and know the going market rate for the position. Only negotiate *after* they have made you the offer.

Do not forget to look at all the non-salary components of the compensation package, especially further training and equity as you become more senior in the organization.

PART II

HOW TO BECOME MANAGEMENT AND LEADERSHIP MATERIAL

WHAT DOES MANAGING AND LEADING MEAN?

When you apply for a promotion, there is a good chance the new position will involve being a manager and a leader of other people. So, in addition to the three main criteria of "can you," "will you," and "will you fit in," there is now the question of "can you manage and lead?"

There is a big difference between being able and willing to complete tasks yourself and being able to oversee staff and motivate them to do the tasks instead.

Therefore;

In order to be a good choice for a promotion, you may also need to provide clear evidence that you can lead and manage.

Let's begin by describing the difference between managing and leading, particularly as this is a common question during interviews for jobs that involve overseeing other employees.

There are literally hundreds of books on these topics. All offer something of value, and I encourage you to read them. Many books will debate whether leaders are born or can be made. Some will emphasize the importance of certain instinctive qualities (such as charisma) and others propose that leaders simply evolve to fill the needs of circumstances.

I have met leaders who came from privileged families, oozed charisma in public, and gave the impression they were born to lead—yet behind the scenes they were as inconsistent as a schizophrenic tyrant. On the flip

seen humble individuals rise through the ranks from all kinds
.grounds, nationalities, and functions to develop into highly com-
.t managers and leaders. My personal belief is that:

People are not born leaders or managers. They make themselves into both!

Therefore, rather than focusing on what leaders and managers are
and where they come from, let's focus on what they **do**. This can be
explained and *learned*.

A key component of **leadership** is having a clear vision of ***where*** you
want to go. Leaders have to have credibility based on deep knowledge,
plus inspirational, motivational, and persuasive skills to convince people
to follow them. For them to be considered good leaders, history needs to
show they led their people to the ***right*** places and do the ***right*** things.

A key component of **management** is having detailed knowledge of ***how***
to get there and ***how*** to do the right things. Good managers have the
inspirational, motivational, and persuasive skills to convince people to
perform their tasks in the ***right way***. They give clear direction and are
good at measuring and checking to ensure tasks are completed on time
with quality and efficiency.

To make this clearer I want to focus on two areas:

1. The actionable differences between leading versus managing.

2. Knowing when to lead versus manage.

I have found it helpful to look at what leaders and managers do in the
context of the Achievement Methodology.

Leaders are good at defining the desired future and building an inspirational vision and a compelling case for that future. They can honestly
assess and face up to existing reality, articulate current or potential future
shortfalls, and suggest strategic ways forward.

Leaders are therefore good at steps 1-4 of the Achievement Methodology.

Managers are good at assessing the practical pros and cons of different solutions. They can define detailed tactical action plans to implement these solutions and execute plans effectively.

Managers are good at steps 5-10.

Leaders and managers are often portrayed as separate people in separate functions. However:

In reality, good leaders also have to be good at managing, and good managers also have to be good at leading.

Thinking about leading and managing in terms of an Achievement Methodology gives you a structure to understand the key activities involved in each. The Achievement Methodology also gives you a structure that helps you balance *when* to apply leadership versus management skills.

However, you won't get through all the steps in the Achievement Methodology and complete any major initiative unless YOU CAN DO BOTH.

Motivating and inspiring are often associated with leadership but, in fact, any situation where you're responsible for the actions of others requires an ability to influence and change how people think and behave to achieve a goal. Leaders pay more attention to the longer term bigger goals while managers pay more attention to the shorter term tasks that are essential along the way to achieving the bigger goals. So both leaders and managers must have the soft skills to be able to motivate and inspire their teams, plus the hard skills to measure progress and make the tough decisions to deliver expected results on time. In the next chapter on attitudes, I specifically cover how to help others overcome inertia, and how to inspire enthusiasm, action, and determination.

BALANCED LEADERSHIP AND MANAGEMENT

With the amount of material being written on leadership and management it is easy to become too focused on any one part. For example, I see endless articles on how to keep your staff motivated but not many articles on getting a major initiative completed. This is why I like to use the Achievement Methodology as a backdrop to this discussion.

At the end of the day, it is about getting things done.

It is about achieving objectives both at the level of each individual reporting to you and all their objectives together as a team to meet your goals as the leader/manager.

In the opening chapters of this book I encouraged you as an individual to;

- Make sure you had the right interpersonal skills and attitudes to *FIT* into the team and culture so that you work effectively with everyone else.
- Make sure you had the specific job skills so that you *CAN* achieve your tasks and objectives.
- Make sure you understand your objectives and the consequences of both success and failure to your boss, colleagues and yourself to ensure you have the motivation and drive to *WANT* to do the job.

Your job as a leader/manager is to *make sure* each individual aligns this way and performs as part of a team to get their own tasks and *YOUR* entire objectives completed.

This means the leader/manager must clearly communicate the objectives and consequences. However, those who only focus on getting the job done, especially if they do so primarily by emphasizing negative consequences, can easily burn out individuals or even the whole team. Those who spend too much time motivating and inspiring at the individual level can create a group of self-centered prima donnas who will only make an effort if it moves their personal goals forward and who won't work as a team. Too much time spent emphasizing the team benefits level can leave individuals wondering how their own personal goals will be met.

Leading and managing is, therefore, a careful balance of paying attention to all three areas of fit, capabilities, and motivation at both the individual level and the team level around achieving specific objectives. *It's about getting everyone to align and shine!*

WHICH COMES FIRST, THE MANAGEMENT AND LEADERSHIP TITLES OR THE EXPERIENCE?

I am often asked,

> *"How do I demonstrate leadership and management capabilities before I get on that first management rung?"*

Here is an important message;

You start by visibly leading and managing yourself.

Show that you apply the achievement methodology to your own development. Demonstrate that you have a clear vision of where you are going, that you have identified your skill gaps and have the discipline to bridge them. Demonstrate that you have the ability to motivate yourself to overcome obstacles to reach your personal and job-related goals. Never give the impression that you do not know where you are going, make poor decisions, or that you are drifting and a victim of circumstances.

If you are not able to demonstrate that you can consistently lead and manage yourself, including during challenging times—how can you possibly lead others?

When you have clearly demonstrated *self*-leadership, management, discipline, organization, and motivation, then talk to your manager and look for opportunities to apply the Achievement Methodology to significant tasks involving other people. Document the process all the way through the steps and you will, by definition, fill your achievement folder with examples of where you have both led and managed. In an interview, this approach will allow you to articulate what leaders and managers do *and* provide examples of where you did so, without necessarily having "manager" in your title.

Another opportunity comes from mentoring. This is worth looking at in more detail.

SEVEN TIPS TO BECOME A BETTER MENTOR

Prior to any official management experience, another way to align with what employers look for when choosing first-time managers is to mentor others. As your mentoring relationship matures with your own boss and you have proven yourself as someone who delivers, ask whether your boss can start mentoring you specifically on leadership and management. Then ask whether you can put what they have taught you into practice by mentoring the next new recruit.

Mentoring means taking on responsibility to provide ongoing guidance, help, and support for another individual. Please note the use of "taking on responsibility" and "ongoing." Anyone can dish out a bit of advice here and there; that's not mentoring.

A mentor "adopts" an individual, takes the trouble to listen to and understand their needs and concerns, and works with the mentee to help them align with the organization. This is a significant responsibility. Your mentee may not officially be reporting to you, but the experience of mentoring others can take you a visible step in the right direction. It's also very rewarding.

Here are some important tips to improve your mentoring.

1. Be selective about whom you mentor. You won't have the time to mentor too many people. Be clear that they must come prepared with objectives and have the discipline to carry out agreed actions. A mentee needs to understand your time is extremely valuable and not to be wasted.

2. Make sure that the objectives are clear; ***to make sure they fit in, can do the job and want to do the job.*** Mentoring is about helping another person through the alignment steps. Revisit these and deliberately create conversations around each step. Without alignment as a backdrop most mentees will focus the conversation on short term issues and problems. These have validity and are worth helping them solve but there needs to be a focus on long term self-improvement too, such as networking, goal setting and targeted skills development.

3. Create a safe environment that encourages an open, non-defensive dialogue. Build trust. Never share the contents of these discussions with anyone unless the circumstances are serious (issues like integrity breaches, substance abuse, or other hazards). Likewise, it is easy to let your own guard down and confide something you should not. *Never* share your opinions on anything that could make you vulnerable if repeated to others.

4. Your key activities are questioning, listening, guiding, encouraging, inspiring, energizing and supporting. Do not spoon-feed and create a dependency.

Above all, you must build self-sufficiency.

Note that I did not list "giving advice" in the above sentence. This sounds so counterintuitive to many people! Sure, there will be times you simply give advice. However, one of the best ways to build self-sufficiency is to refrain from giving advice as your first immediate response. Start by asking good questions. Use open questions such as "why?", "what causes this?" and "what would be the impact of...?" - to get to the root of any discussion. Then coach your mentee to ask good questions themselves. Ask your mentee to come up with multiple answers—themselves. Then ask them to select the best option and state their case for why.

This can be easier said than done because we all want to provide value by solving and fixing problems as fast as possible, especially when we are under pressure—which is all the time! This requires a bit of patience, but it's the only way to encourage the ability in other people to think things through for themselves. The danger for you if you fail to learn to do this, is that you will risk becoming a bottleneck to your team once you become a manager. It will limit the number of people you can mentor and ultimately manage as they all wait for instructions from you. Your day will suffer from endless interruptions from people wanting advice.

Note: Make sure you are clearly demonstrating an ability to think for yourself in your mentee relationship with your boss!

5. From time to time, celebrate achievements. Spring for a meal, give an award. Communicate that the mentee's efforts are worthwhile. *Expose their achievements to your boss.* It is hugely beneficial for your mentee, who will always remember what you did for them. It also shows the boss you are grooming a fellow employee, are successful at it, and positively impacting the business. All of which helps to position you as a potential leader and manager.

When you, your boss, and the mentee can clearly see a benefit from your coaching (a new skill with improved results, for example) make sure you document it so that your mentee can put it in their achievement folder. Put a copy in yours too.

6. Be careful that your boss doesn't perceive your successful mentoring as undermining them.

The objective of your mentoring should always be to help people improve themselves in order to better accomplish their tasks for the department, your manager, and the organization.

Do not allow mentoring sessions to become complaining or venting opportunities, and **NEVER** participate in any behind-the-back criticism of your boss or any other part of the organization. Lead by example and discourage *any form* of disloyalty.

For your boss to be comfortable with you as a mentor, they must have complete trust in your loyalty.

7. Mentor students. When you receive calls from students looking to build their network *DON'T* just automatically turn them down. Remember how important this was to you when you were looking for a job! In fact proactively make yourself available. Contact your local colleges and reach out to the most relevant faculties. Ask to be a speaker.

Mentoring students can be a great way to line up potential candidates for your team as you move up the ranks.

When you mentor someone through a targeted skills development process while they are still at college, you gain a good insight into their likely fit, ability, and motivation. You are much more likely to land an effective, happy and loyal team member in the subsequent recruitment process than selecting a complete stranger after only meeting them for a few hours in an interview.

Mentoring can give your employer a healthy glimpse of your leadership and management potential. If your mentees turn out to be effective, worthwhile employees who demonstrate clear loyalty toward you and the organization, it becomes an easy decision to promote you. Make sure your manager mentors you in the process of mentoring others. This makes them fully aware of your efforts, particularly if you give them credit for your new leadership and management capabilities!

Mentoring helps demonstrate that you *can* lead and manage and that you *want to*. Now you have to demonstrate you *will fit in* at a higher level. This is where your personal brand comes in.

WHY YOU SHOULD CREATE A NEW PERSONAL BRAND

Once you are clearly performing well in your current job, the better you do it, the more your reputation can become associated with that position. Your name can become synonymous with the job. "Oh James, yes he is that really good sales support guy!" Your success can be a trap.

This does not mean you stop striving to do your job better every day.

It means you have to take additional, very deliberate steps to ensure your image within the organization does not become trapped in your current role.

Research what the right image should be for the promotion you want and start building it in advance. This is often also referred to as building your personal brand.

Your targeted skills development actions will ensure you can provide more value in the higher role than your current role. This will already start to shift your image in the right direction. However, you also need to make sure you pass the "will you fit in at a higher level" question. This is basic aligning exactly as you did to get your current job.

This means you need to stand out in terms of how you appear, behave and communicate at all times.

"Every time you speak you are auditioning for leadership."

James Humes

A good strategy to do this is to;

Appear to "be like" the people in the jobs you want rather than blending in with your peers.

Some people find this difficult as it can isolate you initially as you try to move from one peer group and join another. As an example, becoming a mentor can help you be perceived as already taking a first step towards the higher peer group. Revisit Chapter Two to refresh your interpersonal skills to connect and build new relationships. Carefully observe the peer group you wish to join. See how they dress, what they do, where they go, what they worry about and talk about and what words they use. As I said above, connect, connect, connect! The more you connect to people at the same level as the promotion you want, the easier it will be to become part of their peer group.

Your personal brand should do the following;

Promise greater value in the higher level position than your current role AND greater value than your competitors for the promotion.

For your brand to achieve this, it must be *visible, differentiated from your competitors* and *consistent*.

If it is not visible and nobody knows that you want the job, are learning new skills, volunteering for relevant extra work, and developing the right attitudes, then by definition you have no new brand. Find subtle ways to highlight what you are doing such as asking for reviews and advice. Thank anyone involved in helping you get new skills and experience, then copy both your and their boss. Talk about your relevant experiences when you are connecting and building relationships at a higher level.

To differentiate yourself, pick something that re-enforces a *specific key required strength* in the next job up and builds a reputation for having it to a greater degree than your peers. Use the above ways to bring it to the attention of management at the next level up. Also, pay careful attention to how your colleagues competing for the same promotion are trying to differentiate themselves. Get advice and feedback on which differentiators are most valued.

Finally, if you are not consistent and you only live up to your desired brand some of the time it will seem contrived, or not authentic and therefore not persuasive.

You have to commit to your brand 24 X 7 in everything you do and say.

You will know that you have successfully branded yourself when everyone, *especially* the decision makers in the selection process for the next job up, automatically associate you with the competencies and personality strengths they are looking for in the promotion you want. There is a key benefit from this.

The stronger your brand becomes, the less dependent you will be on your performance during the interview for the promotion.

A strong brand can help you cross the selection thresholds before an interview. In fact, if your personal brand is really well aligned you may even get the promotion without an interview. However, you should still prepare for the selection process, especially the interview as though your life depends on it!

Note: A personal brand contains both static and variable components. Once you understand the corporate mission, values and culture, pick attributes such as ethical, straight talking, loyal, and ownership attitudes that are aligned. These should not change much. However, each time you target a new role you may add or swap out different attributes that are more aligned to the specific role you are after.

You optimize your brand for the job you have, and after a period of success, you start optimizing it for the job you want.

STAY ALIGNED AS YOU RISE AS A LEADER

REMEMBER TO FOLLOW

Unless you are a sole business owner, chances are you will spend the majority of your career moving up as a manager and leader but *still* reporting to someone else. Even as the president of a company you serve your team and usually a board of directors.

Many first-time managers are a little overwhelmed by the day-to-day management side of their responsibilities. In fact, some find themselves in a prolonged state of what feels like crisis management. As a result, they have less time to make sure they stay aligned with *their* managers and can lose touch with their expectations.

This can evolve into a tendency to focus on what is best for them and their team rather than what is best for the objectives of their managers and the overall company. A manager can be particularly prone to this behavior when their boss works in a different location, such as a head office.

Managers who have strong leadership skills but who are out of alignment with their bosses can create significant problems. Their entire department can become very difficult to work with for the rest of the organization.

Such managers often have to be realigned or removed quite suddenly, either of which causes stress and disruption for everyone else. Neither is good for the career of the manager in question.

It is worth revisiting your own attitudes from time to time. Think about the ideology behind "I serve!" as described in the next chapter. Go over your alignment steps.

In the context of being a manager and a leader within an organization, being a good follower is just as important. Otherwise, your manager will ask; "WHERE are you leading your team?"

This becomes increasingly important the more senior you are because you have greater influence on a larger part of the organization.

Always stay aligned!

SUMMARY

Excelling in your current job is essential before any employer will consider you for promotion. However getting promoted will *not happen automatically* as a result of doing your job well. In fact the better you do it the more you can get stuck.

Getting promoted requires the execution of proactive strategies. You have to target specific opportunities and apply all the skills in the job cycle.

To trigger a strong "This is who we want!" reaction at the next level up, you will need to understand the top priorities and consequences of failure in the promotions you want.

You will need a targeted skills development plan to learn any new required skills including how to both lead and manage. Your efforts and progress in executing the plan must be highly visible to those who will decide on whether to promote you. This is because they must have *clear evidence* that you can provide *more value* to them and the organization in the *higher position* than the one you are in now.

Developing a well aligned personal brand that draws attention to your targeted skills will help you become more visible and help you stand out from your internal competitors in your drive to move up.

Now let's talk about the top attitudes you will need.

CHAPTER TWELVE

TOP TEN ATTITUDES FOR SUCCESS

"Nothing can stop a man with the right mental attitude
from achieving his goal."

Thomas Jefferson

Your attitudes are the foundation of your life. *They affect everything you do!*

Yet most people are not very self-aware in terms of their predominant attitudes, how those attitudes affect their behavior *or* how they affect the behavior of others they come in contact with.

This section will help you understand, develop, and demonstrate the attitudes you need to perform effectively in the workplace—the ones employers specifically look for.

Many organizations now believe employees' attitudes are just as important as their skills.

All three criteria we've outlined (whether you will *fit in*, whether you *can do* the job and whether you *will do* the job) are heavily influenced by your attitudes.

Interviewers will routinely ask candidates to give examples of their attitudes to the following;

- Being part of a team
- Helping others
- Being loyal
- Motivating yourself and others
- Committing to challenging goals
- Working hard
- Taking orders
- Accepting criticism without getting defensive or sulking
- Enduring difficult circumstances
- Persisting on difficult challenges
- Bouncing back from failure
- Coping with change
- Learning new skills

There are many, and since these attitudes are commonly looked for, it is worth preparing relevant examples of your behavior that demonstrates them. (Remember to use S.O.A.R.)

However, there are some primary, "foundation attitudes" that need to be in place for you to be able to consistently succeed throughout your career and upon which many of the above attitudes are based.

Furthermore, a good interviewer will look beneath the standard attitudes above that most candidates have prepared for. They want to see if these "foundation attitudes" are genuinely there.

Let's start with what attitudes are and how they are formed.

PART I

THE BASICS

WHAT IS AN ATTITUDE?

Attitude is defined by both Google and the Oxford Dictionary as:

> **"A settled way of thinking or feeling about someone or something, typically one that is reflected in a person's behavior."**

The way you think leads to attitudes such as whether you like or dislike, whether you believe or disbelieve, whether you consider something achievable or unachievable, and ultimately whether you will or will not take action. Attitudes are often described as your *disposition* toward something.

Attitudes are a key contributor toward how people are perceived by others, and they are the reason people get tagged as:

- Friendly or unfriendly
- Positive or negative
- Can-do versus can't
- Will-do versus won't
- Action-oriented versus lazy
- Self-sufficient versus needy
- Persistent versus quitter
- Flexible or inflexible
- Enthusiastic or cynical
- Trustworthy versus untrustworthy

Again, there are many such examples. In fact;

Whether you realize it or not, you have an attitude about EVERYTHING ... and it is usually quite visible to others!

Your facial expressions and body language, along with your choice of words, your tone, and the actions you take (or don't) are pretty good indicators of what you think and how you feel. You will often hear people say he or she has a "great attitude" or a "bad attitude" but usually without any specifics. This leaves us to draw our own conclusions, which has the following effect.

It takes CONSISTENT good experiences across ALL of the above labels with EVERYONE you come into contact with to earn you a "great attitude" label.

However;

It can take only ONE bad experience for ONE person with you in only ONE of the above examples—for ALL your attitudes to come into question.

This is especially true if a bad experience is with your boss or an internal or external customer. In this way with just one incident you can earn a generic "bad" attitude label which can be *very hard* to shake off.

You, therefore, have to be aware of a range of specific positive attitudes employers expect from you and make sure you demonstrate them at all times.

HOW ATTITUDES ARE FORMED.

From an early age, through general conditioning from parents, teachers, family members, and friends, we develop ways of thinking about ourselves and our world. Life experiences will further shape our thoughts, either challenging or reinforcing them into attitudes. Once developed, these attitudes become second nature, and we tend not to question them.

By the time we reach early adulthood many have settled and are as hard to break as concrete in some cases!

Parents, relatives, and teachers usually do their best to instill good attitudes, but sometimes they have their own issues and as a result will hand down "attitude baggage." For example attitudes toward other races and religions can be passed on for generations. Peer groups, colleagues, prominent entertainers, bosses, and the media also help shape us, often subconsciously, and not always in positive ways.

ATTITUDES ARE BOTH SELF-FULFILLING AND SELF-REINFORCING

Once your ways of thinking become habitual, consistently triggering the same emotional response, they become attitudes. At this point, most of us accept information only when it *supports* our attitudes. We often fail to even notice any contradicting information or will just dismiss it.

For example, once people decide they are doomed at public speaking, they usually make much more effort to avoid rather than improve their speaking skills. The belief that they have poor speaking skills becomes a self-inflicted, self-sustaining reality.

THE GOOD NEWS

You can learn to change your thinking and keep your emotions in check and, as a result, change your attitudes which in turn will change your behavior.

Using the above public speaking example, proper training, preparation, and some constructive coaching from a good presenter can result in a much-improved performance *from anyone*. Such an experience can totally turn your attitude around. (It can also totally change how management regards you.)

Deciding that you CAN control your thoughts and therefore change your attitudes is THE most important first step you need to take.

So let's start with that. You should note that many of the 10 attitudes are related, depend on, or impact another attitude, which I will point out as we go through them. ALL of them, however, depend on having the first attitude below that *you can develop the right attitudes* and that they are not set in stone.

PART II

THE TEN ATTITUDES EMPLOYERS LOOK FOR

1 - I CHOOSE MY ATTITUDES

Some people believe that how they feel is beyond their control. They think that emotions like anger, jealousy, love, hatred, and fear come and go entirely as a result of *external* events. These people are very vulnerable to the consequences of emotion-driven behavior, such as poor decisions and impulsive actions they later regret. In addition, studies have shown that traditional measures of intelligence, such as IQ, *decrease significantly* during strong emotional moments.

Your ability to think clearly, speak clearly, and make rational choices based on sound logic deteriorates when you are under the influence of strong emotions.

It is therefore highly desirable to avoid letting your emotions get the better of you.

How?

Psychotherapists and psychologists such as Aaron T. Beck realized that the root causes for our attitudes are our thoughts. They proposed that our thoughts, particularly our assumptions, lead to attitudes. The attitudes with which you view external events determine your emotions which in turn trigger certain behaviors. In particular, they found that when we let our thoughts build visions in our heads, those visions amplify our attitudes and consequently also our emotions. The stronger the vision, the stronger the emotions, and the more likely a behavior will be triggered.

So, in the words of Allan Lokos;

"Don't believe everything you think."

It was successfully demonstrated that if we become conscious of our thoughts, challenge our assumptions, and build new attitudes and visions, we can leverage them in very positive ways. This is now a common technique with athletes. They replace negative thoughts and repeatedly visualize themselves succeeding. This triggers positive energy and emotions that greatly enhance their performance. The first two steps in the Achievement Methodology are specifically designed to leverage this.

YOU CAN CHOOSE WHAT YOU THINK AND HOW YOU REACT

Self-aware and self-controlling people believe it is not the events themselves but their attitudes toward those events that determine their subsequent reaction. Doctors, nurses, police officers, soldiers, pilots, and many others have been trained to control their thoughts and consequent emotional responses in very extreme situations. You can learn, too.

If you don't, your thoughts will control you.

Poor thought and emotional management is a sure way to collect negative attitude labels. Coworkers may perceive you as impulsive, moody, bad-tempered, self-indulgent, quick to quit, tantrum-prone, volatile, or even unstable.

Meanwhile, deliberate self-awareness and control will earn you labels such as cool under pressure, balanced, analytical, and logical, which are critical for being considered both employable and promotable.

Here is an example of the strength of the causal relationship between what you think, the visions those thoughts create, and the consequent emotions and physical behavior.

Imagine what goes through the mind of a first-time parachute jumper versus that of an experienced skydiver. The former can be very preoccupied with thoughts and visions of what could go wrong. These visions can be so graphic and vivid that even previously eager jumpers will absolutely refuse to jump when the aircraft doors open. In fact, in some cases, they are literally paralyzed by fear.

Experienced jumpers are energized by visions of soaring and incredible views. They cannot wait to jump. It's an extreme example, but the same principle applies to public speaking. It is the negative thoughts and the visions of failing and being ridiculed by the audience that can paralyze inexperienced speakers. Replacing these thoughts and visions with positive ones is a critical step for change.

INFLUENCING THE ATTITUDES OF OTHERS

In his book *Emotional Intelligence,* Daniel Goleman describes how you can understand and manage not only your *own* behavior through managing your thoughts and attitudes but the behavior of *other people*, as well.

Understanding the attitudes of people such as your boss, colleagues, and customers enables you to predict their typical reactions. We touched on this when we looked at the four personality types. This allows you to align your behavior and your approach to them to ensure your interactions go well. Knowing that certain situations cause certain reactions, you can either leverage or avoid them. You can also learn how to influence people's thoughts and assumptions and reshape their visions to trigger the behavior that you need in order to move forward with something.

Causing positive emotions in this way is the basis for motivating, inspiring, and persuading, including professional selling.

Note; These are *TOP sought-after skills* for getting things done and earning promotions into leadership and management positions.

STRUCTURED THINKING

Seems logical, right? But controlling your thoughts and emotions, especially under pressure, is not easy. As we just said, how you think and the types of assumptions you make settle into patterns over time.

The stronger the pressure of the situation, the more likely you will revert to your old thinking habits.

It is therefore very advantageous to adopt "thinking structures" to combat this tendency. These structures will prompt you to focus on *positive action* rather than wallow in negative visions.

Thinking structures guide you to concentrate on the desired outcomes. They help you to visualize them and leverage the positive emotions and energy they create into taking constructive actions.

The Achievement Methodology is an ideal example of such a structure.

Going through the first steps of the Achievement Methodology to build a clear vision of a positive outcome is a practical way to motivate yourself and others. This is especially true when confronted with a problem.

Describing these steps using an example is a compelling way to demonstrate in an interview how *you* are *self-motivated.* Solving a problem or helping a colleague through the use of these steps is a great way to demonstrate your ability to stay balanced, motivate and inspire others. It will immediately set you apart as a potential leader.

Meanwhile, watch out for fear. It is one of the strongest, most common, and most disruptive emotions.

Remember, it is not the events themselves that produce fear. It is caused by your thoughts, assumptions, attitudes and consequent visions.

Learning to challenge your assumptions and to replace your attitudes and visions will have a huge impact on your ability to conquer your fears.

ACTION

1.1 Identify a work-related attitude that results in you fearing something. Common examples include public speaking, dealing with angry clients or bosses, taking on tasks you think you may fail at, or simply trying something new.

Examine your attitude and subsequent visions of a negative outcome and challenge your assumptions about why you believe they will happen. Use root-cause analysis to go down through several layers of "why?" Then use the steps in the Achievement Methodology to replace the vision that is causing your fears with a new desired vision, and then follow the steps to turn it into reality.

Building positive visions supported by proven, well-thought-out action plans will energize you. Successfully executing those plans will give you a sense of accomplishment which will boost your confidence and performance even further.

Common interview questions

"How would you describe your worst and best attitudes at work?" (trap question – focus on *positive* attitudes and how they helped you achieve relevant top priorities.)

"Have you ever changed your attitude at work? How and what was the impact?" (Pick one that helped you exceed expectations)

"What causes you to feel fearful or angry at work?" (trap – explain how you do not let external events drive your emotions. You focus on root causes and actions to resolve any issues.)

"What new attitudes have you developed in the last year at work?" (Pick one you know they are looking for)

"Can you influence the attitudes of other people at work? How and what was the impact?" (Pick an example – use S.O.A.R)

2 – I WANT TO

Once you have decided you *CAN* develop and alter your attitudes – you have to *WANT* to do so.

Your DESIRE powers your perseverance, and determination to do anything!

People want to do all sorts of things. Some never start, out of fear, and others give up at the slightest difficulty. They rationalize why they do not start or why they quit, but the true cause is usually a lack of genuine desire.

This is why your desire to do the job is one of three things employers look for.

To achieve anything important, you must carry out various tasks. There are two important attitudes toward these tasks: *"I like or dislike"* and *"I can or can't."*

If your attitudes towards these tasks are both "I like" and "I can," there is a high chance that you will accomplish them. This is also when you are most likely to demonstrate a good "will-do" attitude to your boss.

However, obstacles can turn these attitudes to "I dislike" or "I can't." This is when reluctance kicks in and commitment fades. Furthermore, when you feel you can't do something, 9 times out of 10, you will dislike it too, which means they have a habit of turning negative simultaneously. As soon as they both turn negative, people begin creating reasons to quit.

Therefore, a good way to keep *both* these attitudes positive regarding any activity is to get better at it.

When an interviewer asks you to give them an example of a task you dislike they do not really want the details of that task. They want the details of how you made yourself better at the task so that you liked it more and therefore did not allow your "I don't like this" attitude to negatively affect your performance. There will be lots of tasks you will not enjoy, especially at first. Employers are looking for people who know how to get past that.

The ability to manage these attitudes is the fundamental reason why some people are wildly successful while others are not. Successful people have strong visions of where they are going, why they want to get there, and what they will *have* to do on the way.

Their vision is so detailed and compelling that it creates an "I want to" attitude that is strong enough to override any thoughts of "I don't like, I can't, or I'm afraid."

Helping you create a strong vision like this is the purpose of the first two steps in the Achievement Methodology. Use the vision to stop yourself from inventing reasons to quit.

Above all, don't vocalize your negative thoughts! It will only strengthen them and intensify your desire to quit.

Vocalizing negativity also affects those around you. You are putting your negative ideas in their heads, effectively de-motivating them too.

You will be perceived as a whiner and labeled as such.

When you hear that whining voice inside your head telling you to quit, say the opposite. Talk about the benefits of succeeding. You will motivate others and be viewed as inspirational.

In some cases, you may have to fake it until you make it!

ACTION

2.1 Have you ever heard the following sports expression?

"They won because they wanted it more."

The exact same principle applies at work. Build and maintain your positivity and motivation to fuel your desire to perform. For anything important, use the opening steps in the Achievement Methodology to do this. Failure to make the effort to do so in the beginning will make you very vulnerable to giving up later.

Revisit your key goals and objectives and make sure you have clearly described what success looks like and why it is so important to you. This is where having goals and making sure your work and personal goals are aligned is so important. (Revisit Chapter 1)

Make sure you can *visualize* succeeding. Know the consequences of failure too.

Common interview questions include;

"What are your job-related goals?"

"Why do you want this job?"

"What are your personal career goals?"

"How do your personal goals help you achieve your job goals?"

"What scenarios make you give up on difficult tasks?" (What they want to hear is why you *don't* give up on difficult tasks.)

"How do you inspire others around you to achieve difficult goals?"

3 – I CAN

We have talked about the critical effect your "I can" attitudes will have on your desire to do something. As a result, many people will advise you to adopt a positive "I can" attitude. However;

"I can" attitudes cannot be based on ignoring reality. Just saying "you can" but then failing will only strengthen your next "I can't" moment.

A genuine positive, confident attitude is built on using a proven process and building a track record of achieving difficult things. Your subsequent lack of fear and visible belief of success affects everything you do and say. Everyone you interact with will feel it. Employers look for it.

Note: Nothing irritates a manager more than an employee who constantly responds to a task delegation with "I don't know how to do that." What they want to hear is "Consider it done" followed by a "whatever it takes" attitude to figure out how to get it done.

When *consistent* achievers are studied, it nearly always turns out that they have a high degree of self-sufficiency, but they are not afraid to *get help* and they *use processes* for doing things well. Because they have a career plan, they look forward and research what they need to become good at. They anticipate and build new skills all the time. They cultivate relationships with people who can help them *ahead* of time. They find out what processes were used by people who have already succeeded before and learn how to apply them.

ACTION

4.1 To strengthen your "I can" attitude, embrace the Achievement Methodology and look for any opportunity to practice it. Start by focusing on achieving tasks that are within your comfort zone to build up your achievement skills and confidence. Then start stretching out of your comfort zone into new territory. Pick a skill or activity where you think you are lacking and use the 10 steps to turn it around.

Pick an activity you don't like and decide to get good at it. Even if you are convinced that you will never enjoy that activity, you will dislike it less and fear it less if you become better at it.

Tip: Try applying the Achievement Methodology to becoming a good speaker. The effort is worthwhile because public speaking is one of the most essential skills required to move up in any organization! It is one of the quickest and most effective ways to gain visibility as management and leadership material.

Common interview questions include;

"How confident would you rate yourself and why?"

"What do you do when assigned a task that you do not know how to complete?"

"What do you do if assigned a task you think you are bad at?"

4 - I SEEK TO IMPROVE

A "seeking to improve" attitude is an essential part of the "I can" attitude.

A history of improving means that although you may not be able to do something now, you know from past experience of getting better at tasks, that you will be able to do it soon.

Managers will see your desire to improve if you are open to criticism and request feedback. Instead of defending yourself or not listening because you think you know better, you *MUST* seek out and show appreciation for helpful critiques and clearly demonstrate the desire to be better today than you were yesterday—and even better tomorrow.

This is also a very important attitude to display when attempting to get your manager to become a mentor.

No one wants to mentor someone who does not listen or take advice.

Eagerness to learn can also give you a cushion if you do make a mistake because your manager will see you as someone who will learn from the experience.

Also, remember that coaching someone to success is cited as one of the most rewarding aspects of a manager's job. It strengthens the bond between you and your bosses, making it more likely they will take you with them as they move up in the organization.

Conversely, believing that someone is not "coachable" and therefore unlikely to improve is one of the top reasons for management to terminate someone's employment.

A key, underlying attitude or mindset is your belief that *you can get better* at anything, *including becoming more intelligent!*

Many people believe that their intelligence is what it is, often based on tests and other people's opinions when they were young. This is referred to as a "fixed mindset," a belief that you either have a natural ability to do something, or you don't. This can be very limiting.

In her book *Mindset,* Carol Dweck, Ph.D. describes the advantages of having a mindset that believes intelligence can be continually developed which leads to a desire to learn. It embraces making an effort to take on new challenges and sees failures as opportunities to learn. Other people's success inspires them. She calls this a "growth mindset". At the other end of the scale people with "fixed mindsets" are more susceptible to fear of new challenges, see failure as a disaster, and are threatened by the success of others.

They say "I can't" with conviction because they genuinely don't believe that they can get better and consequently will not make the effort to do so.

It's easy to understand which mindset employers look for.

Note: People with fixed "I can't" mindsets tend to also have fixed mindsets about the abilities of other people including what is or is not possible for the team, even the whole organization. They tend to bring problems and reasons for why objectives *can't* be met rather than constructive proposals to ensure that goals *can and will* be met. Managers will do everything they can to ditch the "I can't or we can't" mindsets as fast as possible. Make sure you are not one of them. Everyone can improve!

An important mindset that goes with this is that YOU OWN your training and education. Don't expect the company to own this for you.

Many companies provide training, and you should take full advantage of it. Take their courses and workshops, show up early, pay attention, and participate (leave your texts and emails alone), and stay late to discuss aspects with the course presenters. Take interesting and relevant topics from the training and apply them to your job. Stay in touch with everyone on the training, especially those giving the training. When you utilize their training successfully, go back to the trainers and tell them your experience. They will appreciate it, and you will put goodwill in the tank of a new connection who may put a good word in for you later when you are seeking a promotion or just need help on a project.

Note: Trainers are often asked by management who the stars on their courses are. Take advantage of this.

However, many companies believe they can't afford too much training. In this case, you need to help identify training needs, help organize it, and ensure the company gets feedback afterward that it was worthwhile. There are many informal and inexpensive ways to get training started such as "learning lunches" where you can organize someone to share knowledge. Having an ownership attitude for learning and development is also very important as a leader/manager when it comes to looking after your team. It is a great way to align and motivate your staff. Taking the initiative to organize training is therefore also a great way to identify yourself as a potential future leader. In the process you will create examples for several of the most common interview questions such as, "give me an example of where you showed initiative, how you improved yourself, improved a situation for others, and showed leadership."

It is your "I seek to improve" attitude that is the foundation for your "I can" attitude. A track record of learning and succeeding at new things will give you confidence that you can turn an "I can't now" into an "I will be able to" in the future.

ACTION

3.1 Set goals to constantly improve your skills. Work with your manager to identify skills you need to get better at, and why. Often this involves questioning the processes around you to look for opportunities to improve the quality and timeliness of what you do and how you do it. Remember, in the quest to grow their profits, businesses are under constant pressure to improve their products and services and deliver them faster and at lower costs. Growth is highly valued *and so will you be* if you can make a material impact on it. Grab every training opportunity the company offers. Then create your own. Ask for lunch and coffee meetings to learn something from other people in the organization. *Treat every conversation as a learning opportunity.*

Remember, asking people for advice and then going back and thanking them after you have successfully applied it, is a great way to build and maintain new connections too.

Common interview questions include;

"What is the most important skill you learned at your last job?

"What skill have you learned in the last six months?"

"What training do you feel you have most benefited from?"

"What training have you organized for yourself and others?"

"What aspect of the job have you most and least improved at?"

5 - I CARE

Caring people believe that what they do matters. Remember General Schwarzkopf 's message that things had to be done well because lives depended on it? People who care have that attitude all the time. They are thinking about what impact their work has on others, not on just putting in their eight hours to finance leisure activities. They are willing to go the extra mile and *take pride* in giving others the best possible result.

Caring means knowing what the consequences of failure are and simply not allowing failure to be an option!

Be aware that this attitude is very visible to others, such as management, colleagues, and customers.

Any appearance at any time that you do not care will always be remembered and can be fatal to your career.

"I care" is also an important foundation for sincerity, relationship-building, teamwork, and ethical behavior. These too will immediately come into question if it is perceived that you do not care.

**"People don't care how much you know
until they know how much you care."**

Theodore Roosevelt

ACTION

5.1 Ask yourself how much you care about what you are doing and why. If you don't care much, perhaps you haven't paid enough attention to how your work affects others. Re-align by examining the results of your performance and how this impacts your boss, colleagues, plus your internal and external customers.

Any interview question asking you to demonstrate how much you care should be answered in terms of the effort you make to understand the consequences of your task and the subsequent effort you make to exceed expectations and not let anyone down.

5.2 This also requires you to be clear about how your personal goals are aligned with your work goals. If they are out of alignment, you may feel that your job is not moving you toward a future you value.

Re-align to establish why you care at a personal level or your performance will suffer.

What if you conclude that your work really does not matter? If after genuinely trying to understand the impact of your work you decide it's not important, you have a problem. Your choices are to hope you can stay under the radar long enough to look for another job, or to start asking for additional responsibilities.

In today's economy, jobs of little consequence are not likely to last long. Once the organization finds out you are redundant, you will find yourself back in the job market with no material achievements or references to add to your portfolio. Go back to the principles of alignment in Chapter One. Be certain your relationships with the boss, colleagues, and customers are rock solid. Make sure that you do everything to the best of your abilities, even if you think it is insignificant. Your employers shouldn't have *any* cause for complaint before you start taking action. Otherwise, it is too easy to just let you go.

Meanwhile, step up your internal networking as fast as you can. Volunteer wherever possible for additional training and assignments. Fill goodwill tanks by helping others. This will increase your employer's perception of your value and start opening doors for other internal opportunities.

Do not make the mistake of believing that it is management's responsibility to sort this out. *You own your future.* So don't just complain to your boss. They may just be grateful to you for pointing out a cost saving opportunity and terminate your employment.

Quietly looking for another job is a good backup plan, but organizations do not want individuals who jump from one company to the next. They want employees who face and overcome their challenges. Every time you do, you become more capable, confident, and in demand. It is much better to reach out to the connections you have built within your organization for advice. See if there are other opportunities internally and find out what you need to add to your profile to make you a suitable candidate. *Don't just jump ship.*

Common interview questions:

"How do you think your job benefits the company?"

"What or who suffers if you don't show up to work?"

"What are you most proud of?"

"What kind of work do you struggle to take pride in?" (trap)

6 - I SEEK TO UNDERSTAND

One of the cornerstone themes of this book is the importance of understanding. It is the second step of alignment in Chapter One. You cannot satisfy those who are counting on you without a thorough understanding of:

- the needs of your manager, colleagues, and customers including their personalities and attitudes
- the impact of your role
- how your performance will be measured and against what expectations
- the skills required for you to perform beyond expectations
- how the organization runs, how things are done, procedures, policies, etc.

Management does not think highly of individuals who don't make the effort to understand and then try to use ignorance as an excuse.

To foster and demonstrate an "I seek to understand" attitude, be curious. Ask how things work. Find out why they are done the way they are. The questioning skills that we covered in Chapter Three are critical. Also, use the Achievement Methodology to structure your questions. The questions listed there can help you understand everything around you. When others talk, *listen and take notes,* then ask more clarifying questions.

ACTIONS

6.1 Set a goal of understanding something new every day, something exceptionally significant every month. Choose things such as:

- Measurements that top management pays the most attention to, and find out if there is anything that you do which could influence those measurements (i.e. customer satisfaction, new sales, cash flow, cost reduction, etc.).

- Areas where your manager feels challenged so that you can add value for them and become a trusted advisor (i.e. new technology).
- Areas of weakness in the department so you can become a source of expertise for your colleagues (i.e. a technology, a process, etc.).
- The top 10 things your customers love and hate and what you could do to impact them.
- Areas where if you got involved could set you up for greater responsibilities (i.e. areas of expertise required by the next jobs up the ladder).

Make a point to meet and question new people every week. By doing this, you will develop new skills, remain mentally sharp, add to your contacts, *and build your value.*

6.2 *Make understanding before speaking or acting a mantra you live by.*

Take note of how many people constantly interrupt one another, without listening. Instead, make space in the conversation for other people's views by asking clarifying questions. In the process, you will learn to understand their thoughts, attitudes, logic, and word choices. As a result, you will be able to communicate your views in such a way that they might actually *listen to you!*

Note:

Seeking to understand is a vital attitude to support your improvement seeking attitude.

Caring, understanding, and desiring to improve are the basis for creativity. This is one of the most desirable attributes employers look for because creativity can add value far beyond your defined role.

Common interview questions include;

"How does your job create value?"

"On what basis was your manager judged to be successful and how did your job impact that?"

"How was your department measured and how did your job impact the results?"

"In what aspects of the company would you consider yourself knowledgeable enough to teach others?"

"Give me an example of a process you improved that impacted your internal or external customers."

7 - I ADAPT

Studies have shown that successful people are specific about what their desired outcomes look like and are relentless in getting there. This does not mean they endlessly persist in doing the same thing in the hope they will achieve a different outcome. However, they *are* prepared to *adapt* and *keep trying different* actions until they get there.

In the opening chapters, I asked why literally millions of people find themselves in a pattern of disliking and not performing in their jobs. According to Gallup polls, some 60 to 70% of employees feel disengaged. Some put up with this for years simply because they are uncomfortable with change.

Many people would rather endure the familiar daily frustrations, whine about them and use them as reasons for their limited accomplishments than face their fears of the unknown and take full ownership of their success.

Until you let go of that fear and see all results as learning experiences on your path to getting it right, you can remain trapped forever.

You have to adapt your way of thinking and alter your actions in order to succeed in your environment.

Your environment is constantly changing. Therefore, so must you. This is basic Darwinian survival.

ACTION

7.1 Pick something that is not going as well as you like and make a very deliberate decision to try something different to turn it around. If fear is getting in the way, go to action 1.1. above. Use the 10 steps of the Achievement Methodology. Do not give up if the new approach does not work. Try another.

Common interview questions include;

"Give me an example of where you changed your approach to overcome a difficulty."

"Give me an example of how you adapted to a change in your working environment."

"Give me an example of where you contributed a new idea and the impact it had."

"What kind of change in the workplace upsets you?" (trap)

8 - I SERVE

Many people object to having "I serve" as a core attitude. They think it refers to corporate slavery.

The employment equation is simple. The value that you provide must be greater than the amount that the company is paying you. Otherwise, you are a simply a cost which will be eliminated as soon as they realize it. This is the core of your relationship with your employer.

An employer's perception of the VALUE you provide tends to equate to their PERCEPTION of the SERVICE ATTITUDE with which you carry out your duties. Much of this is driven by the "customer service experience" you provide to anyone who is dependent on your work.

As we covered in Chapter 7, you can significantly erode the perception of your value even though you are doing your job, simply because you don't provide a positive customer experience.

Note: If even *one person* cannot deliver their top priority results because of you, your value will instantly and drastically decline!

Finally, it is worth remembering that everyone serves someone!

Even the top person on the corporate ladder is serving board members, investors, customers, and even their staff. In addition to serving those above them, managers serve those under them by inspiring, guiding, mentoring, developing, and supporting them.

If you show resentment at being told what to do, you will make yourself and those around you miserable.

Nothing irritates a manager more than having to beg staff to do something. You will rapidly earn the "diva" or "prima donna" attitude label.

ACTION

8.1 Revisit Chapter 7 to refresh yourself on what it takes to maximize the customer experience for your manager and anyone at the receiving end of your work.

8.2 Examine your attitude toward serving and, if necessary, adjust it! Read up on famous leaders who were known for their commitment to service. Be thankful (especially in tough economic times) that you are part of a company where you can provide a service, add value, improve yourself, and create opportunities to better your life.

8.3 Look for opportunities to offer help to people at any level in the organization. Some people think that doing a task that is below their pay grade will degrade their status. In fact, the opposite is generally true. No matter how important you think you have become, being seen as willing to help anyone at any level actually *improves* your image.

Ultimately you will find that providing a genuinely valuable service to someone is the most fulfilling and satisfying thing you can do.

Common interview questions include;

"Where, how and to whom do you think you have provided the best service?"

"How have you helped your colleagues?"

"Where have you volunteered to help outside of your role at work?"

"Under what circumstances do you struggle to provide your best service?" (trap)

9 – I TAKE OWNERSHIP

High performers take ownership of their work.

They see finding a way forward as THEIR responsibility.

If something is important to them, even if it is someone else's responsibility, they will ensure it gets done either by helping out or doing the job themselves if necessary.

Low performers typically blame their circumstances, other people, or bad luck for their failures.

Management detests excuse-making, finger-pointing, and a lack of effort to reach a successful completion of a task because of an attitude that says, "This is not fully under my control, and so I cannot be held responsible for the result." They want the opposite attitude, which says:

> *"I own this! Regardless of circumstances,*
> *I have to find a way to succeed."*

To help you develop an ownership attitude, try this exercise:

First, make sure you have total clarity over the desired result and the consequences of both success *and* failure of the task in question. This helps fuel your own drive and commitment *plus it helps you explain it to any others on whom you depend.*

Then make two lists of tasks and factors that can affect your success, those clearly within your control and those you think lie outside of it. Go through the first list and ask yourself if you are doing everything possible to maximize the end results. Really think it through and then take the appropriate actions and follow up to ensure those are successfully completed.

Now, turn to the other list of the dependencies you believe lies outside of your control and use root-cause analysis and ask yourself why you think you do not have control. What could be changed to increase your control or at least your influence? With help from your manager, if necessary, find out who *does* have control. *If it's important, don't just send them an email and think you have taken care of it.* Pay them a visit and discuss your dependence on any issues within their responsibilities. Explain the consequences of any failure of their part of the task, not just to you but to everyone else in the company and the end customer. Make sure deadlines are set, understood and agreed to. Remember the principle that a task without a deadline loses priority to all tasks that do have deadlines.

Gain their commitment to a coordinated plan with synchronized deadlines. Ask for progress updates and make contingency plans to compensate for their failures or delays. Check up and follow up relentlessly!

This process should help you develop a mindset of doing all you can to follow up and influence anything that could become an obstacle to success.

You will also *feel* more on top of your task.

Everything important in organizations is done through the management and coordination of multiple tasks by multiple people in cooperation.

Short of holding a gun to people's heads, you do not have full control over anyone. This is where the interpersonal, persuasive communication and influencing skills we covered in Chapters Two and Eight come into play. Take the time to develop a positive relationship with goodwill in the tank with anyone who has an impact on your ability to deliver. Do so in advance of the task. Don't leave it until things go wrong and everyone is on the defensive!

Assuming accountability means never using the "out of my control" escape clause.

Those who take ownership see themselves as captains of their own fate. They generate their own luck using the Achievement Methodology in the previous chapters. The opposite attitude is often referred to as having a *victim mentality*. This is a belief that you are the victim of your circumstances. Every failure is blamed on someone or something else.

It is very beneficial to your career to gain a reputation as being a "chaser" as a result of your diligence in following up because you take ownership. The opposite is being seen as complacent, as someone who just assumes that everything will be fine without bothering to foresee or check for problems.

Andreas Andreades, chairman of Temenos, a global leader in the provision of banking software, once criticized me over this. I had taken my eye off the ball in a sales situation. I had simply *assumed* something had been done by someone in another part of the company who did not report to me. When it became clear that it had not been done, I blamed the department involved. Andreas was not about to tolerate this.

> *"Alex, YOU were responsible for this sale! You were complacent, which always leads to disappointment— followed immediately by victim and blame mentality.*
>
> *"Take ownership!"*

The criticism was justified, and I have never forgotten it!

Your ownership attitude has a massive impact on the likelihood of you getting the job done, especially when the outcome is dependent on the efforts of others.

Without an ownership attitude, you will certainly not get promoted.

ACTION

9.1 Look at your top priority results and make sure you have taken full ownership. Be clear about which aspects are dependent on other people. Put mutually agreed and *committed* plans in place. Relentlessly double check and follow up on everything.

9.2 *NEVER* blame others. Blaming creates resentment and destroys your likability and trust ratings. It is very damaging to your key relationships. If you feel the urge to blame, turn it on yourself and ask what *you* could have done better and what *you* have learned from the failure.

9.3 To show that you have the right attitude, use phrases like "I own this" or "I've got this." When you volunteer, change your words from "I can help you with this" to "I will take care of this for you." Make these phrases part of your day-to-day vocabulary. It will also subconsciously strengthen your attitude.

Common interview questions include;

"How do you go about making sure an important priority is achieved when not all the resources are under your control?"

"Give me an example of where you were unable to complete a job because it was not fully under your control." *(Trap - What they want is an example of what you did to take ownership and make it happen anyway!)*

10 - MY INTEGRITY IS SACRED

This attitude has two essential components: telling the truth and doing the right thing.

A. I seek and tell the truth.

Almost all of us have been taught to tell the truth. Some of us have been threatened with having our mouths washed out with soap for lying. Then, at some point, we discover the very same people who brandished the soap telling "little white lies." Sometimes we even catch them telling big fat ones!

Most of us feel a small lie can be justifiable to avoid hurting someone's feelings or to sustain our likability. But it is only a short step from there to hiding the truth or manipulating the facts for our own benefit. Very few of us can claim to be entirely free of this behavior.

However, management wants black or white. Did you complete the task or not? Waffling or lying will *ALWAYS* get you into trouble. If you have made a mistake, the quicker you alert your superiors, the more time there is to fix it. Conversely, covering up will only extend the time your mistake impacts others and makes things worse.

Do not live in fear of making a mistake. If you never make any, you are probably not challenging yourself enough. However, managers want people who will be honest about their slip-ups and demonstrate a willingness to immediately resolve problems, plus keep trying and learning.

Those who do cover up and manipulate the truth may get away with it for a while, but not for long. Once discovered, they are *NEVER* trusted again.

Most managers are pretty clear which of their employees they trust and which they do not.

They do not promote or give references for the latter.

Worse still is an ethical breach. Deliberately misleading for gain, such as miss use of expenses or stealing materials or cash, is corporate *and* social suicide. Your chances of getting away with anything these days are slim to none.

You will get caught!

You must have a firm, unshakable commitment to truthfulness. Keep it at the forefront of your mind at all times.

It is important, even with the small stuff. Anyone who observes you telling a white lie will wonder what else you lie about. There's no need to be brutally blunt, but it is better to gain and maintain a reputation for honesty than to hide the facts. Sometimes you can find ways to be gentle without lying, such as asking questions that make people come to their own conclusions as we covered in Chapter Two.

It is equally important for you to show a desire for the truth when dealing with others. Do not fall for the first sound bite as people try to manipulate the facts. Good manipulators will play to your emotions. Digging deeper to get to the facts will help you make better decisions and show you to be a person of integrity and depth. These are the kinds of people whom employers like to hire and promote. People who are easily fooled or manipulated do not make good managers or future leaders. Good questions that focus on root causes and effects are your tools to help you do this.

B. I do the "RIGHT" thing.

Integrity also means respecting others and treating them fairly. You may be confronted with ethical dilemmas in your career. For example, your commitment to treat a customer fairly may cost money and conflict with short-term profitability goals. These pressures are very real especially in publicly traded companies who are under pressure to report maximum profits around quarter ends and year ends to keep share prices up. Maintaining high ethical standards may not always be easy, but identifying, openly discussing and doing your best to live by moral principles will protect your reputation and serve you well in the long run.

ACTIONS

10.1 Ask your boss about the organization's and the department's key principles of integrity. Are they all in sync? What are the priorities in case of conflict? Walk through some examples such as short-term profit versus customer satisfaction. This will position you as a person who cares about both integrity and the organization's objectives. This discussion can provide you with valuable guidance in the event of such a conflict. It is also a common subject for interview questions. Be prepared.

Common interview questions include;

(Note these are particularly tricky. All are potentially fatal traps! Discuss these situations with your connections. Clarify and *get the interviewer* to provide examples and context.)

"Under what circumstances would you consider keeping quiet, not telling the whole truth, or covering up?"

"Have you ever heard your manager not tell the truth about anything and if so what did you do?"

"Would you always tell the whole truth to a customer?"

SUMMARY

I am often challenged as to which attitude is most important. Integrity is the one that immediately springs to mind for most people, and I would agree.

> **"Somebody once said that in looking for people to hire,**
> **you look for three qualities: integrity, intelligence,**
> **and energy. If they don't have the first,**
> **the other two will kill you."**
>
> **Warren Buffet**

Beyond integrity, the most important underlying attitude you need is that you *CAN* change your attitudes and develop new ones.

You can eliminate negative attitudes that will hinder your progress. You can develop and strengthen the ones you need to succeed. The attitudes in this chapter are specifically sought after by employers when recruiting and promoting. However, there are many others. Each employer and even each manager will have their own list. Become aware of your current attitudes and constantly check they are aligned with your current or your targeted employers. Think about the most common questions they will use to look for these attitudes and prepare answers with examples of the situation, what you did and the impact it had. (S.O.A.R.)

Becoming aware of your attitudes and their impact, and developing the right attitudes - WILL transform your life!

CALL TO ACTION

I have introduced you to the job cycle and the skills you need to succeed in it.

Hopefully, you will have gained an insight that these skills are every bit as important as graduating with a degree.

Going through the cycle, I have shown you how to find jobs and employers that you are likely to enjoy working for. This includes how to develop the interpersonal skills you need to uncover the qualities an employer is looking for and how to develop yourself to align with their requirements. I have taken you through the skills you need in interviews to cross the "This is who we want!" threshold and the skills you need during the negotiations to get the salary you deserve. I have shown you how to start a job on the right foot and develop the ideal professional relationship with your boss. I laid out an Achievement Methodology for how to get things done which includes how to solve problems, create new ideas and implement them. It also provides a structure for making informed decisions and shows you where to lead and where to manage. Lastly I covered how to get promoted and the top ten attitudes employers look for.

However;

None of this will make any difference unless you take the risk, no matter how uncomfortable it feels, of actually putting these ideas into practice.

The only purpose of this book is to help you take *ACTION*.

Therefore, the test is to ask:

"What have you been able to DO differently since reading it?"

Please talk to me.

Email me your stories from the front lines as you apply these ideas. With your permission, I will post the most informative ones on my website and incorporate the best of the best in the next revision of this book.

Let's hear the good and the bad. What worked for you and what did not? What are the most common difficulties? What were your most spectacular failures? We can learn as much from situations that went horribly wrong as we can from the ones that worked flawlessly to plan.

Likewise, if you have questions or comments, send them! I will do my best to get back to you. Any criticism is welcome as I am sure the book can be improved forever. Again, any such comments or questions that would benefit a wider audience, with your permission, I will share on the website.

Lastly, if you think there are any useful tips that could help anyone you know, please let them know about the book. It could make a real difference to someone who needs to land a job, improve their success in one, or wants to get promoted.

Please connect with me on LinkedIn. You can use alex.groenendyk@ yahoo as my email.

ABOUT THE AUTHOR

Author, mentor, speaker, business leader and investor. Throughout his career, Alex has employed more than 3000 staff in projects in over 50 countries. He worked in multibillion-dollar organizations such as Fiserv, where he was twice voted business unit President of the year.

After a career providing complex information technology solutions to major financial institutions around the world, Alex started Goal Consulting to help individuals and companies set and achieve their strategic goals. Alex is also a board member of the award-winning venture fund venVelo, who both mentor and provide financial capital to entrepreneurs in early stage startups.

Alex's mission:

1. *Coach and mentor individuals to enter and succeed in the workplace.*
2. *Invest in and mentor early stage start-up business ventures to help create wealth and more opportunities for individuals to enter the workplace.*

Favorite quote:

> *"The best way to predict your future is to create it!"*
>
> *Abraham Lincoln*

CPSIA information can be obtained at www.ICGtesting.com
Printed in the USA
LVOW10s1656270616

494272LV00017BA/139/P